XOXY

Kimberly M. Zieselman

Jessica Kingsley Publishers
London and Philadelphia

First published in 2020
by Jessica Kingsley Publishers
73 Collier Street
London N1 9BE, UK
and
400 Market Street, Suite 400
Philadelphia, PA 19106, USA

www.jkp.com

Library of Congress Cataloging in Publication Data
A CIP catalog record for this book is available from the Library of Congress

British Library Cataloguing in Publication Data
A CIP catalogue record for this book is available from the British Library

ISBN 978 1 78592 837 6
eISBN 978 1 78450 990 3

Printed and bound in the United States

"You will laugh, cry, and get furious alongside Zieselman as she beautifully shares her raw and unbelievable story, which will change everything you thought you knew about bodies, identities, and the white, straight, well-to-do mother next door."

—Georgiann Davis, PhD, sociology professor, scholar-activist, and author of Contesting Intersex: The Dubious Diagnosis

"In *XOXY* Kimberly Zieselman engages and inspires by sharing the intimate details of her burgeoning awareness at mid-life that she was born intersex, and the incredible journey she has been on to help herself and others. It is a gripping narrative that explores how having had information withheld even more than her unique biology has impacted her life. It also chronicles Zieselman's tireless efforts as an advocate and leader to educate those unfamiliar with intersex, and to eradicate the shame, stigma, and discrimination that the 1 in 50 of us who inhabit intersex bodies experience almost daily. She documents how organized medicine continues to perpetuate secrecy and shame by performing harmful and largely irreversible cosmetic surgeries on intersex infants with the singular objective of making their bodies conform to gender norms.

Zieselman is a caped and capable crusader for change, and her book is filled with glimmers of hope for the current and future generation of intersex children. This book is for anyone who has ever felt different, or has stood up against judgment or intolerance, and for anyone who wants to understand what's at stake."

—Sherri Groveman Morris, Founder, AIS Support Group USA

"*XOXY* makes clear how binary notions of gender and sex embedded in U.S. healthcare contribute to life-long harms of intersex persons. This candid personal narrative shows us an intersex woman who refuses to be erased and chronicles the flourishing of an intersex movement that she helped build. An important and engaging read."

—Charlene Galarneau, associate professor emerita, Women's and Gender Studies, Wellesley College; and senior lecturer, Department of Global Health and Social Medicine, Harvard Medical School–Center for Bioethics

"Zieselman's riveting account of secrets and their consequences should motivate physicians to end the damaging, nonconsensual approach to intersex management of children, and inspire many who have endured similar medical trauma. Her turn to activism for intersex people everywhere as director of interACT is nothing short of remarkable."

—*Elizabeth Reis, PhD, Professor of Gender and Bioethics at the Macaulay Honors College at CUNY, and the author of* Bodies in Doubt: An American History of Intersex

"An intimate, searing memoir of an intersex life, *XOXY* lays bare the trauma of being betrayed by the medical profession, and details how one person finds empowerment through community and advocacy."

—*I.W. Gregorio, urologist and author of the Lambda Literary finalist* None of the Above

"In *XOXY* Kimberly Zieselman details the shame, secrecy, and lies she's faced as an intersex person since her childhood. Her perseverance and strength in the face of the powerful medical establishment makes for an astonishing story that you won't be able to put down. Kimberly played an essential role in helping me tell my own story to the world, for which I will be forever grateful. This book will help readers understand intersex, and the need to protect the bodily autonomy of all intersex children."

—*Hanne Gaby Odiele, internationally renowned model and intersex activist*

"When learning she was intersex, Kimberly Zieselman was told her condition was so rare she would never meet anyone who shared it. That doctor was dead wrong! Not only has Kimberly met countless other intersex people, she now stands at the forefront of their mission to be heard. Reading Kimberly's evocative memories of her journey from cheerleader to soccer mom to national intersex advocate and activist spoke to me on a deep, universally human level. After all, we're all longing to understand who we truly are, and be accepted and loved unconditionally. Kimberly is helping to lead a revolution that will change the world for the better—not just for intersex people, but for everyone."

—*Carter Covington, executive producer, writer, and showrunner of MTV's* FAKING IT

"Early in *XOXY*, Zieselman writes, 'I felt a rush of anxiety, but there was a simultaneous emptiness that was settling into me.' That poetic tension is threaded subtly throughout the book. Zieselman tells her own story mellifluously, but with a sense of palpable unease. After all, the narrative arch is of a woman in her forties learning how she was lied to most of her life, and then learning how that lie was part of a spectacular web of medical misinformation and ill treatment.

If you know the story of how most intersex people have been systemically abused by modern medicine, this will be a read laced with foreshadowing for you. If you don't, some of the most eerily familiar and quotidian passages will expose you to an important, often misunderstood narrative about what it means to be different in this world. There are vignettes about the typical childhood discoveries—the anticipation of getting a period, being studied by classmates at a new school as if an exotic artifact, doing drugs, and shoplifting.

Zieselman is brutally honest about the vulnerabilities of adulthood, too—from Imposter Syndrome at work to anxieties over the chaos of parenting kids with disabilities. These stories all take on a new, textured meaning when the truth is revealed. And then there are plot twists that seem ripped from a science fiction film—Kafkaesque half-truths from your parents and that nagging feeling that, even as you get older and wiser, what seems to be everyone else's reality isn't quite the same for you. Even in these moments, Zieselman delivers her story of trauma with alacrity. At one point, the teenage author–narrator is told there's only one other person in the world like her—a mysterious woman in Canada. She becomes a minor character for the rest of the book—at once desperate and comedic.

And in joining Zieselman on her journey in *XOXY*, you get to take one of your own, and meet the intersex community. A community formed around trauma, strengthened by validation, and liberated by too-often still-elusive truth and justice. This book is part not only of an individual's life, but of a movement. It's a movement demanding the simplest of things—truth, autonomy, dignity.

You'd be forgiven for assuming the memoir of a white, straight, cisgender woman in suburban Massachusetts wouldn't be a story of profound self-discovery in a marginalized community; you'd also be wrong. Therein lies the power of *XOXY*—in a raw narrative, Zieselman delicately guides you through her own journey as an intersex woman, a mother, a lawyer, and perhaps a not-so-unlikely activist."

–Kyle Knight, senior researcher,
Human Rights Watch

of related interest

A Comprehensive Guide to Intersex
Jay Kyle Petersen
Foreword by Christina M. Laukaitis, MD, PhD
ISBN 978 1 78592 631 0
eISBN 978 1 78592 632 7

Raising Rosie
Our Story of Parenting an Intersex Child
Eric Lohman and Stephani Lohman
Foreword by Georgiann Davis
ISBN 978 1 78592 767 6
eISBN 978 1 78450 652 0

He's Always Been My Son
A Mother's Story about Raising Her Transgender Son
Janna Barkin
ISBN 978 1 78592 747 8
eISBN 978 1 78450 525 7

Straight Expectations
The Story of a Family in Transition
Peggy Cryden, LMFT
ISBN 978 1 78592 748 5
eISBN 978 1 78450 537 0

How to Understand Your Gender
A Practical Guide for Exploring Who You Are
Alex Iantaffi and Meg-John Barker
Foreword by S. Bear Bergman
ISBN 978 1 78592 746 1
eISBN 978 1 78450 517 2

*To all children born with intersex traits, and
to the families who love them, and to the brave intersex
activists who blazed the trail before me.*

Disclaimer

I have tried to recreate events, locales and conversations from my memories of them. In order to maintain their anonymity in some instances I have changed the names of individuals and medical practitioners, as well as some identifying characteristics and details. Notably, my daughters Alexandra and Charlotte have generously granted me permission to share some very personal details about their lives herein.

Contents

PART III: BECOMING

PART IV: FULFILLMENT

Preface

The term "intersex" refers to someone born with one or more physical sex characteristics (such as genitals, reproductive organs, hormone levels or chromosomes) that don't line up with what is typically considered either a male or female body.

There are many different variations of intersex, and my story is just one narrative. One thing many of us have in common is the experience of medicalization, and the attempts to erase our healthy, non-binary bodies.

Our bodies are just another example that life is not so black and white. Much beauty exists in the infinite shades of gray. Intersex babies—as with all human bodies—exist in a wide spectrum. My hope is that readers will learn about, accept and support intersex children and adults, and respect that we have rights to truth, freedom from harm, and bodily autonomy—just like everyone else.

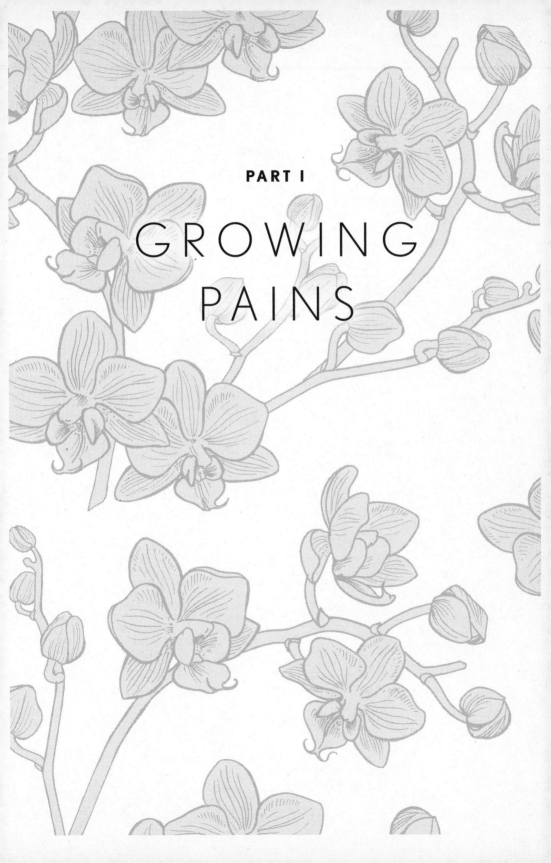

PART I

GROWING PAINS

Male Pseudo-Hermaphrodite

I poured another glass of wine for my sister Tara, and then refilled my own—we would both need to soften the rough edges of the day a little. It was only the third Thanksgiving since my parents' divorce. My twin girls were off playing Nintendo Wii with my nephews. My husband and my brother-in-law were in and out of the kitchen and the living room: monitoring the progress of the dinner, keeping up with football scores, and roughhousing with the kids. We were all tense, waiting for my dad to arrive. He was bringing his girlfriend, Caroline.

"He's been all riled up about next year's elections," Tara said, but I already knew. He kept sharing posts on Facebook filled with "evidence" of how the country was going to hell because of the latest left-wing conspiracy. He had always been on the conservative side, but recently he seemed to be increasingly staunch in his views and more than eager to share them.

"We'll just try to keep him on baseball." The Red Sox had just won the World Series. My dad was thrilled. So was I—after all, I'd been watching Sox games with him since I was a toddler, cheering along with my dad whenever Carl "Yaz" Yastrzemski was at bat.

Tara lived only a few minutes from him, and I was an hour away, so she took the brunt of hosting family gatherings, although we didn't have many more than these holiday get-togethers.

"Did you call Mom?" Tara asked. I'd talked to her in the morning. She was going to be spending the afternoon at a neighbor's in Naples, Florida, where she'd moved full-time shortly after the divorce. She'd asked if we'd be seeing our father, and I'd told her that we were, but I didn't mention who'd be joining him.

The doorbell rang, and my husband met Tara and me at the door. He rubbed my back, just enough. I knew he always had my back. My dad gave hugs all around, and then Caroline followed suit. She put her arms around me before I could process the act, and I cringed, though I gave her a stiff hug in reply. Tara and I knew that Caroline was involved in the breakup of my parents' marriage. Caroline knew that we knew. Everyone was polite. Three years may seem like a long time to take to get over something, but when that something is the complete understanding of the first 38 years of your life, three years is no time at all. There were still plenty of exposed, raw nerves.

My parents made a big deal about holidays when I was growing up. Our family was small—my parents each had a sibling, and I had a few cousins, but we rarely saw them. So before our husbands and kids came along, holidays had been the four of us—me, Tara, my mom, my dad. My dad worked so much that my strongest memories of him were at holidays or on vacations. He loved to buy gifts and gave us anything we needed. I was grateful to him.

But now there was an asterisk over our entire history. So much of what I thought I knew was only a half-truth. It felt like he'd been living another life, separate from us. I sensed their marriage hadn't been good for a while and they both seemed to get on each others' nerves. But I never imagined it would end the way it did.

Now that it was out in the open, I wasn't sure if the two halves had come together, or if there was still another version of my dad out there. Someone I didn't know at all.

"Everything smells so good," my dad said, and he made himself at home, trying to get Caroline to do the same. He smiled, and his eyes twinkled under his long eyelashes. You couldn't deny my dad had charisma. We were all adjusting.

Tara's husband asked my dad about his new iPhone—the original version had just come out that year, and my dad always had to have the latest and greatest of whatever was out there. "I just wish I'd gotten stock sooner," my dad said.

"Although, who knows? The Dow's been dropping."

"It could never stay that high," my dad said, "but it will right itself. Everything will be fine. There's always a dip before elections anyway."

"I just can't wait to get Bush out of there," my husband said.

"I kind of like Romney, but it's going to be McCain," my dad said. "I know it's going to be McCain. Then he'll take Hillary in a landslide."

"I don't know, Dad," I said, "Barack Obama has a shot at the nomination." I'd just watched his transformative speech a couple weeks back. I liked the idea of having hope again. I felt like I needed it. I know people's parents get divorced all the time, but the way it happened—it was rough on all of us.

My dad snorted. "That guy. He's got no experience. He's another unrealistic liberal."

"Please, no politics at Thanksgiving," Tara said. She leaned in while I set the table. "I just want to get through this day."

I nodded. I looked at my father, who had been such a presence in my life: the great big teddy bear. He'd aged, his full head of hair now gray. Now he was always railing about politics, about how his stocks were going to come back up.

"Caroline, can I get you anything?" I poured out some wine and tried to think of something to say to her. I didn't want life to feel weird or fraught, but I was uncomfortable. We all were. This was a great dance of politeness.

"Thank you, sweetie, everything is just...lovely." She spoke slowly, as an affectation. She was a nurse, so I knew she must be sharp. But she seemed to have cultivated a style of speech designed to make a certain type of man feel at ease; telecasting how receptive she was to whatever brilliant thing the big, strong, and wise man had to teach her. I could see why my father—12 years her senior—was drawn to her. The long blonde hair and nice figure didn't hurt.

We ate the food, and it was as good as ever, but my tastes were off, and melancholy had seeped into every dish. My girls asked if they could have a second helping of pie, and my dad gave a wink and served each one an extra-large slice.

"Not too much, Dad," I said. But I smiled—my dad had always been the one to sneak us sweets and indulgences when my mom wasn't looking. I kept this to myself. My dad, however, did not.

"I don't know about you, but I'm going to have a third piece of pie. Any other takers? Now that your mom's not around, there's no one to stop us!" My dad laughed, and Caroline was quick to add in a light chuckle, although I suspected that was for my dad's benefit. She looked uncomfortable. I raised my eyebrows and gave a flat *"huh."*

Tara cut in. "Ugh, Dad, don't bring Mom into this."

"Oh, lighten up, girls, I didn't mean anything by it," my dad said. Both he and my mom were carrying grudges, and it made both my sister and I very uncomfortable.

I felt a tightness in my lower abdomen. There had been a slight tug throughout the day, but I tried to overlook it. I had loaded up on stuffing, and I hoped that I was experiencing indigestion, discomfort from overindulging and the tension of the holiday. But no.

I touched the source of the pain, my lower left abdomen, underneath the old hernia scar.

No, no, no. Not this again.

Maybe it was nothing. I would wait.

We said our goodbyes at the end of the night, packing up our leftovers, loading the girls in the car, and driving the hour back home.

"That went...well," my husband said.

I shook my head.

"It's going to be hard for a while. But eventually, it will just be the new normal."

"I know." I felt a tingle in my eyes and knew if I didn't squash it immediately, I wouldn't be able to control the tears. Only one. I wiped it away.

I'd been going to therapy since my parents announced their divorce. I probably should have gone much sooner, though. I had spent so much time in my youth retreating into myself, and it had become impossible to live that way anymore. It's hard to keep tabs on repressed feelings when you discover much of your happy childhood was a lie. I rubbed my sore spot, adjusting in my seat. The tugging was still there.

"What else is it?" Steven asked.

I winced. I didn't want to worry him, but I was nervous. "Just a little twinge."

"Gas twinge or something else?"

"Not gas," I said. "It's probably nothing." Our girls had dozed off in the backseat, full and wiped out. "I'm always a little nervous if it feels like the hernia. And because the doctors had been worried about cancer..."

"But the surgery you had—wasn't that supposed to prevent any possibility of cancer?"

I checked the girls in the backseat again, then turned back to Steven and smiled. "I'm probably freaked out for no reason." I didn't want to be the hypochondriac who cried *crisis* at every twinge or pinch.

"Still, it would be good to check."

The pain was still there the next morning. Again, I convinced myself it would go away. After all, my surgery when I was 15 should have been an end to my problems. But why this now? Could it be the cancer I had been warned about as a teenager? Was that what this pain was? Did I have cancer? I had spent plenty of time in hospitals and around doctors when I was younger. Since my surgery, though, I've felt uneasy around them, which has only increased with time. Even the thought of going to the doctor can make me nauseous, which often has led me to put off seeing a doctor until my need becomes urgent. Plus, I had been gaining weight again, and everything felt *off*. I'd been on hormones since my surgery—for almost my entire life, I'd been living as a menopausal woman. Now, everything was getting harder, physically. I'd put on a lot of weight after my parents' divorce, and adopting

19

my daughters. But since turning 40 I'd lost 60 pounds and was making a concerted effort to stay slim. Still, though, I was aware of my body changing all the time.

After a week of this pain, I came to terms with the fact that it was urgent. I finally called Dr. Bingley, my primary care doctor. I'd been seeing her since I was 27—the year I got married. Despite the 14 years of going to Lydia Bingley, who had been recommended to me by the surgeon who had performed my teenage surgery, I entered her office feeling anxious and upset. More than usual. I didn't like that her office was in Mass General—a hospital I had grown to dread—and I was uneasy entering around so many patients waiting to be seen. I didn't feel like myself, and I couldn't articulate what was wrong.

When Dr. Bingley walked in the room, her assessment must have been the same. "What the heck is going on? You don't seem yourself!"

I felt the tears forming in my eyes as I explained about the uncomfortable pulling in my groin area. Then, I couldn't contain myself. I burst into tears. "I'm so afraid something is really wrong this time—maybe it really is cancer!" That was what had concerned my surgeon when I was 15—the possibility that my defective reproductive organs would develop cancer when I got older—which is why he recommended a full hysterectomy on an adolescent girl. A surgery that took place at this very hospital.

"No, no, from the way you describe it, I highly doubt it's cancer. Why would you think that?"

I had never fully described all my past surgeries to her, though she was aware of my hysterectomy, so, doing my best to stifle my crying, I told her about my two hernia operations. She gave me a quick examination, then said, "You may have a small inguinal hernia. If that's what it is, it's no big deal. A day surgery would fix it. I'm going to refer you upstairs to our urologist for an examination. Then you can come back here, and we can discuss the plans."

The urologist examined me as well and determined that I did in fact have a mild inguinal hernia and scheduled me for an outpatient surgical procedure the following month.

I went back downstairs to inform Dr. Bingley.

"You know, you are likely suffering from PTSD[1] from your previous experiences," she said. No kidding, I thought. "I think it would be worthwhile to give you a prescription for anti-anxiety medication."

I exhaled. Okay, I thought. This will be good. Everything will be okay. I'm in therapy, I'm getting medical help, these are all the things I'm supposed to be doing. I could be rational. I was a lawyer, for crying out loud. I had to be rational.

"Also, maybe it's time we dig out your old medical records so that you can better understand the surgery performed and put your fears of cancer to rest."

I nodded. "That would be great—thank you, Dr. Bingley."

We agreed to meet a little over a week later and, when I returned, she was ready for me with a manila envelope in her hands. It felt all so dramatic, when really, it was only stuff I had already known about. This was to give me peace of mind.

"I have to see another patient in the room next door, but I'll be back in to check on you, okay?"

I held the folder in my hand. My name was written on the side of it, and several papers were tucked inside. I sat at her desk and pulled out the contents. There in the file, on my records, were the words *Male Pseudo-Hermaphrodite*. Wait—what? My eyes raced over the document. More phrases: *Testicular Feminization. Androgen Sensitivity Syndrome*. Why was my name on this file? I didn't understand what was going on. I flipped through the photocopies of handwritten reports, and I found a postsurgical pathology report:

> Removed testes from patient's body. Testes both healthy and showed no signs of malignancy.

But—no! My surgery was to remove partially formed *ovaries* and a small, underdeveloped *uterus*. That's what had been done. That's what the doctors told me. It's what my parents told me. None of this paperwork referred to a hysterectomy or ovaries or a uterus.

One of the forms was the informed consent to the surgery. It was handwritten by Dr. Morrow, my surgeon:

June 27 1983

The procedure, risks, benefits, and alternatives to it have been discussed.
All questions answered; patient and parents have consented.

Just underneath Dr. Morrow's signature was my father's, and then my naïve
not-quite-16-year-old's signature. I had no memory of signing this form. This
little handwritten note. As if it was excusing me from school for a doctor's
appointment. What was this saying? What was any of this saying?

Male Pseudo-Hermaphrodite. Testicular Feminization. I searched the
papers in a desperate attempt to find something that would talk about my
hysterectomy, that would say I'd had ovaries and a uterus removed because
of a potential for developing cancer.

Hermaphrodite—that sounded like a mythological being—born with male
and female parts. *Testicular Feminization*—what the hell was that? Why wasn't
Dr. Bingley here in this room to explain this all to me? How could she leave
me here alone to find all this out, with no one to help me sort this all out?
When she finally came back, she had this sympathetic, concerned look on
her face, and I would have been annoyed if I weren't so in shock.

"Do you have any questions for me about your files?" she asked.

Was she kidding? Of course I had questions. But I was still trying to
process this. I was...a "male pseudo-hermaphrodite?" Was that like a real
hermaphrodite? I'd had testes? What the hell was "testicular feminization?"

As I started grappling with the reality that this was not a dream, that I had
had testes that required removal, it hit me—I had testes that were removed
but was never told about it. Why was I never told? How could I be finding out
at 41 years old?

I felt a rush of anxiety, but there was a simultaneous emptiness that was
settling into me. I had spent 41 years trying to find my place in the world,
to make sense of who I was and where I fit, and that had been challenged
throughout my adolescence and again—even harder—over the last three
years. Now it seemed as though my very identity had been a lie.

"So...do I have XY chromosomes?" I finally blurted out. I realized my file had said nothing about chromosomes.

"What we can do, if you want, is order you a karyotype test to determine your sex chromosomes."

"Yes, yes—I want that!"

She started filling out the form to send me downstairs to the blood lab at the hospital, but then seemed to change her mind, because she reached for another slip. "I'm going to fill out this request for the karyotype test, but I'm going to give you the contact information for a private lab. It's out in the suburbs."

"Why?"

"Well," she said, hesitating, "if the hospital here has on record that you have XY or typically male chromosomes, your insurance—someday, in the future—might deny you coverage of certain tests. Like mammograms. You still need mammograms. If the test is done outside, I can have the results sent directly to me here, where I can keep them private."

I was grateful that she was thinking ahead to insurance coverage, but was I that much of a freak? I couldn't even have a blood test taken at the hospital? All of this would have to be kept secret?

And I thought of my husband, my daughters, everyone in my family. What would I say to them? I started to hyperventilate.

"How could I not have known any of this?" I said.

"Well," Dr. Bingley said, "I did try to bring it up, but it was almost like you were putting your hands on your ears and saying *unicorns and rainbows, unicorns and rainbows.* I just don't think you were ready to hear it."

Unicorns and rainbows? What was she talking about? I didn't remember any hints, certainly not anything that would direct me to this.

"It's okay," Dr. Bingley said. "You'll get through this. And maybe I can prescribe you stronger anti-anxiety meds for the time being. If that sounds beneficial to you."

What would be beneficial to me is if my doctors had been upfront with me for the last 25 years.

I drove home thinking about the files, the appointments ahead of me, the secrets. Had my parents kept this from me? What would I tell my husband? *Honey, it turns out I'm a hermaphrodite and what I thought was a hysterectomy was actually a removal of testes.* Oh God, what would he think of me? I was terrified. Dr. Bingley was sending me out to the boonies to get my test done where no one would know me. Was I a man, then? I didn't feel like a man. I felt like—well, a woman. But...

But...it wasn't just my hysterectomy. I felt like I was different, I guess, from other girls. There had always been a deep, gnawing feeling that there was something about me that wasn't typical. I've always felt *female*—sort of. It was like a knowing without an understanding of why. But I knew. Not the kind of knowledge you get from books or lectures or Judy Blume, but that deep gut-level kind of knowing. Now, in December of 2007, at 41 years old, I finally knew why.

CHAPTER 1

CHRISTOPHER

Once, when I was about eight or nine years old, I asked my mother what she and my dad would have named me had I been born a boy. Without skipping a beat she said, "Christopher." It's a question I'm sure a lot of kids ask, but I had wondered if my parents had wanted a boy, and instead, they got me and then my sister.

There was nothing remarkable or different about my birth. I was two weeks overdue on a Sunday evening, August 14, 1966, when I was delivered by Dr. Wainer at University of Vermont Medical Center in Burlington, the same doctor who delivered my mother a little more than 21 years earlier at the same hospital. Although my father expressed concern over my pointy "Spock" ears, I was a healthy five-and-a-half-pound baby girl.

That same year, what would become my favorite television show, *Family Affair*, first aired. I can't say when I started watching the show, but seeing Buffy carry around her Mrs. Beasley doll, I had to have one. Mattel's Mrs. Beasley with her short, wiry yellow hair, rectangular glasses over brilliant turquoise eyes. Mrs. Beasley was an old woman with the face of a child, and the soft parts of a rag doll coated in blue with white polka dots. Like Buffy, I cherished this doll and slept with her every night. Life felt as simple and reassuring as it appeared on television.

My early childhood was TV-show-normal for a middle-class white kid in upstate New York in the 1970s. Just before my birth, my very young and struggling parents, who had been living in Cambridge, had decided to temporarily move in with my mom's parents in Vermont for a variety of reasons, but especially the extra help and support. Soon, we were back in our apartment in Cambridge, then to another apartment Newton, where Tara was born. About a year later, we moved 40 miles west, into our first single-family home among the apple trees of Harvard. While my mom stayed home and took care of us and the household needs, my dad commuted over an hour to work at a life insurance company every day in Boston. The commute for my dad was grueling, and he would leave early in the morning, well before I got up, and wouldn't be home until it was almost my bedtime. His presence in my day-to-day life was fleeting, and I craved the vacations and holidays where Tara and I had his complete attention and devotion. Otherwise, my parents' traditional arrangement was what I knew, and so I never thought to question it.

Then, as often happened in those days, my dad put in enough time and work and got a promotion to General Agent, running a whole agency in Syracuse, New York. We moved from the Cape Cod style house in Harvard to a large brick-front colonial with a pool in a suburban neighborhood called DeWitt, just outside Syracuse. It was the kind of neighborhood perfect for kids.

My younger sister Tara and I hung out in our driveway with our Hippity Hops and Big Wheels, until we were old enough to wander further down the street, or we'd spend hours in the backyard pool doing handstands and playing Marco Polo with our friends. Our house was the perfect strategic point for access to neighborhood fun—we lived directly across from the elementary school, which also gave us easy access to the playground, where we bounced balls in a few rounds of Four Square or attempted to maintain a volley across the cracked concrete tennis court.

Every July 4th there was a bike parade and all us kids would decorate our bikes and ride around the neighborhood in a parade that ended with a cooler full of popsicles. At Halloween, hordes of kids dressed as Snoopy, Casper the Ghost, the Bionic Woman, or one of the apes from Planet of the Apes, making the rounds collecting candy and occasionally getting spooked by an overachieving parent at the door dressed like a witch doling out an abundance of M&Ms, Hershey Bars, and Reese's Peanut Butter Cups.

In the ample snow of wintertime, we'd trek across the street in our snowsuits, dragging our Flexible Flyers to the top of the hill behind the schoolyard. Christmastime was also special in our neighborhood. One of our neighbors dressed up as Santa Claus and walked door-to-door through the snow (there was *always* snow at Christmas) visiting children and delivering trinkets, and groups of carolers made the rounds knocking on front doors and treating us to Christmas songs. I think my favorite neighborhood holiday memory though was the lighting of the luminarias. Thin white paper bags partially filled with sand and a candle were placed up and down the side of our street and lit on Christmas Eve, burning through the night and well into Christmas Day.

My dad was thriving in his business, and he and my mom had come a long way from being the young couple who needed help from my grandparents. My mom was now the "executive's housewife," and it was her role to throw cocktail and dinner parties for my father's business associates and their wives. It was exactly like the show *Mad Men*. I loved watching my mom prepare for these parties. Normally, she dressed almost like a tomboy—preppy New England, but always practical. Though she was only 5'1"—a cute, petite blonde—she rarely wore heels. In the summer, she might wear the occasional espadrille wedge, but that was it—she didn't feel the need to compensate. The dinner parties were the few occasions she would put on makeup.

I'd watch her apply the mascara, then squeeze her lashes between a lash curler, then frost her lips with a light pink before applying one spritz of Chanel No. 19—always Chanel No. 19. All the while, her wrist would jingle with my favorite piece of her jewelry—a gold charm bracelet my dad had given her. Over the years, she would add new charms, and the jingling grew fuller.

She moved with such ease through the house. She was always active—she did all the house and yardwork, including mowing the lawns, never hiring anyone to help. Though my mom tended to be shy, she had a likeable personality that was the perfect accompaniment to my father's charisma. They made a very handsome young couple. If the cocktail party at the house was a pre-dinner party, the group would snack and drink before leaving for some nice restaurant nearby. As soon as the house was empty except for us and the babysitter—a teenager from the neighborhood—we would go downstairs and cruise the kitchen, eating all the leftover pigs-in-blankets, stuffed mushroom caps, deviled eggs, scallops wrapped in bacon, and bowls of nuts.

The day after the parties, my mom would spend the morning cleaning the house. Then—at least in summers—she'd spend the afternoon relaxing by the pool, holding a sun reflector to maximize tanning, her pack of True Blue cigarettes at the ready next to a glass of TAB, a separate container of ice on the side. On sunny weekends, this was both my parents' natural state.

Every February, my parents would travel to a resort such as The Breakers down in Florida for my dad's company's yearly convention. They would be gone for five or six nights, so Mrs. Frick would move in for the week to take care of us. Mrs. Frick was our next-door neighbor. She was a kind, elderly Irish widow who always kept a dish of Circus Peanuts or homemade molasses cookies waiting for my sister and me when we would come over for a visit.

The first time they left us for that long we were still young, and the absence was difficult, even for my mom. Being away from us, especially at a place with a lot of strangers she'd have to mingle with, made her eager to return home. The next year, my mom came up with something to appease both her and our separation anxiety.

"Okay, Zimmo, Bug," the nicknames she and my dad had given us, "I have something special planned out for you." She had bought gifts for the both of us, one for each day she and my dad would be gone. "Mrs. Frick is going to give you one each day to unwrap. That way, you have something to look forward to."

This was huge. Our mom didn't usually spend money on frivolous gifts. We didn't get extra candy or games or comics at the grocery store checkout lines. Because she had lived through hard financial times with my dad, she was sure that money could evaporate as quickly as it had come in. So although she liked nice things, there was no excess, no waste.

Mrs. Frick was a comforting presence, but I preferred to go visit her house, usually when her granddaughter Susan was over for a visit. Susan went to school in Fayetteville, a neighboring town. The first time I saw her at her grandmother's, playing in her backyard, I was excited to see another girl my age just next door. But I was shy. It took me all morning to get up the courage to cross Mrs. Frick's yard and talk to her. Once I introduced myself, though, Susan and I became fast friends.

Susan was the youngest of four girls. Sometimes, all the sisters would all be over at Mrs. Frick's house, but generally, Susan spent a lot of weekends there on her own. When I was old enough, I had my first sleepover at Susan's house. She shared a cramped bedroom with her three sisters—Mary, Julia, and Mariah—all loaded up on bunk beds and dressers on either side of the room. Going there was like going to camp for a night.

In my room, on the other hand, I had my own queen bed and twin closets that flanked a dormer window overlooking our front yard and the playground across the street. Childhood was idyllic. At least until I was six.

One night, after my bath, as I was getting ready for bed, my mom noticed a slight bulging in my groin area.

"Sweetie, let me take a look at that." She pushed a finger into my soft flesh, still warm from the bathwater.

"Ow." She hadn't pressed hard, but whatever was pushing around in there was painful. The next day, my mom took me to the doctor, and after a flurry of questions and tests, and it was determined that I needed to be rushed to surgery to repair a double inguinal hernia.[1] I wasn't scared, though, as I was wheeled into surgery, clutching Mrs. Beasley. When I was four, I'd been in the hospital to have my tonsils removed, and then before that, I was hospitalized with pneumonia, sleeping alone under a sick tent for several nights. This surgery was just one more "thing" that needed to be done for my health. I didn't understand what a hernia was; at six, I didn't even know much of the basic biology of intestines and abdominal walls. What I knew is that the surgeon fixed the problem by pushing my small intestine back into place and then sewed me back up.

I had a hernia; the doctor pushed it back in. He didn't say anything else about it. In the three nights I stayed at the hospital, the doctors and nurses didn't explain anything else to me. The surgeon didn't explain to me or my parents that close to 30 percent of males get inguinal hernias in their lifetime, but only about 3 percent of females do. The surgeon didn't explain the fact that the bulging hernia was caused by my internal testes moving around my lower abdomen. The fact that my body was not "typical" of most girls—yet very common in girls born with Androgen Insensitivity Syndrome.[2]

I didn't think much more about my surgery. I had a long scar, which was sometimes painful, but soon I grew used to that too.

* * *

I was ten years old, at a sleepover at Susan's house, when I learned that girls got periods. Mary, Julia, and Mariah were having their periods at the same time—as young women living among and on top of each other, their cycles had synced—and complaining about their cramps.

We were camped out in the girls' bedroom, Susan and I scrunched up on her top bunk, listening to terms be defined.

"As long as I'm not still on the rag on Friday," Mariah said. "That would be the worst."

"At least yours aren't as heavy," Mariah said. "I just feel like I'm gushing."

Susan laughed, a wide-eyed, nervous laugh. "Yeah, and now the bathroom stinks because of all your bloody pads wadded up in the trash. You need to take them outside."

Mary's face got serious. "We can't," she said, her voice quivering, "that's how the bears will know where to come for their next kill."

Susan's body jerked upright, but then she relaxed when she realized the joke.

"Just wait," Julia said, looking at Susan and me. "You'll see."

"When do they start? When did you start having periods?" I asked.

"Eleven...twelve," Julia said. "I was almost twelve."

"I was thirteen," Mary said.

"I guess that means we were just more gifted than you," Mariah said, and Mary threw her pillow across the room, landing on Mariah's head. "Seriously, though," Mariah said, "there's a girl in my class who was eight when she got hers!" That truly was news, and all three of the older girls agreed that would be horrible, and I was inclined to side with them.

"By the way," Julia said, leaning out of her bottom bunk to call up to Mary, if you're still having that time of the month on Friday and can't go to the dance, can I wear your blue dress?"

Mary leaned over. "Touch my blue dress and die!"

Though I remained a shy observer to most of it, I learned from Susan's sisters all about periods. I learned that teenage sisters fought over their clothes, that teenage girls had dates with boys, that teenage girls had boyfriends, and that teenage girls had periods. I couldn't wait to be a teenage girl.

Although Susan's sisters occasionally complained about their time of the month, they were also proud to have them—menstruation was the necessary rite of passage to becoming a woman, and that made them almost worldly. I looked forward to my own and couldn't wait for Susan and me to get our periods. I felt like I'd be admitted into the club for young women once I did. I imagined being able to share stories—someday—with Susan's older sisters, at least if I wasn't too embarrassed to talk about my experiences with them.

As I turned eleven, my mental countdown began: I thought that I could potentially get my period at any time. Sure, I could be like Mary and maybe have to wait until I was thirteen, but there seemed to be a good chance it would happen this year. It was my first year of middle school, and suddenly I felt like not such a child. I hardly spent time with my Mrs. Beasley doll, although she did hold a special place of prominence on my bedroom doll shelf.

But then, just as I was on the cusp of joining the womanhood club with Susan's sisters, according to my projections, my father was offered a new job in Boston, and so we had to move in April, over my spring break. The news was crushing. Being shy, the thought of starting over with friends and acquaintances was a form of torture. Leaving our beloved friends was upsetting for my younger sister Tara as well. We had loved our home and our lives, and the upheaval, especially in the middle of the year, was brutal. I tearfully promised to write Susan as soon as I got to our new historic suburb just west of Boston.

We packed the house and sent off a truckload with some movers, then loaded up our final suitcases into my parents' station wagon. Some of our furniture would be sent to a storage facility—my parents were having a house built, but in the meantime, we would be living in an apartment. Not being able to get settled right away made me anxious and even more sad at the loss. I tried to touch all the walls of my house as a final goodbye, and as I walked out of the door for the last time, I felt a deep pit in my stomach.

My mother consoled Tara, who was sobbing. "It'll be okay," she said to my sister, and then to me, when I walked up to her, pushing my body to my mother's side for comfort. "It's hard for us all, but we'll make this an adventure, okay?" My mother, always with her New England waspy pragmatism and tough love. I wiped away my tears with my sleeve and sniffed, but that didn't stop the tears and snot from flowing.

"Can I sit in the way-back?" Tara asked, referring to the very far back of the wagon. Because of the suitcases, there was only a small space just big enough for Tara to lay her petite, newly-turned-eight-year-old body back there.

"But I wanted the way-back!" I said, feeling injustice well up inside me.

"But I wanted the way-back!" Tara mimicked in a whiny voice.

"Shut up!"

"Hey!" my mother roared at me. "Never say *shut up*. Now apologize to your sister. And Tara, don't tease your sister." My mother tried to negotiate turn-taking, but neither of us was completely satisfied, especially me, since Tara would get the first turn in the way-back. She'd get to look back at our house as we drove away for the last time.

My mother reminded us that we'd be getting to start all over. "It's like getting a new life," she said. "A lot of people don't get that chance. You can make your life whatever you like."

I had a notebook on my lap, already composing a letter to Susan so she wouldn't forget about me, reminding her of all the fun things we had done, while my parents smoked their True Blue cigarettes and rotated their collection of eight-track tapes. Their selection was limited, so I was privileged to a loop of Beach Boys, The Carpenters, Barry Manilow and—my favorite—Captain and Tennille. "Love Will Keep Us Together" was of little comfort, though, as I felt torn apart from so much of what I loved. I signed the letter to Susan *XOXO, Kim*.

I desperately wanted to fit in at my new school, which was a difficult prospect in the middle of the school year. It's particularly difficult to fit (or blend) in when everyone knows you as "the new girl." I felt eyes on me at all times—when I sat in the classroom, when I walked down the hallways. It was as if I was some anthropological curiosity to be studied, figured out.

Meanwhile, I was playing my own Margaret Mead, trying to figure out this drastically different type of school. There were very few walls in the school. Most of the classrooms in my new school were separated by short bookshelves. Rather than having long hallways, lined with student lockers, the lockers at my new school were stacked in the back of the cafeteria. There was no indoor pool at my new school. The foreignness of everything, on top of my shyness, on top of my lack of friends, was isolating.

Then, that summer, I met Kelly, whose family had just moved to our apartment complex from another state when her father's job was relocated. They too were awaiting their new home's construction, although it was going to be in a different neighborhood from our home. Kelly also had an older sister who was more than willing to impart her knowledge on all things womanhood.

"Getting your period really means becoming a woman," she told us. Because there would only be three of us—not an entire gaggle of teenagers, as there had been at Susan's—I felt like I could ask more questions. Like how much that time of the month hurts, how much blood comes out. Kelly's sister answered everything for us and more. Kelly and I had a certain, and appropriate, amount of fear but also plenty of excitement when we talked about getting our own periods, finally becoming women.

We talked about becoming women when we secretly dressed up our Barbie dolls after school, knowing we were too old to still be playing with dolls but taking delight in the dressing and undressing as if it were the last hurrah of childhood. We talked about becoming women as we hovered over Judy Blume's *Are You There God? It's Me, Margaret* in the school library, giggling over the parts about periods, and breasts (*I must, I must, I must increase my bust* we chanted, almost as a coven).

More girls in our class were starting their periods. Some arrived in the morning, pronouncing their step into womanhood at the lunch table; others of our comrades didn't have it so easy, and had an accidental gush all over themselves and their clothes in the class for all to see. That was the kind of mortification to be avoided at all costs. We asked our friends if they knew right before that they were about to get their periods.

"Obviously not," said one of our friends, who had gotten hers while at school but had caught it during a trip to the restroom, before disaster had struck all over her white shorts. So while Kelly and I navigated 7th grade, preparing for whatever trials of adolescence would strike next, we came up with a plan against our biggest fear of unexpectedly getting our period during class.

"We need to be ready at all times," I said. "And those dispensers in the girls' bathroom seem sketchy." We knew them to be unreliable, and sometimes we found unused sanitary napkins unwrapped and stuck to the walls of the bathroom, or tampons pushed out of the cardboard applicators and shoved into the drains of the bathroom sinks, for inexplicable reasons. Adolescence is a very complicated endeavor. Kelly solved this problem by swiping some of her sister's sanitary napkins from her stash in their bathroom, and she gave me some. We kept them hidden in our canvas book bags, tucked beneath our Bonne Bell Lip Smackers.

Some of the boys in our class could be especially brutal, so the key to addressing the DEFCON levels of midday menses would be avoiding attention.

"Here's what we'll do," Kelly said. "We'll write notes ahead of time. To the teacher."

"Are we going to say we got our periods? To the teacher?"

We decided on bracketing a typographic period—a sanitized pictograph. We wrote identical letters, explaining, *I've just gotten my [.] and need to be excused to the girls' room.* Short and sweet.

"Perfect. And now we fold them up and keep them with our bookbags at all time." We were prepared.

By the end of 7th grade, I hadn't gotten my period yet, but I did

feel that familiar uncomfortable tugging in my groin. I pushed where
it hurt, and sure enough, there was the slight bulge and the sharper
pain at the touch.

"Mom?"

"What is it, Zimmo?" I pointed to my groin. "I think—I'm having
that pain again. And there's a lump."

She took me right to the doctor, and within a few short weeks, I was
wheeled into surgery at our community hospital. The doctor called it
"a double hernia repair operation."

In my post-op visit, the doctor came in, seeming genial enough, but
was all business when he said, "We opened you up and pushed the
small intestine back into place." That was it. No mention of anything
irregular.

No mention of testes.

This was now twice that I was cut open, at two different hospitals
in two different states, and was not informed that I had testes. Was
it possible for two surgeons in different places at different times, who
had opened me up and had time to really look inside my body, to not
see that I had testes where I should have had ovaries and a uterus?

My little scar that ran east-west along my groin was reopened, and
then stitched back up—this time its size increased by at least an inch. It
was now bumpy and red again, even worse than it had been before. My
biggest concern with the surgery was how ugly my scar was. I didn't
want to wear a two-piece bathing suit in the summer.

I didn't tell Kelly or any of my new friends about my surgery. I was
too embarrassed—my second inguinal hernia seemed like it should be
a secret. It made me different, and that was the last thing I wanted
to be.

CHAPTER 2

SYNCHRONICITY

As I turned 13 and started 8th grade, my scar faded, little by little. I grew accustomed to it, watching the progress as the skin softened, the bumps flattening, the red line turning pale. Soon, it was just another part of me.

Otherwise, I was still adjusting as the newcomer to school. I did have a few friends, and now they were getting boyfriends. These were the flirty, popular girls who giggled about their first kisses at their lockers or during recess and exchanged gifts with boys on Valentine's Day. I was too shy to have a boyfriend, but that didn't stop me from desperately wanting one. I wasn't getting that type of attention from boys. Instead, Marty from my class would call me Madam Ape Face and give me a big grin whenever he saw me in the hallways, and he once stole my Bonne Bell Lip Smacker out of my book bag, only to return it later, a pencil jabbed through the middle. At the time, I told myself he must have done it because he liked me. Of course, I had no interest in that kind of attention.

I spent a lot of my free time babysitting kids in the neighborhood in order to make easy pocket money. I liked the kids I watched, and I also felt like I had these small human beings looking up to me, caring what I thought about their interests, hoping I liked the same things they liked, wanting the cool teenager to play games with them. I remembered back to the good babysitters Tara and I had when we were younger and how validating it was when one of the "big kids" treated us with respect. When they acted like what we said mattered to them. Babysitting also helped put all the trials of adolescence into perspective, at least a little bit.

The next year, though, I entered high school, and life changed for the better. I had many friends, and I even hung out with boys, going on the occasional date. I made a friend, Bess. Since she and I had gone to different middle schools, we didn't meet until 9th grade. She had an older brother named Bobby—I thought he was cute, and so she introduced us. He was a senior, and that was a big deal in terms of coolness. We dated for most of that year, though it was tame, and we mostly just hung out. When he graduated, he went off to college, and that was the end of the relationship.

Also that first year, I joined the field hockey team. I loved it, but my dream was to make the freshman lacrosse team in the spring, though I had never played before. I spent several weeks in the cold of February and March practicing with my wooden lacrosse stick in my front yard to prepare for tryouts. I did not make the team, and I was devastated. But then a few weeks later, I came down with mono and missed school for several weeks that spring. I felt somewhat better realizing there had been a physical reason why I had performed so poorly at tryouts. The next year, I dropped field hockey and tried out for the JV lacrosse team, and not only did I make it, but I was named co-captain despite not having played the previous year.

I wasn't the best player, but I took the sport seriously and was supportive of my teammates. I loved the sport and being active. I'd gotten the bug seeing the older kids in my neighborhood carry around their lacrosse sticks, but it otherwise hadn't been pushed on me by anyone in my family. They were supportive, though. My mom came to nearly all of my home games, and though they were always on a weekday afternoon, my dad would do his best to get there after work, showing up in his suit because he didn't have time to go home and change.

Tara was active as well—she was a cheerleader, and she loved going to aerobics classes. Sometimes, especially in the off-season, I would join her in our finished basement, which had been our playroom, mirroring the leotard-clad Jane Fonda in the workout videos playing on VHS. More often than not, lacrosse practice was enough of a workout for me, though.

I stayed friendly with Kelly, although she could withdraw and be moody, and in the first couple of years of high school, we started growing apart. But I made new, wonderful friends. One was Nancy. Her mom, Ellie, taught social studies and political classes and was by far my favorite teacher. Nancy was co-captain of the cheerleading squad as well. She and I resembled each other physically, to the point where teachers and students alike regularly confused us. Lenore had been my friend since my one year on field hockey. She played lacrosse as well, and we spent much of our time together. Lenore's father was a principal at a high school in a nearby town, but he was the outdoorsy type and took us on day-long hiking trips in the White Mountains. I had a group of loving, supportive friends with great families—it was an idyllic time.

Sophomore year was also the year I started dating Rick. He was on the football team, though he wasn't my first football player. At the beginning of the year, after saying goodbye to Bobby, I'd gone out with Fred, the quarterback. We met at a student council meeting, where I right away was drawn to his attractiveness and his sharp intellect—the strong, silent type. I told his friend I thought he was cute, and then Fred called me, and we hung out a few times. Mostly we kissed, but nothing more. As the holidays approached, Fred called me to say that he liked me, but he couldn't keep going out with me because he needed to focus on school and getting into college, so he couldn't be distracted.

He didn't date for the rest of high school, ended up at Brown and became a successful lawyer afterward.

Rick, though, was most definitely not a rebound. I'd noticed Rick in science class. He was good-looking, and he was noticing me, too. The flirting began, and we started hanging out during our free periods. Rick was smart, but because he hung out with other football players, he pretended that he wasn't good in school. Weekends were usually spent hanging out together, just the two of us, or sometimes with the group of our friends partying, more often than not at a house where someone's parents were away.

To all the world, I was a typical young woman in New England. I had a boyfriend who was my first love. In addition to Nancy and Lenore, I had a tight group of girlfriends who meant the world to me: Monica was a cheerleading co-captain with Nancy, Cassy was on the lacrosse team with me and was a much better player as well as an artist. Julie's dad was a business executive like my dad, and our families were better off financially than a lot of our friends. We acknowledged our privilege and preppiness to the degree that we (privately) nicknamed each other Muffy and Buffy. Caitlin was a real stunner, the petite redhead with a perfect figure, and Karly was funny as hell—everyone loved her. She came from a big Irish Catholic family, and her father happened to be our town's chief of police. In fact, senior year, we would even coin a name for our group of girlfriends: The Senior Bitches, shortened to SBs.

I was fairly popular and athletic and doing well in school, knowing I would go to college though not sure what I wanted to do with my life. From the outside, I was about as typical a preppy, upper middle class New England high school girl as you could get. Yet there was still a difference I felt deep within me. I was a girl—that I never questioned. But I wasn't the same as my girlfriends.

When I was the only one of my friends not to get her period, my mom told me that I was just a late bloomer. "Also, girls who are active sometimes get their periods late. That's a fact."

"But Tara got hers already," I said. "A couple of years ago." She worked out as if it was going out of style.

Menstruation wasn't the only difference, but I couldn't totally pinpoint what separated me from all the girls I knew. The only noticeable physical difference was my lack of pubic hair. In the gym locker room or at sleepovers I made great efforts to hide this fact from to the other girls. I felt ashamed. I wanted to look like all the other girls. At least I had developed breasts and grown hips—I was sure that meant my period would be coming any minute. Instead, I was a bystander as Nancy and Lenore complained about the "time of the month," doubled over in cramps and upset that their parents wouldn't let them stay home from school. At least I didn't have to deal with that yet, I conceded to myself, though I was disappointed. What they were experiencing was alien to me. I couldn't imagine what it felt like, except for maybe bad gas—or my hernia. "Is it a pulling kind of pain?" I once ventured to Nancy.

"No, it's a squeezing, like someone's taking your insides in their hands and wringing them out."

"For me, it's like being stabbed with hot knives," Julie, another of our friends, jumped in. Though it sounded horrific, they also shared a delight in telling their misery. Their complaints of pain were ritualistic; I was left out of the temple.

Then, my girlfriends were visiting their doctors for birth control prescriptions. They were freaking out if a period was late one month. I didn't know what that meant for me. While they shared concerns and remedies, I was relegated to the role of silent bystander to my friends' lives. Part of me was relieved to not experience the pain—but either it was something I had "to look forward to," so to speak, or there was something wrong, something much worse, ahead for me. Either way, it seemed like there was some kind of countdown underway to an explosion—I just had no clue what minute I was on.

That's not to say I wasn't living an otherwise-similar life. One night junior year, at a friend's house party, Rick and I had sex. The parents had gone away for the weekend, and Rick and I sneaked into their bedroom (because teenagers often do things that make their adult selves cringe). We hadn't talked much about "it"—our friends were having sex, and Rick had dated a few girls before me, including older girls. He seemed to know what he was doing. I, on the other hand, did not, having been told next-to-nothing except for some vague general tidbits from our friends or what was discussed in movies. In hindsight, I was so vulnerable. There was pain, which I'd heard people talk about before, but it wasn't a dramatic pain. Just a kind of stretching. A first time can't help but be a somewhat alien experience. I both couldn't believe it was happening and was simultaneously relieved that it finally was.

Did Rick feel that anything was different from the other girls he'd been with? He must have, though he never said, and his enjoyment did not appear at all tempered.

Though my mom didn't say anything directly, she must have suspected that Rick and I had taken our relationship to the coital level. When he was about to arrive to pick me up for a date, she took to saying *Be true to thine own self*. She always said that, I think as a way of saying to be careful. But that was it. I would laugh, roll my eyes, cringing a little on the inside but appreciating her care as well as her discretion.

I didn't expect sex to suddenly trigger menses, but questions of protection came up, and I had no clue what was going on with my body. My biggest concern now was that something was wrong with me.

"Mom," I finally said one day in spring of my junior year. I'd been feeling anxious and uneasy, despite enjoying school and thriving with sports and babysitting and friends and Rick and the rest of my life. "Tara got her period when she was 11." She was now 13, and I was going on 16.

My mom nodded. She made some calls, and then, a couple of weeks later, my parents drove me the 45 minutes to Mass General Hospital in Boston. It was a Harvard teaching hospital. They had to have answers for us. The flash of doctors and nurses administering physical exams, tests, and asking questions left only a vague impression on me. While my parents were out of the room, the doctor asked if I was sexually active. I hesitated. "I assure you," he said, "your response is kept confidential."

"Yes," I said, "my boyfriend and I recently started having sex… sometimes."

"Okay," he said, making a short note on my chart, but otherwise, he didn't act as if it was a big deal. Beyond that, there was nothing memorable about anything that day. The whole process seemed ordinary, cursory even. One doctor said that I'd likely get the results by the beginning of June. Okay, nothing to do but wait.

I hadn't been paying too much attention to dates, other than focusing on the end of the school year. It was a sunny Saturday morning, and I had a day of studying and lounging planned before I was scheduled to babysit that night.

"Hey, Zimmo," my mom said to me as I rummaged for cereal in the kitchen.

"Morning, Mom."

"Kim, your dad and I want to talk to you. It's so nice out today, why don't we go out by the pool."

The pool sparkled in the early morning sun. The air was still cool, but I could already tell the day would turn hot in a couple of hours. What a great Saturday it would turn out to be—for other families.

"The doctor called back…with your test results," my mom began. I had completely forgotten about the test results coming in. My dad was leaning his elbows on his knees, his hands folded. He looked at me, then down at his hands.

"There's no easy way to say it," she continued. "You were born with partially formed female reproductive organs. The doctors say they could become cancerous if they aren't surgically removed, and soon. It's a procedure called a *hysterectomy*."

All I heard was *cancer*. I could have *cancer*. My thoughts flashed like lightening. I could get cancer and die. Would it be soon? What if they take out everything and I still get cancer? Do they know for sure I don't already have cancer?

Hysterectomy. Removing all my reproductive organs. Then it hit me—if I didn't have reproductive organs, I would never have biological children. I would never be pregnant.

"Who's going to want to marry me?" I blurted. Tears streamed down my cheeks.

"Someone who loves you for you," my mother replied. I don't know if she had already planned what to say or not, but it came out so readily that at the time, I thought it must be the truth. And though it was the perfect thing to say in that moment, she followed up with, "Don't feel sorry for yourself. You have so much to be thankful for. Remember, it could be much worse—it's not like you're losing an arm or an eye."

My mom was giving her typical stoic New England waspy tough love again. She meant well. But what I heard was, "Grieving the loss of fertility and feeling sorry for yourself is not acceptable and will not be tolerated."

I had to be a good girl. In that moment, I began the process of burying my emotions. Bury the anguish of my heart. Bury the fact that I had taken for granted I would one day have biological children. Now, I had to reconcile myself to that fact before I even had a chance to process that I wouldn't, and that the reason was something beyond my control.

Don't feel sorry for yourself. Remember, it could be much worse. You have so much to be thankful for.

My mom hugged me, but I needed to get out of the sun and hide in my room where I could flop on my bed and sob to myself. I lay on my bed, looking up at my ceiling. My Laura Ashley wallpaper was entirely too cheery. Everything mocked my despair: the Steiff puppets I had collected and stuck atop each of my bed's four posts, the bulletin board over my bed tacked with pages ripped from magazines, photos of my friends and me, my varsity letter and pins, award ribbons.

Maybe I didn't really want kids, anyway. I'd never get to do what I wanted if I had kids. For the years of their infancy and toddlerhood, you're pretty much tethered to them. They're messy and expensive. There would be so much I could do if I didn't have kids.

Soon, I would become an expert at talking myself out of things I had once wanted but couldn't have.

I reached for the phone to call my neighbors. How could I babysit that night? I hung the phone back on the cradle. I was a good girl; I didn't cancel. I sat with the kids I used to enjoy. And I was miserable the entire time.

I never babysat ever again.

* * *

My surgery was scheduled, and soon I was back at Mass General, checking into a tiny private room in the cancer ward. Rick came with us. After babysitting, I had called Rick to tell him what the doctors had told me. He felt bad for me and was supportive, but we didn't spend much time discussing my condition or the ramifications of it. I was grateful when he offered to come to the hospital with us to help me get settled in the day before my surgery. My parents were staying at the Holiday Inn next to the hospital, and Rick would be taking the train that evening back home.

After checking in, Rick went with me to the lab and sat with me while the nurse drew blood. I squeezed his hand as we walked—a vice grip. This was the part I already knew I despised.

"Ah, here's the woman of the hour," the nurse said. "I'll be so quick—just a little blood so we can check your levels. We'll leave you plenty!"

I was fasting and hungry, and seeing the needle go in only made me more lightheaded than I was before. But the nurse was beyond friendly and considerate, and having Rick there made everything feel normal—I wasn't going through this in isolation. His presence also took off some of the pressure from my parents, who I'm sure were nervous wrecks.

Then, I received my plastic identification bracelet, and Rick kissed me goodbye. "I'll come back to see you soon, okay?"

I put on my hospital gown and climbed into the hospital bed, spinning my ID bracelet around my wrist. My parents had already bought flowers and a small mylar balloon to cheer me up.

"Everything's going to be fine," my mother said. One of the charge nurses then called her out to fill out additional paperwork. "I'll be right back, Zimmo."

Another nurse came in and smiled at me. "You have the best room in the house," she said. "Now, what are you in for today?"

"A hysterectomy," I said.

She chuckled and reached for the chart on my bed. "Oh no, honey, that isn't right, you must be confused."

At that moment, my mother reentered the room. "Excuse me," my mother said, in her most deep and serious mom voice, "can you please step outside with me for a moment?"

The nurse followed my mom into the hall, and my mom closed the door. All I could hear was my mom's voice, muffled but unmistakably angry. I couldn't imagine what the nurse had done to upset my mother so much. She had been friendly, even if she didn't seem to know why I was there. I reasoned that my mom probably didn't want me to have to answer any questions that might upset me before surgery. She and my dad had been doing everything they could to keep the mood light and cheery.

I was wheeled into the operating room the next morning. Though I was familiar with the routines, I was scared nonetheless.

"Dr. Morrow?" I asked in a rush of panic. "Could you try to stay inside my existing scar line? I just—I want to be sure I can still wear my bikini."

He laughed. "I promise I will, Kim."

The anesthesiologist placed the mask over my nose and mouth, and I realized this was it—I would wake up and not have reproductive organs.

"Count backwards from ten, now," the anesthesiologist said. *Ten.* I wouldn't ever be pregnant. *Nine.* Forever, something would have been taken out of my body. *Eight.* This was the "before" and "after" moment of my life…

* * *

I spent the next several days in the hospital recuperating. My parents had given me a brand-new yellow Sports Walkman to use for running, and I brought it with me to help the hours pass and dull out the hospital din. A few weeks before I was admitted for surgery, The Police released their album *Synchronicity*. Tara had had Rick drive her to the mall specifically to buy it for me as a gift before going into the hospital. I lost count of how many times I flipped over my cassette. When I was tired of watching bad TV, I listened to that album. Though I was restless for my friends, the tedium wasn't terrible, and I knew I would be out of the hospital in a few days. The worst parts were the frequent visits from the doctors. Most of these were residents, young doctors in training, usually two to five at a time, and almost all of them men. They proceeded with awkward enthusiasm to lift my bedsheets to "examine the surgeon's handiwork," while one of them recited details to the others with terms that made no sense to me. Nothing was explained to me about their visits, and I felt little more than a science experiment as they prodded me and discussed me as if I wasn't even there. For a teenager already self-conscious about her surgery and burying any ancillary trauma, this was mortifying. By the end of the second day, whenever I would see them coming in for teaching rounds, I learned to put on my headphones and play The Police, doing my best to ignore their investigations. While they were treating me like a specimen, I would be drifting off with Sting, Andy Summers, and Stewart Copeland, and soon be many miles away.

These young men in white coats would likely have been fully acquainted with my condition and procedure.

At my post-op consultation with my doctor, he explained that my condition was extremely rare. "There's nobody else like you in the world. Except, perhaps, some woman in Canada I once read about in a study."

Only one? Who was this woman in Canada? How could I talk to her? Did she know exactly what was wrong with her, why we developed the way we had?

"Now," the doctor continued, "there are other surgeries that we want to think about." He looked to my parents. "During surgery, we noticed your daughter's vagina has a blind-ended pouch. Very short. Too short to accommodate her future husband's penis. We could do another surgery to create a new vagina, using a skin graft from the buttocks to create a new vaginal canal.[1] Some results have been found using pig intestines, but it's better if it comes from the patient."

I heard the words, but somehow Dr. Morrow seemed so far away. So did my parents. I didn't hear what they said. *Blind-ended pouch?* What the hell did that mean?

Fortunately for me, my parents interceded at that point and nixed the idea. "She's been through a lot," I heard my mom say. While they may have been in the dark about a lot of things, when the doctor described the process of cutting skin from my butt to surgically construct a new vagina, they fully grasped the severity of the procedure and its likely toll on 16-year-old me.

"But it's something she can elect to do when she's older?" my mom asked. If I were to guess, a large part of their hesitation was that they were not ready to deal with the idea of their daughter having a vagina ready for penetrative sex.

"Oh, well, of course," Dr. Morrow said. "In the meantime, there is one other thing we can do," he added, sighing. He told me he would bring me a special device. I was struck with its banality—it resembled a plastic test tube, even with measurement lines on it. "What you want to do is insert this into yourself and push, as often as you can stand it, to stretch your vaginal canal."

Push down the emotions. Don't be emotional. Make things easy on your parents and the doctors. Be a good girl. "Do I…have to do this right now?"

"Oh no," Dr. Morrow said. "But start it in a few weeks, once you have recovered, and continue it regularly."

* * *

One day, Nancy, Monica, Lenore, Julie, and another couple of our friends took the train to the city to come visit me at the hospital. It felt so great to see them. They knew I had had some sort of "female" surgery to prevent cancer and that as a result, I would never menstruate or have biological kids. Like Rick, I'd told them what I was going through, and they were sympathetic, but since we never discussed my surgery on a deeper level, they blithely swept in as if I'd had a tonsillectomy or wisdom tooth removed. They asked me questions, how I was doing. Talking to them now, after it had happened, now that plan had become fact, only underscored how different I felt from the rest of them. They seemed as awkward as I felt. They switched the topic to fill me in on the summer gossip that I'd missed in the last few days, but only stayed for half an hour.

"Well, we'd better let you rest," they said, almost as if it was a code between them, a signal for them to leave. They told me they were taking advantage of the rare freedom to go hang out in the city. The hospital was in walking distance to Faneuil Hall Marketplace, a touristy area with shops and restaurants.

"Oh. Already? Okay, no problem."

My heart was heavy at their quick departure. They all got to go traipse around downtown Boston, and I was stuck in here, prodded multiple times a day, a childless and possibly loveless future ahead of me. No big deal.

After they were gone and I was alone in my hospital room, I couldn't help but question whether visiting me was their primary motivation for coming to the city. It was just as likely I was the excuse they gave to their parents to get permission to come hang out in the city. I couldn't blame them, exactly—I probably would have done the same thing. Still, that didn't stop the loneliness. Not only because I was in the hospital and they were cruising Faneuil Hall. I pressed play on Side B of my cassette, listening to Sting's voice on "King of Pain," plenty of circles turning in my brain.

CHAPTER 3

DISORDERLY CONDUCT

I sat on the edge of my bed, holding the medical dildo Dr. Morrow had given me. The plastic was cool and disconcerting. I inserted it and immediately it felt wrong.[1] I tried to push, and the sensation was pure awfulness. I cried, feeling like a freak. I rinsed it off and shoved it to the back of the bathroom drawer. My mother would occasionally ask if I had been using it, telling me, "Just give it a shot—it's what the doctors recommended. And it's better than surgery." But even her suggestion felt half-hearted. Rick hadn't had any problems, so why was I even trying to torture myself now? I'd told my surgeon I was sexually active—clearly, we had figured things out. Maybe that information was forgotten. Eventually, the horrible device was forgotten.

What wasn't forgotten was the woman in Canada who was like me. Someone else in the world had known what I was going through. There was no way for me to talk with her, at least not now, but I liked to imagine her, sometimes lying on her bed, imagining someone like her, or else she was exploring the world, or maybe even space, untethered by the constraints of motherhood, not having anyone tell her what to do, making a life for herself her own way. For brief moments, I felt not so alone. Afterward, however, I would think that I was the only person in the United States born this way, and I felt even more alone. I was a freak. Every day, these feeling raced through me, and I'd be able to talk myself up by thinking of all the opportunities ahead of me, but those highs would inevitably crash as I told myself how weird I must be, how miserable I was, how no one would love me, how every possibility I had envisioned for my future was now over. With no one to talk to about the complexities of my feelings, my depression, my loss, and being instructed not to feel sorry for myself, I pushed down everything. Soon, all feelings would learn to become suppressed.

What I also didn't understand was how I was affected by the hormones I was now required to take. Dr. Morrow prescribed birth control pills in order to provide my body with the right amounts of estrogen to do all the tasks they're famous for doing, such as keeping women's bones strong (thereby avoiding osteoporosis), keeping the vagina lubricated, and the moods steady.[2] My doctors now treated me as a post-menopausal woman.

I hated the pills, but I took them like a good girl despite the mortification of picking up my prescription every month in my small-town pharmacy, where everyone knew me. I was now "one of those girls" taking birth control, a scarlet letter on my chest, though I wasn't sure if it would be a *P* for "premarital sex" or *L* for "loose woman" (oh, the irony), or even a big *S* for "sexually active." Sex wasn't something that was ever addressed in my household. However, Rick and I continued to have sex.

The last weeks of summer were spent yearning for my senior year of school, where I could go from being a patient to being just Kim, high school student. I threw myself into my school work and college applications. I was on the National Honors Society, and I joined the yearbook committee and even the French Club. Since Rick played football, and Nancy and Monica were cheerleading co-captains, I joined the cheerleading squad that fall for my first and only season.

I was not a natural cheerleader, but I had a blast. My true love was still lacrosse, and I was named captain of our varsity team that spring. My schedule was packed, and I pushed myself to excel in each of my activities. Hindsight might say that the corresponding letter for this behavior should have been *O* for "overcompensating for feeling so different" or *D* for "desperately trying not to be a freak."

Indeed, I was the perfect girl, but that too felt false. Since my real feelings were buried down, I was left with a gnawing dissatisfaction of being known by everyone as the "perfect girl." My feelings couldn't be discussed at home or with friends—good New England wasps keep our private lives private. Between the pressures to succeed and the pressures to fit in, and the agony of not feeling like myself, I was nearing a self-reflexive standoff. Emotional duel at high noon.

So what *is* the appropriate response to buried pain and a frenzied masking? If you're response is to act out in subversive ways such as trying cocaine and shoplifting, you would be wrong, and yet that's exactly what I did. The cocaine was a one-off, which a friend had gotten from her older brother, and I only did it to do something bad. The shoplifting started off as an accident (I'm sure many criminal statements to police have begun the same way). But starting in the spring of my senior year, I worked part-time at a women's clothing and gift shop in our town. While working, the store would let employees wear the costume jewelry and other accessories to showcase the goods. A couple of times, I accidentally went home still wearing the jewelry. The next day at work, no one asked for it back. I hung onto the pieces, ready to say I'd completely forgotten but I could bring them right back—but that never happened. I realized how easy it was to repeat the process. I wore the jewelry home, not every day, but more than a few times, and I never returned any of it. I didn't need any of it. Being bad felt good, even if nobody knew about it. Especially because nobody knew about it. Being bad went against everyone's image of me as the good girl. I thrilled at the act of doing the opposite of what

Perfect Kim would do. Afterward, naturally, I was wracked with guilt. Confused. And then—I would shut off, as if numb. Thus I was back to diligent Kim, and I immersed myself in college applications.

My plan was to major in psychology. I applied for early decision at Bowdoin, a tiny liberal arts college in Maine, my dream school, but I didn't get in. Then, the acceptances came in: Colgate, Boston College, University of Vermont. My grandmother, my aunt, and other cousins lived near UVM's campus in Burlington. I loved the college town atmosphere, and it felt like the right place for me, so to Vermont I'd be headed in the fall, days after my 18th birthday.

Throughout this year, Rick and I continued our relationship. Prom was the perfect cap to my final year in high school. I wore a simple white strapless tea-length dress, with tiered layers from the waist down. Around my neck, I tied a pink ribbon in a bow as a choker. Perfect '80s femininity. A year earlier, I was recovering from surgery. This year, Rick and I were sneaking off after the dance to have sex—I felt a smug satisfaction toward Dr. Morrow and the other prodders making the rounds. My vagina worked just fine, no pig intestines necessary. That night, Rick and I went with Nancy and her date, a friend of Rick's, to Nancy's dad's house in Marblehead, right on the ocean. We had a wonderful night, tinged only somewhat by the impending separations once we all graduated. We would all be going to different schools. The separation would be hardest on Rick, who was planning to do a gap year at a private boarding school to get his grades up before applying to college.

After graduation, Nancy's mom rented a flat in London for the summer, and they invited me to come spend a week in July with them. However, just before my trip, my parents had gone into the trunk of my car for some reason, where they happened to find a lot of jewelry with tags still on, and they confronted me about it.

"What could you even be thinking?" my mom asked. I was so ashamed.

"Zimmo, you have everything you need," my dad said. "There's no reason to steal anything." The disappointment and confusion were all over their faces. I couldn't give them an answer to why I had shoplifted. My "I don't know" was frustrating for both them and me. They hit me with "Do we even know who you are?" and plenty of other well-deserved admonishments. I was shattered because they were so upset about it, and because even I hated myself for stealing.

"If this is who you are," my dad said, "I don't know if I want you going off to London. Maybe you've been taking too much for granted."

My mom agreed, and the trip was touch-and-go for a couple of days. I returned all the jewelry, never taking anything from there again. Eventually my parents agreed to let me go to London, though I carried the weight of their disappointment with me. Maybe I'd been carrying it around long before they found out.

London, though, felt like a turning point. I wanted it to be the beginning of all my fresh starts, finishing out high school and the trauma of my surgery and the hormones, and entering a future in which so much more would be based on what I wanted. And in hanging out with Nancy and her mom, I got to have plenty of the family feel with a parent who wasn't mine and who wasn't upset with me. We went to Wimbledon, saw Little Shop of Horrors in the West End, and hit a few of the other touristy sites. This was the first time I felt the freedom of adulthood. Nancy and I took the Tube on our own, going here and there, including to a night club to go dance. We were both of legal drinking age in England.

Back at home, I continued to work at the clothing store, though I'd gone straight, and my criminal life was over. Rick and I spent as much time together as possible, ramping up for my move to Vermont. When it was finally moving day, we packed up my parents' Jeep Grand Cherokee to the brim with my clothes and pillows and blankets and supplies for my dorm. Rick came to my house to say goodbye—it was tearful and gut-wrenching. My dorm, I'd learned, had one payphone at the end of the hall. We would send letters and have the occasional call once we'd learned our schedules, nailed down the timing. Each of us would have to be waiting at the payphone at a predetermined time. I didn't know the next time I would get to hear his voice. As the car pulled away, he stood waving in our driveway, while I waved through the back window. *XOXO*.

* * *

Move-in day, I met Derek. He was a sophomore and a lacrosse player from Connecticut. Within two weeks, we'd gone from chatting, to casual flirtation, to dating.

After moving into my room, another freshman girl in my dorm noticed my lacrosse stick and asked if I wanted to go outside and toss the ball around. So we went outside, and that's when I saw Derek —and he saw me. He introduced himself, using lacrosse as the instant connection point, and I introduced myself as "Kimberly," my full name, for the first time. I'd graduated with five other Kims in my class, and this was yet another change I was ready to make in my life.

Derek and I flirted a bit, and then we bumped into each other two days later at Red Rocks, a beach just beyond town on the shore of Lake Champlain, where a bunch of kids on my floor and I were taking advantage of the warm early September day. Derek and I ended up taking a walk and wound up sitting on a rock high above the water, talking for over an hour. That was the beginning of what would be a long-term relationship.

The problem was that I didn't officially break things off with Rick. On my trip home for Thanksgiving, Rick was also going to be home and was looking forward to seeing me for the first time since August. I had to break the news to him about Derek and me. We were watching a movie in my parents' finished basement, and he could sense my increasing distance and discomfort. I finally told him we needed to break up, and then things got intense, lots of crying, while he tried to figure out what went wrong, feeling guilty for being apart. He didn't want to accept it was over, but I knew in my heart it was the right thing to do, even though it was one of the hardest things I'd ever had to do. I was ready to move on. I was in college, and I was Kimberly now, not Kim. It's not as if I was a different person, but my life was refocused, and there was a freshness to that difference. I didn't have to challenge anyone's preconceived ideas about me—we were all at UVM to have some fun, study, and get a good job afterward.

Aside from the typical stress and occasional heartbreaks, college was a wonderful time in my life. After giving psychology a try, I settled on a double major in Political Science and Communications. Burlington is the quintessential college town, and in the early '80s, Vermont was one of the last states to still have the drinking age at 18. With no internet, no mobile phones, and with being over a three-hour drive away from home, I really was away from home, which gave me a sense of independence I'd never had before. Though high school was a great experience, I was happy to put that period of my life behind me, keeping my fond memories and staying in touch with my old friends through letters and the occasional phone call. I went through rush my freshman year and joined Alpha Chi Omega by the end of my first semester. Frat parties and weekend nights spent at the downtown bars became the norm, but I still managed to stay focused on schoolwork and maintained a 3.5 GPA throughout my four years. I didn't drink much or smoke pot, but because it was college in the '80s, I occasionally did cocaine—I liked the way it made me feel *über* alive. However, after graduation, I never touched the stuff again. In the fall of my junior year, Playboy came to campus to recruit female students to pose for photographs—all appointments were held in a local hotel room. I never even considered it, but I had friends who went. Several months later, leading up to my senior year, Playboy released its list of best party schools in the country, and UVM was ranked number 4, which seemed about right from my experience. The '80s were definitely a different time, and sometimes I look back on some of those frat parties and all I can do is cringe—they were as bad as one might imagine. If not worse.

By senior year, Derek and I had broken up, things running their course, and it was the first year of college that I was single. I made full use of that, having as much fun as I could, though I also worked part-time as a waitress at a popular bar downtown. So even if I was working on a Saturday night, I was around a lot of the kids I knew from school and never felt like I was missing out.

By the end of my senior year, I was determined to pursue a career in advertising, though I struggled to find a job after graduation. Stacey— one of my best friends from UVM—and I got a tiny apartment on Beacon Hill in Boston. We had no money and shared a bedroom. For six months, I worked as an assistant for the Sheraton Boston Hotel in sales and marketing. But that had not been the dream of my future throughout college.

One thing I couldn't escape, however, was the thought of my infertility. A few months after my graduation, one of my former classmates came to me in tears, asking if I could help support her as she got an abortion. Staunchly pro-choice, I didn't question her decision, yet it stung with a little irony that she would come to me when exercising her choice regarding her pregnancy. I would never be given a choice. I was not given a choice to remove my reproductive organs. There were many choices that were denied me.

What I could choose, needed to choose, was my next course of action. What did I really want to do with my life? Always looming was the idea of law school. Since I could afford to go, thanks to my father's generosity, I wanted to give law school a try. While studying for the LSATs and then applying to law schools, I found a job as a legal assistant, then as a paralegal, working for a solo practitioner who specialized in civil litigation. My first choice was Northeastern University in Boston because of their emphasis on social justice and public interest law, but once again, my first choice didn't accept my application. Disappointment was mitigated by being waitlisted at Boston College Law and admitted to Suffolk University Law School on Beacon Hill, which was where I decided to go. After 18 months of working in the field, and nearly two years after graduating from college, I began law school.

I found that I loved the law—the complexities of it. During the summer after my first year, I started clerking for an attorney who specialized in family building, which included the complexities of adoption and assisted reproduction technology such as IVF, egg donation, and surrogacy. Having been so focused on my situation, my body, and perhaps with a curious eye toward my own future, I was drawn to legal work involving infertility and how the abilities of science had been outpacing the law. The case law was new and developing with fascinating precedents and monumental rulings. So many people would be seeking expertise in this field. Maybe one day even I would.

PART II

THE NEW
WORLD

Reckoning with the Truth

I made dinner for Steven and my daughters. We talked about their day, about kindergarten, about schoolyard and stuffed animal politics. They both were in therapy for speech and language delays, and there always seemed to be a fight with the school district about services for children with special or additional needs. I had two meetings lined up in the next month, and my daughters' care was constantly on my mind. For whatever reason, I hadn't mentioned my doctor appointment to Steven beforehand. Mostly, I didn't want him to worry about me. Or to sound hysterical for worrying that I might have cancer if it turned out to be something trivial.

Male pseudo-hermaphrodite. Testicular feminization. What was inside of me? What had been taken out when they removed my testes?

"You okay, hon?" Steven asked me. "Still thinking about Thanksgiving?" Nothing bad had happened with my dad and Caroline that day, but the overall tension had worn me down, to the point where some days I felt like an eraser nub, or the cart grooves in a cobblestone street.

"I'm okay. Just tired."

"Are you still having the pain? Because if it's another hernia, you want to get that checked out by the doctor."

"It's—I'm okay."

"If you're worried it's cancer," he said, "which I'm sure it isn't, but you should get peace of mind."

I nodded. What was I supposed to say to my family? I didn't even understand what was wrong with me. I had a blood test scheduled, but when would I find out for sure? What would Steven think of me?

We cleared the table and washed up while my girls got ready for bed. I tucked them in, kissing each of them. I was so grateful for their smell, their softness. Was I still their *mother*? Was I a *wife*?

"You coming to bed?" Steven asked.

"I have to work on some photos for a client. I'll be up in a bit."

I climbed the stairs to my third floor—we had converted the attic to be my home office, where I ran my small business of taking photos of family and children, a new creative outlet I'd taken on in the last couple of years. I powered up my iMac and looked up the terms written on my medical records. The initial Google results were terrifying to me. There were images of mythical creatures known as hermaphrodites. There were drawings from medical books, some with up close sketches of body parts. There were photos of children's genitals. There were black and white photographs of naked children with black bars over their eyes to conceal their identities. There were links to horrible websites making derogatory comments about celebs who were really hermaphrodites, not so much outing as bashing people with no proof. This was the treatment of people who were like me? Was I like them? My head spun and I wanted to shut down the computer and bury my head in a pillow. Maybe I could forget this day happened. What if I could erase this?

Yet—I was curious. I was able to discover facts about myself, things that finally made sense. One link led me to a page that discussed Androgen Insensitivity Syndrome. The page explained what was previously referred to as testicular feminization. AIS occurs in babies born with testes and one X and one Y chromosome, the typical pattern in boys, though the body doesn't respond to or in some cases is immune to androgens such as testosterone. Babies' genitals don't diverge until after seven weeks in utero, after which testosterone kicks in to form the penis and testes, and in girls, ovaries appear between 11 and 12 weeks. The penis and clitoris are roughly the same for the first 14 weeks, until the penis lengthens and the testes descend. However, this process is triggered by the Y chromosome, which releases testosterone into the male body. Partial AIS may lead to incomplete formation of the penis and testicles, or they may have genital ambiguity. With Complete Androgen Insensitivity Syndrome, the body has no response at all to the testosterone and appears typically female—except for a typically shallow or non-existent vagina. So many parts of my story were crashing on top of me, like storm waters preceding a hurricane.

So there were levels of AIS/CAIS. That meant there was likely more than just one other woman in Canada somewhere, as my surgeon had so cavalierly referred to her.

I did a deeper search into AIS. Since testes do make some estrogen, and the body can turn androgens into estrogen, children with AIS may have female development from their own hormones.

This sounded...familiar.

Then I read about surgical removal of the testes, known as a gona-dectomy, and how it was recommended for people with AIS because of a potential risk of cancer developing in the testes. However, the risk of cancer development before puberty in CAIS is actually very low, and more than one progressive doctor was now advocating leaving the testes in place for a more natural puberty.

Wait. I was almost breathless. I had been lied to? My testes had been perfectly healthy, at least according to the surgical records. Why had this happened?

Soon, I discovered an online group called the AIS Support Group for Women and Families.[1] A support *group*. For *people*. *Plural*. I read stories that sounded like mine. There were actually women out there like me. I devoured these stories. Some of these were shocking, far more than my own, although I was still raw from the discovery. But this was a light, a beacon.

The AIS Support Group also had a private electronic mailing list group[2] solely for women with AIS. There was a form to sign up for the group, and I entered my information. As part of the vetting process to be admitted to the group, I would be interviewed on the phone by someone in the organization to be sure I was authentic and not a poser or a troll. I was aware of how these groups were set up, as I was already part of several Listserv-type groups for adoption and adoption from China, which had been particularly helpful during our process of adopting our twin girls seven years earlier. I set up an appointment for the phone call a couple of days later.

I spent most of the next day online, hunting for stories of people with CAIS and similar conditions. There were other conditions that were also once classified as "hermaphroditic," though the term was now considered derogatory. So many people had gone through surgeries that had left them in pain, deformed, had changed their lives, and had been done without their consent. This was almost too much to bear.

The dissociation began to set in. Those first couple of days have black patches around them. It had been happening for years, now. Steven and I would have an argument, I would withdraw, and five minutes later, I wouldn't even remember the subject of our argument—I only had the feeling of mutual anger and that whatever had happened had been bad. I couldn't remember the first moments I met Alexandra and Charlotte in the orphanage. I couldn't remember Steven proposing to me on bended knee in the Boston Public Garden. If there had been a rise in stress or adrenaline, negative or positive—it didn't seem to matter—I withdrew and blocked my consciousness.

But there are flashes. There was anger at having been lied to by my doctors and possibly even by my parents. How could my parents not have known? Is that why my mother had gotten angry with the nurse the day of my surgery?

There was fear at what my family would think of me. Feeling like I had spent much of my life as a fraud, and now I was somehow responsible for the ultimate con job—posing as a woman when really I was...what *was* I?

Two weeks after the initial discovery, my clandestine blood test revealed that my chromosomes were in fact 46, XY. I had what the medical community referred to as a "disorder of sex development." It was real now, as if I needed the blood test to confirm what I knew in my heart. It was time to talk to Steven, but the shock of the discovery still needed to settle. I was afraid of what he would say, what he would think, but I couldn't spend much more time alone in this knowledge. I trusted Steven and needed him desperately to help me navigate this. He came home and I told him, "I have something I need to tell you. I did go to see Dr. Bingley."

"Are you okay? What is it?"

"I found out something. Something that I didn't know until Dr. Bingley gave me my records. You know how I had surgery when I was 15? Well it turns out that wasn't a hysterectomy." I took a deep breath. "I have XY sex chromosomes. What the doctors removed were internal testes. All this time, I had no idea." My tears burned while I waited for a response. I hated every one of those doctors.

Steven hugged me. He remained calm. "Well," he said after a pause, "that doesn't change anything. You are still you."

His response was lovely. It's what most people want to hear. I needed to hear it. But what I wanted in that moment was for him to be as upset as I was, that this discovery was a huge deal.

"So that's it?" I snapped. "This is a huge part of my identity and it's been hidden from me by doctors for my entire life!"

"I know, that's terrible. But that doesn't change how I feel about you." Steven was doing his best to be a calming, stable presence, and I knew it was for my benefit. He was showing me he loved me regardless. The poor guy couldn't win.

"We don't even know what this means for us, legally!" The lawyer in me started to take over. Also, the hurting Kimberly pushed hard for a reaction. I wanted him to feel my hurt and my fear, and he didn't. "Do you realize that some people would consider us in an illegal gay marriage?" It was a fear that was newly swirling inside my brain, but this was the first time I had given voice to it. My whole life could be ripped apart because of this. Maybe that's why Dr. Bingley wanted to send me away for the blood test. Would I be declared a man?

"There's a lot to figure out and digest, I know," Steven said, still trying to calm me down. Ultimately, he gave me my space and tried his best to be supportive as I careened on my emotional roller coaster. Which continued for a couple of weeks.

I needed more help.

When it was time for my vetting call for the support group, I was contacted by the president at the time, Mandy. "Thank you for your interest," she said. "You can imagine that we have to take our members' safety and privacy very seriously. Many of our members are, for the time being, keeping their AIS a secret."

"Of course, absolutely," I said.

Mandy and I started with a simple chat—I'm sure she could tell I was nervous. She and I were about the same age, and she lived in another nearby New England state. I told her about my recent discovery, about my past surgeries. I told her how alone I had felt then, and how freaked out I was now, and upset at my husband's nice-but-too-relaxed reaction. And then something almost magical happened. Mandy shared with me her story, and how it was so similar to mine, and how her emotional responses had been the same. I was not singular in my struggles. As I listened to her speak, I realized that this was the first time I was knowingly speaking to another intersex person—someone like me. Maybe I had spoken to one and hadn't realized it. But now, I was finally talking to someone who knew how I felt. For the first time in my entire life. She wasn't a lone unicorn or yeti off in Canada.

After my conversation with Mandy, I was added into the group. I didn't post right away, but I read through every email I could. My conversation with Mandy, and now being part of a group—even if I was still on the periphery—gave me the courage to talk about having AIS to Leslie, my therapist. I'd been seeing her the three years since my parents split up, since we had all discovered that my dad had been living a secret life that included affairs. Leslie had been great to me. I came to my appointment armed with information printed off the internet from the AIS Support Group.

"You know, like a hermaphrodite, but not really," I said. And then I sat there in disbelief—such a term was now applied to me? I already hated that word.

"Wow," she said. "This is incredible. First, I'm so sorry this happened to you and you had to discover the truth in this way."

"You know, it sucks that it happened this way, but then—it makes sense. My whole life, I knew there was something different about me. This explains it. It's like I'm validated now, knowing there was something more than what I was being told."

"I'm impressed with how well you're handling the news."

"Honestly, it varies by the hour. But thanks. Yeah, I'm angry, and I'm feeling it, but I'm also relieved. I'm both things." Like being Kimberly, an XY woman. Yeah—exactly like that.

My hands shook a little as I handed Leslie the information from the support group.

"Thank you for bringing in this information. The truth is that I've never heard the terms 'AIS' or 'disorder of sex development' before. But I will learn all I can about this so you can get the support you need. There is still going to be so much to navigate as you continue to learn more."

I was so relieved to have her, someone who already knew me so well before this information bomb was dropped on my life.

"Do you think my parents knew all this time and didn't tell me?" I asked.

"You won't know until you talk to them. And even then, you may not know for sure."

"My father signed the medical consent form."

"And so did you. Maybe they are in the dark about this. Maybe they should have asked more questions. Until you talk to them, though, it's only conjecture. But do it when you are ready. There's no rush—you are in control now."

* * *

My first call that day was to my mom down in Florida. "So, I recently saw my medical records for the first time." I was in a hurry to get it all out. My hand shook as it held my phone. "I found out I did not have a hysterectomy. They removed testes. And I took a test and I have XY chromosomes. I have something called AIS." And then I asked her point blank, "Did you know this? Did you keep this a secret from me?"

"No, Sweetie—I remember being told you had partially formed

reproductive organs that would become cancerous if left inside, and they had to be removed surgically ASAP." Her voice was calm. She didn't seem as shocked as I was and not nearly angry enough.

"So you didn't know or didn't suspect?"

"Nothing. Not at all. But you know, this doesn't change anything. You are still you."

What was wrong with everyone? Why weren't they as shocked and outraged? My call with my dad didn't go much better.

"I swear, Kimberly, I didn't know anything other than they said your organs were partially formed."

"And they never said which organs?"

"It was a long time ago. They said they were giving you a hysterectomy."

"But how could they do this? You weren't given full knowledge of what was being done, so how could you possibly consent to it? That's illegal!"

"Things were different back then. That's the only thing I can think of. But you know your mother and I were doing what we thought was best for you, right?"

How was this not turning their world upside down? This should be their discovery as much as it was mine. Both of my parents denied knowledge of my testes, my gonadectomy. Neither of my parents seemed shocked. They didn't express anger. Would they lie to me, even now? I wanted so much to be able to trust them and believe they knew nothing, but I couldn't shake the feeling they'd known more than they were letting on. Plus, I now knew my father was an expert at keeping secrets.

Tara was equally shocked when I told her over the phone, but she gave me total support. "I love you so much, Sissy."

"I can't believe it, though. And I can't shake the feeling that Mom and Dad knew more than they were letting on."

"Well I don't know anything about that," Tara said. "But I remember vividly when you had your surgery back then. Mom and Dad were upset—especially Mom. I didn't tell you this, but the day you went into the hospital, I saw a flask in Mom's purse."

"What? Our mother?"

"That's what I mean. Our mother was freaked out. She seemed really worried about you."

I'd never seen our mom do anything like that before.

"And of course this sounds so stupid now," Tara continued, "but during that time, I actually got a little jealous of you. The weeks leading up to your surgery, and then through your recovery, Mom and Dad were doting on you. No matter what, you could do no wrong. And I was kind of mad because I guess I felt a little neglected.[3] I feel a little bad about that part."

"Oh my gosh, you shouldn't. I get it."

Tara was quiet before asking, "So what next?"

"I still have to have a friggin' hernia operation! Next week. Fortunately, it'll be outpatient." But it was just adding insult to injury—another surgery.

* * *

I made it through my third hernia operation and the holidays. My mom came up from Florida and stayed with my sister, but she also stayed with me for a couple of days to help out and spend time with my daughters.

In the meantime, I found I was ready to tell my best friend, Ellen. We'd met four years earlier at the playground when our kids were in preschool. Our houses weren't far away, and we talked nearly every day. Ellen was a person I could trust to be accepting and understanding. This was rare for me. My Boston suburb was small, very homogenously Irish Catholic, well off, and they valued keeping things the same, orderly, without change or disruption. Though I had several good "mom friends," I still didn't feel like I ever fit in. Certainly, it had been a challenge with my daughters being adopted twins from China. I had just been named the head of the Special Education Parent Advocacy Committee because I had to fight to get my girls any of the special services owed them by the school. I ruffled feathers now and again. Could this community accept me *now*, with *this* news? Ellen was the only one I even wanted to tell, at least for now.

She came over to my house and we were having coffee. She was sitting at my kitchen counter, and I stood across from her, tapping at my cup, until

I finally spilled everything I'd found out, while she sat there, open-mouthed and riveted. The act of saying I had AIS, a disorder of sex development, was still new, almost foreign. I'd told Steven, my sister, and my parents, plus Leslie, but each iteration was a new struggle. When I finally got the words out, Ellen hugged me. "I can't believe no one told you!" She was incredulous. "How are you doing, are you okay?" She took turns railing against the medical community, saying there needed to be some kind of litigation, and making sure I was really okay. It was exactly the reaction I had been craving. She recognized what a big deal this was. "This has to be life-changing for you."

"It is. It does explain so much, though—and it validates my feelings of being different when I was growing up."

I upped my appointments with Leslie so that I could get a handle on my emotions on a weekly basis. The new discovery was causing me to dig up other things about myself, the way I reacted in certain situations, as well as my relationships with my parents, and it was overwhelming. For several weeks after my discovery, I saw Leslie twice a week, driving 45 minutes each way into Brookline to her brownstone office on Beacon Street. It was a big time commitment, but I needed to be able to re-examine everything I'd previously thought and understood about myself and my parents with this new information. My appointments were always in the middle of the school day, while the girls were at school, as I didn't want them to know anything was wrong. They'd been making such good progress on their development, and I was aware of the potential effects learning about my trauma could have on them. Their mother couldn't fall apart on them.

While looking through my old scrapbooks and photo albums from my high school era, just to see what I had, I came across my plastic hospital bracelet from my gonadectomy. I had totally forgotten I had kept it as a memento. With it was a picture from my stay, of me in my private hospital room, surrounded by flowers and balloons. My smile is like a homecoming queen smile. If you didn't see the hospital bed and equipment on the periphery, you'd think this photo was taken in a lovely home during a celebration. I had forgotten the detail of the fireplace that was in my hospital room. Several years later, I asked my dad why I would have had a hospital room with a fireplace of all things. He told me it had been a renovated wing of the old hospital, reserved for VIPs.

"I was doing very well in the '80s," he said. "We could afford it, and I wanted to make the experience as easy as possible for you."

I distrusted everything—had he felt guilty, and that's why? Or was he just trying to compensate because his daughter had to have what he thought was a hysterectomy and would never have biological children? This girl in this picture seemed like some other me in a distant lifetime. Pieces of her body had been taken away in a fiction that had been made up for her.

There was so much to wrap my head around, and I could feel the disconnecting flutter somewhere inside me, flickering like black hole that wanted to suck up everything, me included. I could picture it there, in the space vacated by my former testes.

I rushed back to my computer, to the search engines, to the AIS-DSD Support Group. There, I found a link to an old episode of Oprah, called "Growing up Intersex." There was an interview with three people who fell under the umbrella term "intersex." Two identified as women, although one had been forced to spend her first 30 years as a man when she never felt like a man. A third didn't identify as either, although Oprah used the pronoun "her"—even though they felt equal parts male and female. Only the first guest had CAIS, like me—Katie. There was even a photo of her in a majorette uniform, which reminded me of pictures of myself in my cheerleading uniform. I felt an instant kinship with Katie. She was young and about to start medical school. She'd grown up upper-middle class. And she was born with Complete Androgen Insensitivity. Her mother, Dr. Arlene Baratz, was also interviewed and seemed so warm and intelligent. So poised on camera for someone whose daughter was being asked to describe her genitalia on national television. While I was taken aback at Oprah asking Katie the intimate details of her biology, thinking of all the giddy, eager doctors prodding at me like a zoological experiment, and the awful plastic test tube dilator, I listened to Katie's words as if they had been my story. She had been told at a young age what her condition was. She had doctors who were understanding and parents who were in the medical profession and understood not to put their daughter through surgery if not medically necessary. Katie then decided when she was 18 that she wanted to remove her testes. I imagined that as my story, what might have been if I had grown up with her experience.

It would be so easy to fall into the pity trap, the *poor me/why me* cycle. At the end of the episode, the person who identified as both genders was grateful that no operation had been performed, no sex modified to fit a gender and wouldn't want to be "a regular woman" if someone paid them. The assertion, the confidence of that assertion, was radical to me. These advocates were blazing a trail for the rest of us, and to hear on the show a declaration of being happy to be intersex blew my mind. More importantly, was there a future for me in which *I* would be happy to say I was intersex? I tried to imagine being an open intersex woman in my family, growing up. I couldn't actually picture my parents explaining my condition to people outside the family. Even inside the family would be a stretch. I pictured my mother telling me to just be strong and not let it affect me. And, as I did, I couldn't help but feel the creep of doubt settle over me—how was it possible my parents didn't know I had testes? How could the doctors legally not tell them?

This was the struggle I'd had for years, maybe even my whole conscious life—as if no one really knew me. Certainly the real me. Had it been all along that I didn't feel like I was a real girl? I kept so much of my personality secret—the shoplifting, the drugs, my romantic life. I'd kept plenty hidden away from myself, knowing parts of myself were lurking in the depths but in a place I didn't have to see them. But this, testes, AIS—there were parts of me even I hadn't known. The real Kimberly was a complete stranger. Maybe she didn't even exist.

CHAPTER 4

SETTING A COURSE

I liked law school. I was good at the coursework. Or, at least, I was fully engaged by it; the ways in which it provided structure and routine, and the way studying law required informed interpretation and translation. How definitive, how important, and still how fragile the whole idea of a rule of law was. Clerking helped me see the real-world importance of the work, and I knew if I wanted a life in which I could actually help people, do some good in the world, the law seemed to be the best field to lay a solid foundation on which to do this good.

Was it the best time of my life? In terms of stress-free entertainment, no. But I was inspired every day. The work was hard, the hours long, but I'm pretty sure I can say that I enjoyed it. One thing that helped me in this time was that Tara and I moved into an apartment together on Beacon Hill; this time each of us had our own rooms. The casualness of living again with family, even if we were both quietly studying, or passing each other in the kitchen, provided a great source of stability and comfort. I never felt alone.

I also had made good friends from law school. Nancy, Debbie, Jen and I had formed a study group the first few weeks of class, and we stayed together well into our second year. Nancy rented an apartment near the school, and we spent a great deal of time together those three years, studying and socializing, and we got pretty close.

One of the benefits of being in Boston was that I was close to my friend Julie from high school. She'd gone to Boston College, where she met her husband, Dan. Every year since graduating in 1988, they had been throwing an annual St. Patrick's Day party. I had never attended before. Though the party was going to be held at the Lenox Hotel, walking distance from my apartment, I was in head-down study mode. There was no way I could make it.

"Please, it's *one* night!" Julie said. "You never come, and I haven't seen you in ages."

"It's just that I'm in the middle of studying for an exam and have a paper due to boot."

"Okay, I understand. It's just that I *really* want you to come. Besides, there will be food, you can take a doggie bag home and then you won't have to cook for a couple of days—coming will actually save you time, in the long run. And if you come, you won't have to feel like you're missing out, which may actually distract you from your studying. Besides, you can walk here from your apartment in under fifteen minutes."

She wasn't wrong. Since the party was on a Saturday, five days after St. Patrick's Day, I would have all of Sunday to recover. Still, I was reluctant as I got dressed in absolutely no green whatsoever, instead choosing a black top and short black skirt and tights. I put on jewelry. I hadn't been out in weeks, so if I was skipping a night of studying, I was going to make it count. I met Julie and a few of her girlfriends from Boston College at the hotel. They'd rented out the ballroom, and already the room was filling up.

"Beer or whiskey?" Julie asked me.

"I'm not getting hungover. I have a full study day tomorrow."

She handed me a mediocre beer. We made the rounds of the room,

Julie introducing me to people, but I didn't know anyone except her. "I'm not going to stay too long, Julie."

"Oh, here, meet Kate. You'll like her." Kate was also from Boston College, as was her boyfriend. Her boyfriend brought his roommate, who shared an apartment in Hoboken.

"I'm Steven—I'm Eugene and Kate's third wheel."

Steven was funny, and as his roommate Eugene and Kate moved to other corners of the party, Steven and I found ourselves in a huddle discussing the sartorial awfulness on display, as well as atrocious dancing by awkward young professionals who were getting drunk on probably-watered-down whiskey and bottles of Guinness and Killian's Irish Red.

"Hey, want to get out, go for a walk?" Steven asked.

We talked about law school and work as we walked down Boylston Street, then ducked into the Cactus Club for a drink. We talked about our families, and Steven was quick with humor, but not in an obnoxious, forced way. His humor came organically, and so did my laughter. We kept leaning close, daring physical contact. Once it happened—either our shoulders touching as we sat next to each other at the bar or maybe it was our knees first—that was it, we didn't have to pretend or feign indifference. There was no reason to shy away. It was late, and we made the required statement that it was time to maybe probably head home. Steven was staying with friends at an apartment in Charlestown, and my apartment was a few blocks away.

"I'll walk you, then," Steven said.

We headed to West Cedar Street. The casual touching became handholding. And then, because so much had already been random and surprising about this night and because we were both feeling the warm and fuzzy effects of a little too much alcohol and because we didn't really want the night to end, when we found ourselves in front of an all-night Copy Cop print shop and copy center, we decided to go in to make a photocopy of our hands. We held hands, and closed the lid, which didn't close with our hands locked together, and we tried not to giggle too much and attract the attention of a tired and snotty clerk. We each got a copy and folded the papers into our pockets. After we left, we cut through the Boston Public Gardens. We meandered, taking in the cool spring night. Near a row of benches, Steven pulled me aside.

"Can I kiss you?" he asked.

Yes. Yes, absolutely, yes.

That was our first kiss, on the night we met at a party we were both talked into attending.

CHAPTER 5

IMPOSTER
IN THE MIRROR

Steven and I were in the throes of coupledom, though we had a me-dium-distance relationship between Boston and New York City via Amtrak. I really liked him, and I didn't want there to be secrets. I had an inkling the relationship might progress, but my biggest fear was: *Would he cut and run when he found out I couldn't have biological children?*

I was back to being 15 again. *Who will want to marry me?* I hadn't let this bother me too much until now. My mother's voice replayed that it would be someone who loves me for me. I would casually mention my surgery to Steven to see his reaction. He might shrug and then pull away, he might say that's fine and then the relationship runs its course, he might say he could never get involved with someone who couldn't produce his spawn—regardless, it was better to know, for him and for me.

As it happened, the topic of birth control came up in conversation, related to some news event. "At least that's a particular area I don't have to worry about," I said. I took a shaky breath. "I had to have a hysterectomy when I was a teenager. Partially formed organs, they said. So, I guess, you know—lucky me." Perhaps I said that part as a question. I let it hang in the air before qualifying it. "But it means I can't have biological children."

"Oh, wow," Steven said. "Well, you know, I'm adopted. Having biological kids really isn't that important to me." Like that, we were past it. Intense relief. The flutter of excitement—it was unspoken, but a future together hadn't been ruled out. I was in a world where I could be loved for me.

Meanwhile, the weight and pressure of law school kept me busy and exhausted. There were plenty of impediments to the blissful stage of puppy love, and we both got tense. I didn't always communicate how I was feeling. I was pretty far on the needle to Type A[1] and focused on graduating law school and taking the bar, not to mention worried about finding a job afterward. Steven could be intense himself, though unlike me, he grew up in a family environment where everyone wore their emotions on their sleeves. He was used to communicating everything, letting his feelings show, and working through them in the open.

I'd never gotten into arguments before. My parents never argued about anything directly and, if they fought, it certainly wasn't in front of Tara or me. Also, I had the great emotional excavator with which I could dig enormous holes to bury my feelings. It was so much easier to do that than to ever engage in conflict. I would probably dig through metamorphic rock with a soupspoon before diving into an argument.

One night, the topic of weekend plans with some of my friends came up. He was upset because I had made plans that didn't include him, and he had assumed we'd be doing something together alone that upcoming Saturday night. I didn't know what to say as his agitation and voice both rose, but I didn't like it.

"Friggin' calm down," I said. Then, there was a feeling. My head pounded from my blood rush of anxiety, and then there was a dark, murky dread that settled inside of me. I was tired, fuzzy, upset. There was only that feeling.

"Please don't walk away from me like that."

"What?" I looked up at Steven. I was in another room, but I don't remember getting here. I had the awful feeling that I was just in a fight—I was grinding my teeth and sweating—but I couldn't remember about what.

He registered the confusion and shock on my face. "What is it?"

"I don't—I can't remember. Wait, what were you just saying?"

"Well, you were just explaining how I was an unreasonable jerk and should calm down."

"What? I never said that." Was I talking at all?

"You sure did."

"But—I don't remember anything." I couldn't remember a thing, other than feeling the anger. I started shaking.

This pattern would be repeated. During an argument, I would forget what we were arguing about, leave the room, and retreat. I would be conscious of the fact that we were having a negative experience, that I was upset, but I couldn't for the life of me remember the subject of the argument. I was blacking out and it scared me. I was not in control of my body, what I was doing, how I was reacting. Being 26, this was beyond alarming.

Eventually, I learned I was suffering from dissociative disorder,[2] known to be a coping mechanism. Whenever I experienced a strong emotional reaction to something, my mind couldn't cope with "feeling" the strong emotion and would dissociate. Any feeling, high or low, would trigger a blackout mode.

It was terrible.

The blackouts were carving out big, important slices of my life. This wasn't true only of the negative experiences, either.

Six months after meeting, on a Friday evening in September, Steven rode the Amtrak from New York for the weekend. When he arrived that evening, I was studying, nursing a cold, and curled up in sweatpants and a T-shirt over my law textbook. I wasn't feeling great at all, though I was happy to see him. Steven, however, was antsy. "I really need to take a walk after sitting on the train for so long."

"I don't want to go anywhere." My trash was spilling over with damp, wadded tissues.

"No, but I think it will be good for you to get out, nothing vigorous. You know how a little movement boosts endorphins, and that helps you heal faster."

I wasn't sure that I bought that reasoning, but I could tell that Steven wasn't going to let up until I got out for at least a short jaunt. I grabbed my coat, and we walked down Charles Street to the end, crossed over to Beacon, to the entrance to the Public Garden. He asked me if I remembered our first walk there, and of course I did—the night we met. There was a soft breeze, and the leaves rustled as we made our way to the row of benches where we had our first kiss. Steven's voice caught as he was saying something about that night. My heart swelled, I had butterflies, I was kissing Steven, we were smiling and laughing—*what had just happened?*

There was a ring on my finger. I was engaged. I had said yes and was celebrating. I felt love and gratitude. My body had a physiological response to the news, to the intense emotions, yet I was unaware of what had taken place.[3] How could it be possible that I was interacting with Steven, seeming conscious to him, and yet have no recollection of the proposal? I was scared and disappointed. This should be a happy memory, and it was not in my brain.

Later, I listened intently as Steven recounted the details to Tara, then to our parents over the phone. He got down on one knee, pulled the diamond ring out of his coat pocket, I said yes. I know the words and can tell the story, but I still have no memory of this event. Steven had no clue I had no memory of it, that I hadn't experienced it. I didn't tell him, either. I asked him to tell me the story again. "I like hearing you tell it," I said. It was true—though I was bothered by the hole, the absence of this memory, this was an important story to me. Now, in Steven's retelling, I could experience it, at least peripherally.

Was this the first time I had experienced emotions this acutely? Had Steven brought out a strong emotional reaction in me, for the first time ever? If so, I certainly didn't have the equipment, or at least, the equipment had rusted through. I'd spent my entire life tempering my feelings, instructed to do so. Steven felt things, he reacted, and this relationship was almost like a permission to feel—unfortunately, my consciousness couldn't cope.

As I grew detached from my strong emotions, a new emotion surfaced. I was preparing to graduate law school, with honors. One day I told Steven, "I feel like a fake."

"What do you mean? You have worked your butt off for this."

I couldn't fully explain, but it was as if I didn't really deserve it. It didn't feel like I was the one who had achieved this, and that Kimberly had somehow fooled everyone into giving this degree, conferring the honors. I looked in the mirror and saw an imposter. Law degree? Honors? Who would have thought I'd be a lawyer? How did I fool everyone? No, I didn't yet know to call it Imposter Syndrome,[4] but it lodged itself deep in my psyche.

CHAPTER 6

LAYERS OF SECRETS

The year I turned 27, I graduated from law school, studied for and took the Massachusetts bar exam, and I married Steven. Shortly before the wedding, I had my final "mandatory" follow-up appointment with my surgeon at Mass General, the doctor who had removed my reproductive organs just over a decade earlier. He tested my abdomen, asked a few rote questions: how I was feeling, was sex working out okay, was I taking my hormones? Before I left his office for what would be the last time I ever saw him, Dr. Morrow asked if I would like a referral to a good primary care doctor in the Boston area. "Since you're getting married and are starting a job in the area." He meant *settling down*. "Here, go see Dr. Lydia Bingley. It will be good to set up an introductory appointment with her soon, and I can forward along your information to keep her in the loop."

That sounded good. Dr. Morrow was being thorough. Okay, I thought.

Steven and I got married over Labor Day weekend. Since so many of our guests, especially his side of the family, would be coming from out of state, we chose to get married at the Andover Inn, on the campus of Phillips Academy in Andover, which could accommodate many of our 90 guests, who could then come downstairs from their rooms and not have to worry about commuting around town. Steven had been raised Jewish, and I was agnostic about the whole thing, so to appease his family we found an ultra-progressive rabbi to marry us outside in the backyard of the inn. I arranged for us to be married under a traditional chuppah—a white wooden lattice archway, completely adorned with white roses. The ceremony was late Sunday morning, and our guests sat in chairs lined on each side of the aisle. Though it rained through the early morning, an hour before our ceremony the sun peeked out from behind the clouds. At the end of the ceremony, I'd chosen to include the Jewish tradition of breaking the glass, though I wanted a twist—instead of just the groom stepping on a glass, I wanted us both to break it together. After we each stomped on the light bulb wrapped in a dishtowel, we kissed and walked back down the aisle among our friends, and into our brunch reception with live jazz. When the party was over, Steven and I changed out of our wedding clothes and departed in an old-fashioned car for the Boston Harbor Hotel, where we'd be staying the night before flying to Bermuda for our honeymoon. The Giants were playing that night—Steven's favorite football team—so the game was on in our honeymoon suite. We were both so tired that we literally crashed.

We arrived in Bermuda the next evening just in time for the beginning of hurricane season. We got more than our fair share of rain, and our large resort lost power one day. Then, Steven came down with a cold. The hotel, the staff, the ambiance, Bermuda were all lovely, but for a honeymoon, we were pretty tame. A highlight, though, was riding on the back of a moped while Steven navigated the winding Bermuda roads, the both of us laughing as we got drenched in a sudden rainstorm. When it was time to go home, I cried in the cab. "I promise we'll come back," Steven said. "Maybe for our 5th anniversary."

He's given me endless gifts and memories over the years, but we have yet to return to Bermuda. Maybe for our 30th.

* * *

Not long after the wedding, I had my first appointment with Dr. Lydia Bingley. "So what do you know about your medical history?" she asked.

"Well, I had a complete hysterectomy my junior year of high school. I hadn't gotten my period, and Dr. Morrow said my ovaries were partially formed and needed to be removed or they could become cancerous. I'm still always a little afraid of getting cancer, I guess." It was true—*cancer* was a word that loomed over my life. My body in some ways felt like a ticking time bomb, although I didn't say that to Dr. Bingley. "Other than that, I also had two hernia surgeries. Double inguinal hernia."

"Okay, yes. I saw that all on your medical records. Regarding your hysterectomy, you're what we call '*über* feminine.' I read a case study about a Miss America back in the '50s who was like you."

I waited for her to elaborate on the Miss America, but she didn't. I thought there was only a woman in Canada like me? Did a Miss America move to Canada? *Über feminine*. What did that even mean? Had she said anything else? I sensed there might have been more, but I think I did what I often did and emotionally checked out of the conversation.

Dr. Bingley had my full medical records back then. Almost 15 years before she handed over my records to me, she, Dr. Bingley, my primary care doctor, had read my records and then asked me what I knew. She has since explained that she "tried to tell me" the truth, but according to her, it was clear I wasn't ready to hear it. "It was like you were covering your ears and tightly shutting your eyes, repeating *unicorns and rainbows* over and over to block out something you didn't want to hear."

But from my perspective: when she realized that I had been told a lie, she then made the decision to continue to keep the truth from me.

* * *

After graduation, I got a job working for the Joint Committee on Health Care at the Massachusetts Legislature. I had interviewed for the staff position while studying for the bar and was offered the job a few weeks before my wedding. My start date was the day after we got back from our honeymoon.

My job was to become a bit of an expert on issues that came before the committee that related to reproductive health, children's health, and eventually also long-term care. I had to be prepared to advise the House and Senate Committee members as they were considering the bills before them. It was a wonderful introduction into the world of legislative policy and the ins and outs of how things get done (or sometimes don't get done) inside the statehouse.

On my lunch breaks, I would often walk to a nearby soup and salad café, and then I'd walk through a couple of the nearby shops in Downtown Crossing. I liked perusing Buck a Book, a discount bookstore filled with discounted and overstocked books. One day in the late fall, I came across a random book on genetic defects. Why I picked it up, I don't know; or, at least, it was not a conscious thought to pick up a book and perhaps find evidence of *über* femininity, or of girls with partially formed ovaries who either lived in Canada or became Miss America. The book wasn't even explicitly on disorders of sex development—it was a curiosity. However, as I flipped through, I landed on a chapter on what was called *Types of Hermaphroditism*. Headings in bold such as *Pathology of Sexual Differentiation and Hypospadias* and *Incomplete Labioscrotal Fusion*. A picture of a man below the phrase *Klinefelter Syndrome*. I closed the book, overcome with a sensation of horror. Beyond feeling intrusive of other people's intimate details, I felt something else more disquieting, though I couldn't put a name to it. Instead, I blocked it out. The book was weird and shocking—that was all. Didn't apply to me in any way.

Again and again, my subconscious went to great lengths in order to suppress any deeper thinking of my history, who I was, what was done to me. A decade after closing the book on disorders of sex development, I read the hit novel *Middlesex* by Jeffrey Eugenides, which had just won the Pulitzer awarded in 2003. Cal, the narrator, was born with 5-alpha-reductase deficiency, a recessive trait found frequently in cultures that inbreed, and is a deficiency of the enzyme that converts testosterone. XY males may be born with atypical-looking genitalia and feminine features, as is Cal, who was called Calliope and raised as a girl. When Cal was 14, still thinking he was a girl, he fell in love with a female friend. Eugenides sometimes writes of *hermaphroditism*, other times using the term *intersex*. Intersex was the preferred term. Apparently, Eugenides wanted to keep the Greek cultural references, and a link to Hermaphroditus. I was fascinated. Cal describes feeling different, not like the other girls. The book was gripping, and I loved the setting and the history, of the Greco-Turkish wars, the industrialization of Detroit and the various declines. *Intersex*. A new term. Maybe I could have examined the connections more closely. I didn't look up intersex. Instead, I thought the book made a strange assumption about intersex identity based on sexual preference—Cal couldn't be a lesbian, so must be a man? The logic seemed murky. Still, I recommended the book to a couple of friends. "The writing is compelling," I told them, "and wow, is it a fascinating story."

Such denials go back to Freud's patient notes, with much subsequent discussion. In her memoir *Inheritance*, Dani Shapiro writes of learning through a home-DNA test that her father is not her biological father. She looks back to all past evidence, things people said to her, everyone telling her that despite her strong Orthodox Jewish heritage, she did not look Jewish, the various signs pointing to the truth of her paternity while being able to completely shut off these signals and believe wholeheartedly that the story from her parents was the truth. Shapiro refers to it as the "unknown known." She knew something was off, that she didn't quite fit into the world around her, yet in the face of any evidence that was brought before her, her brain shut it down. Or put another way, like the Pearl Jam song "Unthought Known," which comes from a term coined by Christopher Bollas to identify an experience in some way that we know in our very core but cannot bring ourselves to think of it. I didn't know my identity had secrets—I believed that I was told everything I needed to know about my history. Were the answers I received unsatisfactory? Absolutely. Why was it I was able to read about intersex conditions, feel a strange connection, but then could immediately shove that connection to the back of my consciousness? Of course, it goes back to being indoctrinated in the practice of burying my emotions, being a good girl, not asking so many questions. *Don't pry. Don't be difficult.* Then, when I developed a relationship with someone who didn't bury every deep emotion, my brain did the work for me. *Disassociate. Black out. This is not something you want to touch. It's too emotional.*

The secrets, the silence, the denials—these will eat away at a person and threaten to devour them—me—whole.

* * *

Because of my experience in working for the government, as well as my background clerking at a law practice that dealt with issues related to infertility cases, I left the Massachusetts legislature in 1996, after not much more than a year, to become Director of Government Relations for National RESOLVE, an organization for infertility patient advocacy. The pay was better, and a year spent working for state government was enough for me to realize that I didn't want to stay too long. While there were some talented and goodhearted people working at the statehouse, there was an overall employee mentality that didn't appeal to me, and I never felt like I fit in. Much of my new job with RESOLVE related to fighting at both the state and federal levels for insurance coverage of various infertility treatments. The people we were helping were infertile and desperate, choosing difficult medical procedures and complex contracts with egg donors and surrogates. All this to become parents. Day in and day out, I was confronted with people who were turning their lives over, with both time and money, to produce biological children. Before long, I was unable to sympathize, mostly because of the total immersion in the turmoil of these people's lives. I couldn't help but think of all the children worldwide needing to be adopted. After about 18 months, I was burned out from this work and the topic—the desperation and conundrums. I needed to separate from this issue completely, and so I chose to work in government relations and policy for an elderly long-term care organization. After all, while working at the statehouse, I had been involved in the drafting and passage of the state's first law regulating a new up-and-coming industry: assisted living. Though this line of work came with its own emotional baggage, it didn't hit me personally, and I felt that here, I could actually improve peoples' lives in a meaningful way without the subject taking the same emotional toll.

Then, after a little more than a year, I was approached by someone I had met while working at the statehouse regarding a new position opening up, and in early 1997 I landed my dream job at Boston Children's Hospital, working in Government Relations and Advocacy. I would be representing one of the best hospitals in the world at both the state and federal levels. In a way, I drank the Kool-Aid—I believed the hospital could do no wrong. They save children's lives every day, and overall, do so many amazing things as an institution. My job sometimes required touring VIP guests, including Senator John Kerry, around the hospital and witnessing the miracles that occur at this institution each and every day. I loved working for Children's Hospital. However, they were also an institution that performed harmful medically unnecessary surgeries on intersex children and have continued to do so.

Ironically, I had been completely unaware of the issue while I worked there. Of course, I was still in the dark about my own intersex body and medical history.

* * *

It turned out that secrets ran deeper through our family that I ever expected.

My parents had their second home in Naples, Florida, and would spend half a year down there. My dad had retired very early from his company at age 55. It wasn't uncommon for my parents to go back and forth between Massachusetts and Florida, torn between escaping cold weather and seeing their family and tending to their responsibilities up north.

Super Bowl weekend 1998, my mom was still in Florida, but my dad had flown back up to their main home in Concord for a real estate deal—he'd gotten into selling real estate as something to do in his retirement. My sister, who was nine months pregnant with her first son at the time, knew that our dad was up by himself for the weekend, so she and her husband decided to swing by on Saturday to see if he wanted to join them for an early evening movie. They only lived one town over—an easy drive to pop over to my parents' house. While her husband waited in the car, my sister let herself into the house and called for my dad several times. There was no reply. She walked through the kitchen, past the family room, then down a long hallway to the master bedroom. "Dad?" she called out. "Dad, you there?" As she turned the corner into the bedroom, she saw him, with another woman.

She tiptoed back out of the room and rushed through the family room and into the kitchen, where she now noticed a pair of women's tall black boots on the floor. An unfamiliar purse was on the kitchen counter. Without thinking, Tara reached into the purse, took the wallet, and opened it to see the Massachusetts state driver's license—her name was Caroline. Tara stashed the ID into her pocket and left the house. She burst into tears as soon as she got into the car, telling her husband to drive quickly—they had to get out of there.

She called me within five minutes. She could barely speak through her sobs, but she finally told me what happened. Steven and I flew into the car and drove the hour from our house in Marblehead to their apartment in Acton. Tara and I held hands and cried into tissues as she recounted the story in as much detail as she could. We were all in shock, not sure of what to do next. We decided we had to confront him.

"Let's drive over there now and ask him what the hell is going on," I said. Tara agreed. But our husbands stepped in.

"It's probably not the best idea to go over there without giving your dad a heads-up," my brother-in-law said.

"Things could get ugly quick," Steven added, "and your dad would be very defensive." They were right—he was going to get defensive no matter what, but we needed to be able to diffuse the blast that was about to hit our family as much as possible. Not that it hadn't already hit, but the confrontation was liable to be even worse than the shock of the discovery.

Giving my dad a heads-up of course gave him time to think up a story, which he calmly gave us as he sat in an armchair in the family room while Tara and I sat together on the couch across from him. He had a full glass of wine in one hand, as if he was hosting a period piece on Masterpiece Theatre.

"The woman—I met her through real estate. Her husband recently died of cancer. I was consoling her, and then one thing led to another, and—it shouldn't have happened, and it was a mistake."

It was a *mea culpa* rife with tragedy and empathy. My dad—a good guy—had gotten caught up in the moment, that's all.

"Okay," Tara said, "but we feel like we need to tell Mom about this."

"Are you kidding me?" Our dad flared with anger and sat up. "If you tell her, you know what will happen? Your mom will want a divorce. And what would happen if we got divorced, hmm? Would it be good for her? Think of her health issues." Our mom had been diagnosed with MS several years earlier, though she was doing very well. "And, sure, she'd get alimony, but she would not have things as good as she does now. Do you want that kind of life for her?" He sat back, sipped his wine. "Besides, if we divorce, her life will be hard, and you don't want to do that to her, do you?"

Who *was* this man? This couldn't be my father. Who the hell was he? He just threatened us with the responsibility of hurting the mother we loved, his wife of over 30 years, if we told her the truth. In that moment, I felt my dad had become a monster. Just like that, the platform of everything I knew about my life gave way from under my feet and I was freefalling. Nothing made sense, and I had nothing to grab onto.

I thought about my dad's secret so much over the next few years, how he had made his secret my secret, my sister's secret. The first few times I saw my parents together after that was excruciating. My guilt at not telling my mom was tremendous. I couldn't wrap my mind around the person my dad had become, and though interactions got easier over time, I was acutely aware of any moment of tension between them. And there were a lot more moments of tension. Nothing was the same anymore.

Though Tara and I talked about it periodically, we continued to keep what we knew buried inside. We didn't want to hurt mom. And, if we were being honest, we didn't want our parents to get a divorce.

Tara had her first son, and the family was able to rally around that joy. Meanwhile, I couldn't let the crumbling dynamic of my parents' marriage undermine my own sense of family. The summer of 2000—seven years into our marriage—Steven and I decided we were ready to expand our family of two. My work in infertility advocacy had only reinforced my dedication to building our family through adoption. We both quickly agreed on international adoption and, after investigating a few different options, we decided to adopt from China. We both loved the idea of parenting a daughter, and the vast majority of babies available for adoption in China were girls.

Okay, we thought. *Let's do it.*

CHAPTER 7

RED THREADS

According to Chinese legend, lunar matchmaker god Yuè Lǎo has a book filled with the names of people destined for marriage. The couple are tied to each other with an invisible red thread, attached at the ankle (or, in Japanese and Korean traditions, at the pinky finger). This is the red thread of fate, the link that cannot be undone. Extending beyond matrimony, the thread can symbolize the connection between two people who are fated to meet one another or provide help to each other in some way. Our red thread led us to China.

Seeking international adoption in China was agonizing. Initially, Steven and I were told to expect the process to take six to nine months between filing the paperwork for both the US and Chinese governments and meeting our child. This waiting period is known in the "waiting parent" community as being DTC—Dossier to China. Chinese adoption law sets certain criteria for what children are available for adoption as well as what potential parents are considered suitable. The Chinese government then requires a referral, and then the referral, once obtained, must be approved by the government. Then, after traveling across the globe to meet your child, there are interviews at Chinese government offices, medical exams, and of course the expected "donation" of several thousand dollars to the welfare institute where the adopted child was living up to the point of adoption.

At the very beginning of our process, I joined an email list group for parents in the process of adopting from China. It was immensely helpful—I learned so much about what to expect and how to prepare, and we parents gave each other continued support and encouragement.

The actual "paper chase" stage, as it's called, really wasn't too bad for us, apart from the energy put into filling out form after form, preparing financial statements, getting letters of recommendation from friends and family members, putting together photos of ourselves and our home, coordinating multiple visits from a social worker who would deem whether we were fit for parenting.

I was resentful of the hoops we were forced to jump through. I couldn't help think about how many people get pregnant by accident, regardless of their "fitness" to be a parent, yet there were so many people like Steven and me who were so ready and able to become parents yet we had to prove ourselves to the governments of the United States and China to do so.

In November of 2000, we were finally DTC. I had made sure we were ready to move quickly once we started the process back in July—I was on a mission. When I initially filled out the intake form with the adoption agency "China Adoption with Love" in Brookline, MA—a short walk from my office at Children's Hospital—I checked the box saying we would be open to twins, though this was a prospect the agency director said was rare. I didn't even tell Steven I had done that. It felt like an impossibility, but I figured the more the merrier.

We started prepping the baby room; not going overboard, but getting the crib, some clothes, other necessities that we'd continue to pick up during the long waiting process. One day, while we were driving to another appointment to fill out paperwork, I asked Steven what names he liked. "I don't know—have you thought of any?"

Suddenly, the book *Charlotte's Web* popped into my head. "Charlotte," I said.

Steven nodded and smiled. "Yeah. Yeah, I like it. Charlotte."

Every so often, we'd be doing something in the house and one of us would say, "Where's Charlotte?" sending out a wish, imagining that she could pop her head around the corner. Wherever she was, she was already our daughter.

However, as we entered into the tenth month of waiting, we grew tense, on edge, especially when we realized the wait would be much longer. Because I worked so close to the agency, I popped in to talk to the staff from time to time, and so I asked them one day if I could see the "Waiting Children" lists—children the Chinese government had deemed less adoptable because of a difference, a special need.

Steven agreed it would be worth looking into alternatives to infant children, and so our agency let me pore through the files of some of these waiting children. I landed on one girl, Li Min, who was about seven years old. She was born with what was listed as a "genetic defect" indicating her reproductive organs were not typical. I felt a tug. I thought that perhaps this could be fate—though I didn't know I was intersex yet, and though I didn't think of myself as having "ambiguous" genitalia, something about her story clicked. Years later, I realized this was like finding the chapter on intersex people at Buck a Book, a recognition I couldn't process but had flagged as important. There was another girl out there who was like me and who might go through what I had already gone through. I made a copy of Li Min's file and brought it home to Steven. "I know her story is different than mine, but I feel like I could relate to it. Would you…consider adopting her?"

Immediately, without an ounce of hesitation, Steven said, "Let's do it." As an adoptee himself, he is very empathetic to needing to be wanted.

The next day, I called the agency director and told her we wanted more information about Li Min, including her medical records. "And see if there are any records of her chromosomes." Why had I asked that question? It was there, at the ready. I must have instinctively thought it might help to understand her diagnosis. A little more than a week later, the director called back to tell me she'd received more information.

Because of our inquiry, the orphanage took Li Min to the hospital for further genetic testing. To their surprise—and to ours—Li Min had XY chromosomes. She was therefore, in their minds, "genetically male." They now were distressed, both the representatives of the government and the adoption agency. "We have been raising her as a girl," the directors said. "Years back, as a baby, doctors performed genital surgery on Li Min to make her appear more female. But all this time, she was really a boy."

"Wait, what happened to her?" I asked. I was stunned.

"Her genitals were atypical," the director explained. "Chromosomally, she is male, but because she otherwise appeared to be a girl, and the penis was not fully formed, they operated on her to reduce the size to make her look more like a standard girl. She would be more adoptable that way. Well, I suppose I should say, 'he.' It seems a grave mistake has been made."

They had cut her genitals for aesthetic reasons? She was actually biologically male but otherwise female? I tried to wrap my mind around this. *Middlesex* had not yet come out and won the Pulitzer, and the term "intersex" was not being discussed.

The unknown known. What did I instinctively understand, even then? I was crushed for Li Min, and I felt guilty, responsible for the agency discovering her XY status. They had taken her chromosomes to mean she was unequivocally a boy, but I wasn't so sure that was the way things worked. Without my request, they would have continued to raise her as a girl with no question. Now what would happen to her? And what did she feel about who she was? Had anyone asked her?

Steven and I discussed it. This girl needed a home. She needed to be loved. "Should we choose her?" Steven asked. Something in our hearts pulled us toward her, though I couldn't say what. I was a wreck already—the process had been filled with so many emotions. There were so many children who needed help—how do you know you are getting your child, the one you are meant to be with? The child who would need you specifically to be their parent?

We had all but decided to adopt Li Min. Steven and I went to my parents' house for dinner, and I thought it was time to tell them our news. "We think we've found our girl," I said, the four of us sitting in my parents' family room. "She's seven. Now, she is on the list of waiting children because she has a genetic disorder. She is actually an XY male, but she had underdeveloped genitals. And…she was operated on to look more female when she was a baby."

My dad and my mom shifted in their seats, then looked at each other. This was not the enthusiastic reaction of people who were discovering they were about to become grandparents again. Their reaction to Tara's news had been very different. Instead, they took turns offering reasons why this was the wrong choice.

"It's just—is this what you really want or what you feel like you should do?"

"Shouldn't you hang on a bit longer and wait for a referral to a baby? Isn't that what you'd wanted?"

"You know, at seven, she's already experienced so much, and it's likely to be a very difficult transition. Are you sure you can handle that?"

My body stiffened as I listened to my parents list off what might have been reasonable questions, questions that I myself might have wondered if they hadn't seemed so…inappropriate. I felt shame thinking about these questions, as if I had a moral obligation now. And why couldn't they have just been enthusiastic about her possible adoption? I was indignant. Would I be able to handle things? I wanted to believe I could. And then—how could I bring a child home that my parents weren't excited about? I felt now the old pull—*be a good girl, do what your parents want, they are wiser, and you should make them happy.*

My face burned when I talked to Steven later on, when we were back at home. "But we have to think, are we best positioned to handle all her needs? We'll already be managing her life as an adopted child from China—but to add the possible complications of gender identity? How would we even navigate that?" The cruel irony is not lost on me all these years later.

I parroted all the doubts of my parents, though in a subtler, gentler fashion. Though I was nervous and already felt the shame that would never quite leave me over this, I made the call to the agency director. I was sorry, but we would ride out the regular waiting time. We wouldn't be adopting Li Min. Even as I said the words, I felt the creep of relief but also something like a shadow, as if I was committing a horrible crime.

Years later, this would be a topic of mental dissection with Leslie. My guilt, lack of confidence in myself, but also my desire to please my parents, even into adulthood.

"Is there a way," I asked the director, "that maybe I can send money to support Li Min…until she's adopted?" I felt responsible somehow. This wasn't out of a savior complex, since all I felt was shame and regret. For a few years, we sent money, and then the agency lost track of her. No one in our family knew we had continued to support her for a while, or that we could no longer find her.

But in November, on Veterans Day, I had the day off and was planning on spending a rare day with my mother, shopping. Steven was also off from work that day and was out at Home Depot, back home an hour after I'd left. On the answering machine—the long-awaited message. Later, he told me his hands were shaking when he dialed my cell phone.

It was late morning, and I had just spotted my mom at our designated meeting place at Bloomingdale's when my phone rang.

"Kimberly?"

"Yeah?"

"There are two of them."

* * *

That day, Steven and I drove to the adoption agency to see the girls' photos and sign a form accepting the referral. We realized in the car—we needed a second name. "How about Alexandra?" I had worked with an Alex during my time at the statehouse and liked it as a nickname. Steven did as well. As if the name had been a part of our lives all along and we had only to call it up. Then, when we looked at the photos, we had to decide which would be which. We looked at a photo of the two of them together, and then we both pointed to the same baby at the same time and said, "There's Charlotte."

Later that day, we drove out to my parents' place to show them the referral photos. My sister and her family came over, and everyone was so excited and happy for us. My mom pulled together a lovely celebration with yummy treats. She even had a few gifts ready for us, including two matching sleepers she bought right after I'd said goodbye and ran out of the mall that morning.

However, a week after getting our referral call, our agency director, Lillian, called to tell us that Chen Hai Hong, our Charlotte, had been hospitalized. "I'm not sure why, but the Chinese government has promised to find us another pair of twins!"

Uh, what? Steven and I were in agreement. "Absolutely not." At this point, both girls were already ours in our hearts. We weren't going to give up on them now.

"I'll find out more, hopefully in a couple of days, and I'll let you know as soon as any news comes in," Lillian said.

How sick was she? We felt so powerless, so helpless. She was no longer an imagined Charlotte, but our Charlotte Hai Hong, a real person, and we couldn't be there to help her and had no idea what was happening to her. Two days were agony.

Lillian called a few days later. "She was just dehydrated, so they took her to the hospital and gave her an IV for a few days. She's fine now."

Wait, so the government wanted to switch out our daughters for some changelings because of *dehydration*? Sure, they must have been worried about another health crisis, or perhaps giving the Americans a bad impression, but come on. She was safe and healthy and still ours, though, and that was all that mattered now.

The other catch we realized all too quick: Charlotte's bedroom was set up for Charlotte—one baby. Steven and I scrambled to get double of almost everything. Within three weeks' time before we left for China to bring home our girls. We had to order Alex's matching crib, which wouldn't be shipped until we were in China. "Don't worry," my mom said, "your dad and I will go over and get it all set up before you get home." I was relieved. Excited. Nervous. It was happening, it was really happening.

I was thrilled to have my mom's help, but disappointed in other ways. My mom and I had thrown my sister a baby shower at my parents' house a few years earlier, when her first son was on the way. I thought maybe my mom and sister would throw me a baby shower, but over the last couple of months while waiting for our referral, she was reluctant.

"I don't know, I just—it feels a little tacky, don't you think?"

For her, Steven and I were well established, and it wouldn't be classy to ask others to buy gifts for our new arrivals. I knew she was genuinely excited to have granddaughters, but still, her waspy hang-ups bothered me. I didn't fight her on it, though. I never did.

I complained about it to my sister, though, telling her that there were going to be certain aspects of being a mom that I was missing out on, and a baby shower was one of those traditions I could do. I wanted to celebrate becoming a mom. My body was not biologically preparing for motherhood, and I didn't suddenly have hormones kicking into gear, triggering an internal countdown clock to set off maternal instincts. But maybe rituals and celebrations could be a surrogate for that.

My mom hemmed and hawed for those couple of months, and finally, when we finally knew who our babies were, just weeks away from coming home, I understood that my mom had no intention of throwing me a shower. I knew she would love these adopted children as much as she loved my sister's two biological sons, that she was excited about the girls coming, but her refusal bothered me. The mental justification I gave myself again echoed my mom's perspective—that Steven and I were both working professionals with the means to buy things we needed, whereas Tara and her husband had been younger and not yet as financially established back when their first son was born. Still. It bothered me.

Meanwhile, when I broke the news of the referral to my friends, a couple of them got together and threw me a very small last-minute "book shower," where everyone brought toddler board books and older children's books. That was a lovely day and meant the world to me that my friends had made this small gesture to show their enthusiasm and support. Even more remarkable, as the girls got older, they loved flipping through those books and would spend hours going through them, pointing out pictures, and reading them aloud to each other. The shower books turned out to be some of their favorite possessions.

* * *

The flights from Boston to Los Angeles and Los Angeles to Beijing via Guangzhou were long, and I couldn't sleep. We missed our connecting flight in Guangzhou and struggled to communicate our way onto another later flight. To top it off, the airline lost one of our suitcases—the one carrying all the baby supplies. All of them. It was stressful to say the least. However, we were about to meet our daughters—Chen Hai You and Chen Hai Hong, identical twin girls, nine months old. That's all that really mattered. But first, the agency had all adopting parents spend a few days in the capital city, soaking in the history and Chinese culture. The idea was that it would help adoptive parents to later teach their children about their heritage. I'm pretty sure, though, it was also designed to have foreigners like us spend more time and money, boosting the tourism economy.

We spent the first few days with others from our agency who were adopting at the same time—our referrals had come in on the same day in one "batch." The agency program took us on tours of the Forbidden City, the Great Wall, and plenty of other cultural monuments in an effort to give us a crash course on our children's heritage. As we climbed a section of the Great Wall, our shoes crunched on the light snow that had fallen on the ancient steps. Here we were, walking the Great Wall when we had just been in Boston, and in two days, we would be meeting our daughters. The other adopting parents on the trip heard about our lost luggage and took up a collection—supplying us with enough clothes and supplies to manage our first couple of days with the twins. It was incredibly sweet. From there, we flew down to Shanghai, and the rest of the group dispersed among several provinces where they would be meeting their own babies.

Then, as if the whirlwind of sights and palaces and ancient walls weren't disorienting enough, in what was a blink of an eye, we were at the children's home, ready to meet our girls. That early December morning, the day after landing in Shanghai, we were met by a guide and driver who took us to the Shanghai Children's Home. Lillian was already there to meet us. She would only travel on one or two trips a year with families, so we felt fortunate to have her with us. My guess is that, after Charlotte's hospitalization, she wanted to be there in person to make sure she was really okay and there were no other crises, medical or otherwise.

The Shanghai Children's Home was a marvel to behold. It was massive—and it had just been open a couple of months. The new orphanage was built to showcase the Chinese adoption system as a direct response to the horrific stories of terrible conditions and abuse and the negative PR the government received in the 1990s, including a BBC exposé called "The Dying Rooms," which highlighted the worst Chinese facilities—including the old orphanage in Shanghai. The old orphanage where the girls had spent the first few months of their lives. The Dying Rooms were where the most challenged orphans—those with special needs, or those who simply became sick—were left to die. It was heartbreaking.

The new facility was a building deliberately designed to wipe away any impression of the Dying Rooms. The walls were painted in vivid colors, the playgrounds were new and state-of-the-art, the lawn outside was lush, the rooms were all clean, and the building was capped with a massive clock tower that included rotating characters that evoked Disney.

We were told that members of the Chinese military were brought in to help transport the babies and children from the old orphanage to the new one. I can only imagine the organization and planning that was required to make that transition smooth. But why did I assume it went smoothly? It may have been chaotic, especially if the outside world wasn't watching. I felt so grateful that my girls survived that time, that we were united before they turned one, and I was ready for us to be a family immediately.

But first, more paperwork, and forms to sign in which Steven and I promised to take care of our new daughters. Afterward, we were led down a ridiculously long and dark hallway, and then sprung into a room full of cribs, playpens, and children, including toddlers scooting around in little Exersaucers.

The orphanage director leaned toward Steven and me and asked, "Can you tell which ones are yours?"

Steven turned and pointed to Chen Hai You, Alexandra, in the far corner of the room. "There. There's Alex." I spotted Charlotte on the opposite side. They were dressed exactly the same, yellow sweaters covered with colorful flowers. Each girl had a red dot in the middle of her forehead—I was taken aback.

"What are—?" I touched my own forehead without realizing it.

Lillian read my confusion. "The red dot? It's a symbol of good luck, placed there by the nannies." The nannies were the caretakers who came to the orphanage, making the rounds with the many, many children in an effort to give them personalized attention and monitor them each day. The red dot—none of the parents on the email group had mentioned it.

The girls were led to us, and Steven scooped up Alex like a pro, bouncing her while a smile crept across her face as she stared into his eyes.

Much of what happened is another experience I can't remember. The emotions of this day surged, and as a reaction—my typical reaction—I dissociated and blacked out. However, one of the other new fathers was shooting a video of his wife meeting their daughter and was kind enough to include footage for us of our first meeting. I have watched it over and over, hoping for a trace of the firsthand experience to blink on in my brain. Instead, I observe myself as an outsider, bending down to pick up Charlotte. Charlotte's face scrunches up, her mouth opens wide, wide enough to let out a roaring wail. The confusion and uncertainty are crystal clear on my face. Though my consciousness had taken a hike, my emotions were there.

Clearly, I have no idea what to do for Charlotte. I remember feelings, a lack of confidence, not wanting to scare Charlotte any further by picking her up. All of a sudden, Steven is beside me, gently placing Alex into my arms. She remains calm and smiling despite the transition. Then, Steven bends over and up comes Charlotte, holding onto Steven. Her crying stops immediately. That moment captured on video, replayed hundreds of times, that moment we stand together for the first time as four, a family.

December 10—that is what we call our "Forever Family Day." We've celebrated it as a family every year since. That day, we all got new names. Chen Hai Hong became Charlotte Hai Hong Zieselman, and Chen Hai You became Alexandra Hai You Zieselman. I became Mommy; Steven became Daddy.

We were meant to be together. I couldn't get enough of them. Suddenly, this felt like our family. Though I had regrets for Li Min, there isn't a second that goes by that I'm not convinced these girls were the ones to complete our family. They were destined to be ours just as much as Steven and I were destined to be theirs. The red thread of fate was going to bring us together. And with the help of our English-speaking guide in Shanghai, the missing suitcase was finally delivered to our hotel.

Getting the girls' travel visas ready took another ten days of waiting, during which we spent time with them when we could, working on becoming familiar faces to them. One day, I popped into a local gift store and purchased a huge suitcase—which cost about fifteen US dollars—and I filled it with little gifts and trinkets to bring home. I'd gotten the idea a couple of weeks earlier that each year, on our Forever Family Day, I would give them each one gift that I'd gotten right after meeting them. I got enough gifts to last until they were 21. While Steven and I were still in Beijing, we visited the local pearl market and purchased Charlotte and Alex a beautiful strand of pearls, which we would give them on our Forever Family Day when they turned 16. Otherwise, the gifts were small trinkets, such as jade chopsticks, *cloisonné* ornaments, and other local handcrafts. Our dollar was very strong at the time, so it was easy to purchase many gifts.

The two-week trip was exhausting for everyone, emotionally and physically. That, and we all had contracted strep throat. Three days before Christmas, we arrived back in Boston and were met at the airport by my parents and Tara and her family, who had ordered a stretch limo to take us back to our house. My mom, dad, and Tara all took turns holding each of the girls. As soon as my mom clutched the babies close to her, she burst into tears. I didn't dissociate, at least not completely, at our arrival and the introduction of our girls to the family, but I remember it most through the pictures my dad took that day. In my defense, I was jetlagged and had strep throat, but emotions were running high, so I'm sure I had my foot in the door to a blackout, just waiting to make a jump for it. I was relieved that my mom was authentically emotional, especially after the baby shower disappointment. Now was not a time for bitterness, though. My mom and dad stayed with us that first night, and then we all went to their house the two days later and stayed over for Christmas. Then, as soon as the holidays were over, they flew back to Florida as the true snowbirds they were becoming.

I was grateful for the maternity leave from my job for four months: we now had two nine-month-old girls. All hands were on deck, except it was only Steven and I who were minding the decks. Tara and her family lived an hour away from us, so once the holidays were over and everyone dispersed, Steven and I were left on our own to learn how to become parents. And we were both on medication for strep, and the girls were also still sick. Steven took off work over the holidays, but the day he went back to work I wound up calling him at his office by 11am, in tears, saying, "I can't do this alone, it's too hard! I can't keep them both happy at the same time!" It was the first time I had been alone with the two of them.

This is where the panic set in—I had girls to raise. How was I going to raise them through puberty? What was I going to tell them about getting a period? I wasn't qualified for this. I was faking my way through everything—first law school, then work, and now being a mom. Then, my daughters would be old enough to see through me. Kids always find out fakes. And freaks. Who the hell was I to raise kids, to take on these new lives?

From the second we met them, I felt that Steven was a much better, more natural parent than I was, and it bothered me. For months, I struggled with feeling like a fraud, like I wasn't a "real mom," that whatever had been taken out of me all those years ago had also stripped me of my natural maternal instincts. I loved them, more than 100 percent, but at times I couldn't shake the feeling that I was play-acting at being a mom, and everything I did was inauthentic. My maternity leave included some dark times. The New England winter was cold, snowy, and dark. The days were short outside, but so long in our house. Caring for two infants at the same time was overwhelming, especially for someone like me with little to no experience with babies. This new frontier was especially lonely, as we had only recently moved back to this new suburb outside Boston—an easier work commute, but I had no friends in town yet, no support system nearby.

There was pressure to return to work, and I was exhausted. I loved my job, but I had no idea how much work it would take to care for these babies. I never dreamed I'd be a stay-at-home mom. My pictures of the future always included a job. Was this further proof that I was a fraud? I couldn't handle both my job at Children's Hospital and motherhood.

Halfway through my leave, I called my boss and told her we needed to talk, so we met for lunch. I asked if it would be possible to figure out something part-time.

"I am so relieved," she said. "I was preparing for you to say you quit. Of course we can work out something." I went back to working 20 hours a week, continuing with that plan for about two years.

I felt shame that I was turning my back on the job that I loved so much, and I wondered if everyone saw that I couldn't hack work and family and this was a sign I hadn't been cut out for this life—again, being a fraud. Instead, I threw myself into taking care of my girls, making sure that I provided them with everything they needed.

And, in a few months, I settled into a routine. I understood what my girls needed and when, and I knew how to give it to them—for the most part. However, I remained as hard on myself as I had been those first few months. Of course, they had been hearing Chinese for most of their life, and now they were in an English-speaking household. Sure they were only nine months old, but I had to give myself a break—everything would sound and smell and look and feel different to beings whose only experience was sensory.

As they became toddlers, though, I noticed certain delays, especially in speech, in language skills. The Listserv parents said this sometimes happens with children adopted from other countries, even as babies. There were other delays, though. Their fine and gross motor skills were delayed compared with most other babies. I understood that developmental delays tend to be more common with twins. Regardless, I was a worried mess because they weren't doing what all the·books told us they should be doing at this age. Even when I thought they should be catching up to their peers with speech, they weren't. I researched what to do, found some therapy options, but I wouldn't be able to manage getting them to appointments and all the extra help I would need to give them while working 20 hours a week. I needed to be a full-time mom to my girls, and so I finally said goodbye to Children's Hospital.

* * *

I had loved photography since high school. I'd kept photo albums and scrapbooks from the time I was 13 and, though I took a photography course in college, I mostly played around with photography as a hobby and didn't do any serious training. Not long after adopting the girls, I bought my first digital camera. Now that I was staying at home with them, I pulled out my Nikon camera and held mini-photoshoots with my girls, practicing with lighting and exposure and posing. There was a greater urgency to my documenting my girls' lives on film because I didn't want to forget some moment in a dissociative episode, and I worried that there might be periods of their lives that I would be unable to recall. Mostly, though, it was a fun activity that kept me interested in something other than childcare. Each year with them, I made a family photo album for the year. Then, friends asked me to take photos of their kids for them, especially at the end of the year for their annual holiday cards. If I knew a friend wanted family photos, I'd offer to do it for them. It clicked that this could be a potential business idea. I enrolled in an adult education class to learn more about digital photography, and then I paid someone to develop a website for my new company, KZ Images. By mid-2007, the site was up and running and I was ready to advertise around town. Most of my clients came by word-of-mouth from friends and friends of friends. That first fall, I worked almost every weekend, taking on-location pictures of families, then coming home and working on the photographs on my computer.

I turned the top floor of our house into an office space. The shoots took me away from my own family on the weekends, which was hard, but I enjoyed working and being creative. I was getting out, being productive for a reason other than raising children; being a mom was great, but I needed something for myself, too. I worried less about being a fraud, though there were still moments off and on. But despite worrying that I wasn't measuring up, I was also overcome with joy at my family. My girls were special, and I felt a tremendous privilege to be their mom. Maybe I had conned everyone into thinking I had this all down, but I would enjoy this, dammit, even if I had to keep everyone fooled.

PART III

BECOMING

Orchids

Seven months after discovering the truth about my body in my medical records, I had a ticket to fly to Dallas to attend the annual weekend conference of the AIS-DSD Support Group, which at the time was specifically for women with AIS. Discovering this group was a watershed moment. I'd chatted with Mandy, and then I reached out to other members of the group. I spent several weeks lurking, reading members' questions and comments. There were so many posts, and I wanted to catch up on things that had already been said. Reading through what these other women with AIS had gone through, I realized how lucky I'd been by comparison. There were horrific surgeries performed, frequently without their knowledge and consent. The *Oprah* episode didn't even scratch the surface of the experiences.

I came close to posting but hesitated. One of my first comments was on someone else's post—I asked what others were taking for hormone replacement therapy. Someone replied right away, and then another woman, and then a group of us started comparing notes and sharing experiences. It turned out that I was on a dose way too low for my needs. The doctors, they said, don't really know what to do with our bodies. (I immediately told

Dr. Bingley what I learned about my hormone dose, and she apologized for not knowing sooner how to help me.)

The group was named New Rare Orchids, and the orchid was the official symbol. *Orchid*, from the Latin *orchis*, the name for the flower, which derived its name from the Greek *órkhis*, which means *testicle*. The tubers of the orchid resemble two testicles. Generally, these are buried and hidden, and all we see is the flower. I loved the symbolism.

Speaking with Mandy was the beginning of finding my tribe.

It was also on New Rare Orchids that I first learned that the organization would be holding their next annual support group meeting in a few months, in one of the many airport hotels in Dallas. There had been no question in my mind as to whether I would be there or not. I was going.

The question I did have, though, was whether I should go alone or bring Steven with me. It could be a great opportunity to include him, and he had been very supportive, happy that I was finding support, and he'd listen whenever I'd learned something new and wanted to share. This was something he could do to actually share in this process of discovery with me. But then I wondered if I would be better off alone, spending time meeting new friends, finally having face-to-face discussions with people I'd only known online or over the phone. I floated my dilemma to the group, and the responses were more conflicted than I was. Some told me that when they had brought their husbands or family members in the past, they got to learn about AIS together, which was helpful. Others told me I needed to come alone—it was time for me and me alone. Finally, one of the members pointed out that this conference would be a special time for me. "You would benefit from not having to think about anyone else but yourself during the weekend," she wrote. Her point was excellent—I had been framing the problem around my husband, but I needed to center my own experiences, since this was going to be new. And the purpose of the conference was to do this for myself. So that's what I did. I went to the web page, though not without nervous tension, and registered.

Other than Steven, Leslie, my mom and Tara, the only person who knew where I was really going was my friend Ellen. Everyone else—my daughters, coworkers, my mother-in-law, and my extended family—all were told that I was going for an annual girls' weekend away with my friends from college. That week, Ellen and I met for lunch.

"I'm so nervous," I told her. "Excited, but still kind of freaked."

"This is going to be such a great opportunity. You already know a lot of these women online, right? Are you worried about anything?"

"Well, no. It's just—" I searched for the feeling.

"It's real now, when you go."

Yeah. Exactly that.

"Here, for your trip. Just a little something." Ellen handed me a gift bag, and inside was a large purse—tapestry style with wild colors in a funky print. It was amazing.

I would be okay at this conference alone. I had Ellen on my side, now with me in spirit. And I had the same with Steven when I packed the bright orange pashmina shawl he had brought back for me a couple of years earlier as a gift from one of his business trips. I figured that July in Texas would be hot, but the AC in the hotel would be on full blast. I'd wear my summer outfits, making sure I felt like a woman in the way I dressed, then have Steven's pashmina wrapped around me and Ellen's purse with me wherever I went. But I wouldn't be bland or try to be invisible. I would be bright and celebrate being part of a community.

And then it was time to get on my flight. In Dallas, I took the shuttle to the airport hotel and checked in. The only indication of the conference going on was a small hotel sign announcing the Orchid Conference registration was scheduled outside the ballroom that afternoon and through the evening. The next couple of hours were spent in my room as I tried to stay calm.

Women like me, I thought. *Women like me.*

* * *

The anxiety didn't set in until the elevator ride down to registration. What would everyone look like? Was I going to fit in? Would they know I was one of them immediately, by looking at me? Would I know if they liked me?

The elevator door slid open in front of the bustling Orchid Conference registration desk, and standing in front was Dr. Arlene Baratz, the mother of Katie, the young woman with AIS I'd seen on *Oprah*. Seeing her standing at the registration desk was akin to spotting a celebrity. I went right up to her, introducing myself. "I recognized you from *Oprah*. Your daughter, Katie, was the first other woman with AIS I had ever 'known.' She's had such a profound impact on me."

"Kimberly, so nice to meet you—and what a wonderful thing to say." Arlene was as warm as she'd seemed on TV. She put me at ease completely. We chatted for a few minutes, and I explained to her I had only just learned I had CAIS and had found Katie's interview while researching anything I could find on CAIS. I told myself not to gush too much, and that I shouldn't monopolize Arlene's time, especially at the beginning of a long conference. I excused myself to register, collecting my information packet, my schedule, and my name tag, adorned with a purple orchid. I slid the lanyard over my head. It was a small action, the movements rote and ordinary—and yet, what a giant leap for Kimberly. As I turned from the registration table, I was waved over to join a group of women assembling in a circle, giving hugs and genuine, happy greetings to one another. All of these women were like me—I was overwhelmed but ecstatic.

The conference was like nothing I'd ever attended before. While the agenda included both plenary and breakout sessions to learn about different topics, as with other work- and adoption-related conferences I'd attended, the vibe of the Orchid Conference was so much more intimate and communal.

Aside from a few isolated moments in my life, I was never much of a crier. Having to say goodbye to friends when moving, losing a grandparent, or being told I had to have a hysterectomy, and of course moments of my discovery that I had CAIS—sure, I would cry a little. But movies or sad songs or holiday Hallmark commercials didn't make me weepy, and I'd spent the better portion of my life burying all my emotions. Here, though, at this conference, and among 80 to 100 other Orchid sisters, my studied waspy stoicism crumbled. During presentations, I found myself clutching at my orange pashmina, my shoulders bouncing up and down in jagged sobs. It was never a hard cry—more like stifled sobbing, which was noticeable to the people sitting behind me. A few years later, a few attendees recognized me, saying they remembered my orange scarf and bouncy shoulders.

I cried harder, though, at the share session. Everyone in the conference gathers in a circle and passes around a "talking stick," giving the holder five minutes of uninterrupted time to share their story, their thoughts, what they're learning or experiencing. The whole process takes an emotional three to four hours. Some were ongoing horror stories—families that wouldn't accept them, lifelong consequences of unauthorized surgery, secrets, and betrayals. Sometimes, the anguish was like a ping that went around the room like an electrical current, burning our hearts and snapping our insides. Not all of it was negative, though. Yet the pervasive themes were of shame and loneliness, fear of intimacy, issues of trust, and anger at being lied to by doctors and parents. I had never cried so hard in my life. It felt good to feel, though—I was having a true catharsis. This was also the first time in my life I felt like I belonged and truly fit in.

In the evening, we were invited into the hospitality suite, a hotel room open to us for socializing over snacks and drinks. I joined a group of women congregating around a small table. Several of us had glasses of wine, and there were plenty of snacks everywhere—and boxes of tissues. "The conference organizers definitely know their attendees," one woman said, and we laughed. We shared stories about our lives, and I brought up my twin daughters, adopted from an orphanage in Shanghai about eight years earlier.

"*What?*" the woman named Marie said, lighting up. She was French Canadian from Montreal, as I'd learned a few minutes earlier. "My husband's job landed us in Shanghai for a few years—we were there then!"

"Wow!" I said, "what are the odds?"

"No, but that's not it," she said, holding out her arm. "I regularly volunteered at the orphanage." She named the one where my daughters had been. "I remember them! You don't forget identical twin girls in a Shanghai orphanage, even if there are hundreds there."

I was aghast. A few months earlier, I thought I was one of two women, alone on the planet, with AIS. And then came Dallas, connecting with women from all over the world who'd had similar experiences and emotions, including a woman who met my adopted twin daughters before I had, at their orphanage in Shanghai. I cried some more. Finding this group proved nothing short of *kismet*.

The hospitality suite dwindled and was packed up, so a few of us new Orchid sisters meandered downstairs to the hotel bar: Lucy, a spunky and attractive redhead who was also an adoptive mom, had traveled from California; Marianne, a young and pretty Latina from Texas; Hannah, who was much younger than I was but had been a cop and served in the Gulf War. Hannah ordered a Blue Moon and, when I asked what it was, she ordered a second one, with an orange slice, and taught me the proper way to drink it. The beer calmed me, as did being among a smaller group. We recapped the day, processing over the information shared. They helped me get a handle on my thoughts. The beer, the quiet conversation, helped distill the shocks, the revelations, the communion with my newfound sisters. My racing mind quieted enough to fall into my exhaustion, overwhelmed with gratitude.

Each day of the conference I relived a hundred lifetimes. That's part of the nature of meeting your community for the first time, forming immediate and strong bonds. I even got to meet Katie Baratz. Her mom, Arlene, saw me by the refreshments and introduced us. Katie was as warm and friendly as her mother, exactly as she had come across on *Oprah*. I was as awestruck as I would have been if I met Oprah. Katie had been a brave young advocate of CAIS and a trailblazer in creating awareness in the mid-1990s.

Katie's family learned when she was six that she had CAIS, when she had surgery to repair a hernia and the doctors discovered internal testes. Her doctors had seen them then—it was impossible or at least highly improbable that my doctors, when I was the same age and having that same surgery, had neglected to see them. Sew me up, kick the can down the road, and let another doctor deal with it.

Sunday morning, the final session of the conference was held in the large ballroom for the group's annual meeting, which was really the business portion of the conference. Already, some of my new Orchid sisters were departing for their mid-morning flights, and I was emotional over leaving my newfound tribe on my mid-afternoon flight. As the conference concluded, Dr. Mark Baratz, Katie's father, set up his computer and projection system for what had become tradition at the conference. Each year someone, often Mark, assembled a slide show of posed and candid photos he and others had taken throughout the conference weekend. He set the slide show to "True Colors," sung by Eva Cassidy. Though I had known the song well, the lyrics took on a new meaning, acknowledging an authenticity I had been seeking for years. Watching these slides, listening to "True Colors," I finally knew and, better yet, accepted who I really was. And as my true colors shined through, I realized that I wasn't invisible; I was seen by and mattered to women I never imagined I'd get to meet. I sobbed so hard I couldn't speak for about fifteen minutes.

On the plane home, I added Eva Cassidy's cover of "True Colors" to my music, which inspired me to create an "Orchid" playlist on my first-generation iPhone. I added Melissa Ethridge's "Precious Pain," Natalie Merchant's "Wonder," "In Repair" by John Mayer, and Coldplay's "Fix You," from the aptly named *X&Y* album.

When I got home, Steven and the girls picked me up at the airport, giving me hugs and asking about the trip. With the girls, I was vague, talking mostly about the weather, the hotel, the food. As far as they knew, I was with friends. Steven had to wait for the full update, but he said I looked good, revived and refreshed.

"It was an amazing time," I said.

"I am so happy that you had this time," Steven said. "I can't wait to hear more."

But first, life happened. The next day, I had to take the girls for their swimming lessons. I sat by the pool, watching them as they got their instructions and bobbed back and forth to the opposite edges, their little girl wiggles as they kicked at the chlorinated water. How was I here when just yesterday I was in Dallas, with my Orchid sisters? Everything was different now. I was different. My girls waved, then dove for rings, then wiggle-kicked the length in their bright bathing suits. Other parents I knew chatted intermittently.

Nobody here knew that I had been through something monumental. To them, I was Kimberly-as-before.

Before attending the conference, my group warned me of the inevitable "crash" I would feel when I got back home, away from the familiar and understanding cocoon of people I'd been with all weekend. Other members reiterated this during the conference, and I took it to heart—that didn't mean the preparation helped prevent any of the crash from happening. Becoming an Orchid sister and being around such support had been freeing, life-changing—all of that. But what did that mean here, poolside at swim class?

I sent a text to my friend Ellen. *This is so weird*, I tapped into the phone. *I had a transformative weekend. Now I'm at swim class like nothing happened. Can I call you later?* Talking about it would keep it real, like it wasn't some dream.

Ellen wrote back that she'd love to hear more. I knew I couldn't just live inside my online community, though I longed for that cocoon. I had to bring this experience to the rest of my life, although I wasn't yet ready to tell everyone I knew. Once again, I had this strange sensation of being an imposter, as if I was never going to be fully myself.

When we spoke that afternoon, I summarized the weekend, what I'd experienced, how I was feeling, how beautiful it was to finally be part of a group, how there were finally people who understood what I was going through. Ellen listened, then she told me how proud she was that I'd been brave enough to go on this trip. "So much of what you said is familiar." She'd gone through AA more than a decade earlier and was still very involved, serving as an active member and role model to others. "It can't be overstated how important it is to have a community of people who get it."

"I'm so glad I have you, too," I told my friend.

What I started to notice more than anything were the friends and acquaintances who seemed to be always performing, whether it was being outright phony or mildly inauthentic. At a school event, I might see someone put on airs to impress colleagues, or the phony backslappers, the sycophants, people trying too hard to be something they weren't. As I became more myself, at least in my private life, I became exponentially irritated with those who weren't authentically themselves. Though I had a couple of friends in my neighborhood, the rest of my community was relatively homogenous. Everything had to be done a certain way, people were expected to behave a certain way, to "fit into" this particular society.

I vented my frustrations to my private group, and once again, I discovered that despite what my doctors had told me all those years ago, I wasn't alone. Doing the hard work of living an authentic life—which we were all trying to do—makes exposure to blatant inauthenticity untenable.

"Yeah," one friend wrote, "it's amazing now how many phonies I can spot within a minute."

This group was my community, but even more than that, I felt us becoming a family, as necessary to me as my own husband and children.

* * *

Private Facebook (or other social media) groups are a powerful tool, not just for the intersex community. Going through a trauma or even a major life change feels less isolating and desperate when you can talk to people who relate to what you're going through. Family may care, but if they don't have firsthand experience with what you've experienced, then it is impossible to offer all the support that you need. Having an online community for overseas adoption, and specifically adoption from China, helped me navigate the developmental complexities my daughters were facing and gave me the tools to be a better mom even though I wasn't from my daughters' race and culture. But adoption, parenting—these topics are far better understood. Though individual complexities may arise, requiring specialized advice, the average person is far more willing and able to offer emotional support and advice in the field of child rearing. This isn't the case for the intersex community.

So many of our experiences have been hidden, buried, dismissed by society, the medical community, even by our families and our friends. We need each other, desperately, for emotional support, as outlets, as sources of information about medical and mental health. In some cases, even a person's survival hinges on having a supportive community. These groups truly are life saving.[1]

Over the last decade, I met or heard stories about hundreds of women with the very same intersex condition—CAIS—discovered when they were children when surgeries on inguinal hernias revealed unexpected testes. Some were like me and didn't know the truth until adulthood. Others who may have known lived in the shadows of an unsupportive family. Like me, so many were told they too were rare, alone. Like me, so many believed they were freaks. Together, we recognize we are us, amazing, and absolutely normal people with bodies that happened to have been born a little bit different, healthy variations of nature. Bodies aren't as binary as we were all taught in school.

I felt gratitude in its purest form. I loved these people on the other end of the internet connection. Some I'd met at the Orchid Conference, others were known only on the screen. After a few months, I posted about a frustration with an acquaintance from my suburb I'd met for lunch who was so focused on appearance and status that I could no longer have a meaningful conversation with her. I was doing a business portrait for her, but I quickly became so irritated with her that I was regretting taking her on as a client. After a short post in which I told my group how special their authenticity was to me, I signed off with my name, but I thought of a new signature, one that would show my affection, as I had in my letters when I was young, but a signature that defined the new, the real me: *XOXY, Kimberly.*

As I clicked post, I thought, *Yes. That is me.* That was my signature, my show of support, of solidarity, of love, for my CAIS sisters. My love for myself.

* * *

My newfound authenticity and ownership of my identity was not without complications or what might be called hypocrisy. For a few years after my discovery, I did not tell everyone in my life about my other world of AIS support groups and Orchid friends. When I made my annual pilgrimages to the AIS conference, there were friends who still thought I was on a girls' trip. I wasn't ready to come out to everyone I knew yet, and I recognized that telling people needed to happen at my own pace. I had little trouble discussing this with strangers—the ones I most resisted telling were people I knew from my high school years. I'm still not sure why, but I felt the most vulnerable when faced with the idea of people from that time in my life knowing my secret. I talked about this with Leslie, and she stressed the importance of this being my information to share when and only if I felt ready. "You are in control of it, Kimberly. But I also believe that sharing with more people may take away some of the feelings of shame and stigma." She acknowledged how difficult this might be to do. "Give yourself plenty of time and space to do it on your own terms, when you're ready." This chat relieved a lot of the burden I had put on myself over the quandary of whether to share or not. I will never not be grateful for having Leslie in my life.

It was a process. I was trying to learn to forgive myself and be patient.

Not long after this, Leslie pointed out that I hadn't reported having any dissociative episodes since my discovery, and especially since my trip to Dallas. Now that I knew my history and my identity and could sort through all my old emotions, and had an explanation for what I'd been through, my mind was allowing me to feel through every part of the process. And I'm pretty sure I never had another dissociative episode afterward.

* * *

In March of 2009, eight months after my first AIS conference in Texas, 15 months after my CAIS discovery, Steven came up to my third-floor office space one Wednesday evening.

"Hey there, you busy?" he asked.

"Just working on some photos. Business portraits." I clicked save on the latest changes and turned to Steven. He was holding a ring box.

It wasn't my birthday, it wasn't our anniversary—it was a random weeknight.

"What's this?" Inside was a simple band ringed with small diamonds. Classic and beautiful.

"I wanted to say how much I've seen you change this last year—in the best way. Since finding out the truth about yourself, and meeting your Orchid family, it seems like you've become more whole. Like completing a previously unfinished circle. This ring represents that circle now being complete—and I want you to realize that every time you look at it."

This time, I remembered everything. Every word Steven said, everything I felt—I was overcome with love and appreciation. I was so lucky to have Steven, to have this life, to have people who understood me and loved me no matter what, to have all the privileges of this life. I knew full well how much I had that others did not.

This ring meant more to me than my engagement ring or any other gift ever would. Steven was by my side, my wonderful partner.

CHAPTER 8

FAMILY TOGETHER, FAMILY APART

Five years had passed since Tara and I had discovered our dad's affair with the woman named Caroline. For five years, Tara and I struggled with keeping our dad's secret, convincing ourselves that the incident was a one-time deal and that our dad wasn't cheating on our mom anymore. Things had gone back to normal, so life would move on.

Except that about 18 months after Steven and I brought the girls home, my mom was up from Naples and wanted to have dinner with Tara and me. "I have to tell you both something," she said. "I'm divorcing your father. I made some recent…discoveries."

These discoveries weren't just the Caroline affair, but there was a list of…grievances. Tara and I broke down in tears. We told our mom what had happened five years earlier. My mom was heartbroken.

"I am so sorry you both had to suffer like that," she said. "But you know, if you had told me back then, I probably wouldn't have been ready to leave him. I'm ready now."

The dinner led to an awful summer. I helped my mom find a good divorce lawyer, and I ended up reading through the depositions given by her and my dad. The proceedings turned nasty and took a year to finalize. I didn't speak to my father, or, rather, he didn't speak to me. Not during the divorce and not for a couple of years afterward.

Something in me felt irreparably broken. I sought out a therapist and that's when I found Leslie, who worked to slowly lead me to a path toward healing. As I would later find out, there was plenty lurking in my subconscious that made it hard for me to trust people, plenty that I had blocked out but knew was there.

For over two years, my dad hadn't tried to talk to me. He was probably afraid, knowing how much he had screwed up, but that was also something he couldn't admit. Finally, after two years of silence, and with the guidance from my therapist, Leslie, I met him for lunch. We talked and tried to get to a place of forgiveness. It didn't happen all in one lunch. Maybe it's still a work in progress. He missed a couple of years of seeing his granddaughters grow up. It was hard not having the father I'd grown up with in my life, or in my daughters' lives. It was hard losing that trust in him, losing the faith in him, feeling duped that he'd silenced me by roping me into his lie, then fooling me by not changing his behaviors. The whole premise of his excuse was a lie: a couple of years later, I even met Caroline's ex-husband, alive and well. She had been no grieving widow, and my father no tarnished saint. If I wanted an apology, I wouldn't be getting one—it wasn't in my dad's nature. If I wanted my father in my life, there were parts of him I would have to accept, however reluctant I was. But he was my family, and I still loved him, despite how broken our family had become because of his actions.

Can you have love without trust? Does it require a different type of love when there is so much to doubt?

CHAPTER 9

ME, AN ACTIVIST?

Well before I learned about my CAIS I was already learning what I could be capable of changing, even of advocating, thanks to my daughters.

When we brought our daughters home, within a few months, their developmental delays became apparent. We weren't entirely surprised—the pediatrician said that delays could be expected since they were twins and likely had been premature and had lived their first nine months in a humble orphanage. I had to figure out how to access both government early-intervention services and private therapy services to help them.

By the time they were three years old, they were eligible for special education services and an Individualized Education Plan (IEP) through our public school system. Our daughters were happy and delightful little girls who brought us endless joy, but neither of them talked much—in fact, they would barely speak at all. Despite such an obvious delay in development, I struggled to get them access to the resources the school system offered, which were limited in number. After jumping through several hoops and pushing my way into a required scheduled evaluation, I got them both enrolled in a half-day integrated preschool. Half the kids were enrolled as typically-developing "peer role models" and had no developmental delays; the other half were like mine, needing various levels of special education therapy and support. And what a difference these special services made on my girls. (It was there at this school that I met other mom friends, including Ellen.)

Alexandra and Charlotte ran in every morning, excited to see their friends and teachers. In the afternoon, to the envy of every other parent in the pickup line, every single day, I was greeted with both of them running toward me, full speed, arms open, smiling and yelling *Mama!* They would fly into my arms, and both my arms and my heart were full. Moments such as those were the ongoing reminders of how lucky I was to have been matched with my girls. This was my family, and we were meant to be.

Still, I worried all the time about their lagging development. Charlotte had shown marked progress, but Alexandra was still lagging noticeably behind. Even Charlotte needed continued speech and language therapy as well as, eventually, support with learning to read. Although each was intelligent, they both had been diagnosed with processing and communication disorders and were on their way to developing diagnosed learning disabilities. I worried when it was time to leave the preschool and enter kindergarten and the administrator of the school told me that, despite Alexandra's needs, there were other kids in her class who had even greater need for the peer-integrated special education kindergarten in the fall. "We just don't have a spot for her." There is a problem with funding and getting the necessary tools for all the students with special needs and making sure the teachers have the adequate support (as well as a manageable class size). But the children who need that care shouldn't pay the price. I was frustrated, and I asked around at the playground after school.

"The school actually can't do that," Bernie, one of the other moms I'd befriended, told me. She was a seasoned special needs mom whose daughter was a peer role model in the preschool but whose older son was autistic. She had been advocating for him for years. "By law, the school is mandated to accommodate every child who has demonstrated a need for special education assistance."

I did my own research and found out this was true. However, an additional complication was that the school district's Director of Special Education had recently resigned, and his replacement was already hired and set to begin work in July. I had no time to lose. On his first day in July, I showed up at his office, which was in the administrative wing of our high school's building, otherwise empty for summer.

Introducing myself, and welcoming him to the new position, I explained my daughter's situation. I told him that I knew he had plenty of items on his itinerary, but that something he could do quickly was to admit Alexandra into the kindergarten program she needed and, in fact, the program she had already been a part of throughout preschool. From July to August, I sent a couple of email reminders, but on the last week of August, days before school was set to start, I received notice that Alex had been placed in the class. Success! Showing up and being the squeaky-wheel parent had made a difference, and I had used my knowledge and privileges to get what my daughter needed. It pained me to know full well that not all families would be as fortunate.

This would be the first time that Alex and Charlotte would be in different classes, but both girls would still receive the necessary academic and therapeutic support, including speech and language therapy as well as occupational therapy. In addition, they were also enrolled in weekly private speech and language therapy sessions outside of school. Both had still had their IEPs, and I continued to advocate for them during the teacher consults and annual official IEP meetings, where the school administration continued to equivocate on my daughters' needs, putting pressure on me to just let them continue with whatever they were doing in their own time, because they needed to cut costs by restricting services. "It's actually a mandate from the new Director of Special Education—he was brought in specifically to cut costs." This of course made me furious, and when I did a quick online search of the new administrator, I learned that this was his specialty—cutting school costs by limiting services wherever the school could get away with doing so. He'd spent the previous seven years at two different school districts in Massachusetts with the exact same game plan.

If this had just been about me, I might have let it go. I was not yet confident in advocating for myself, as I had spent all my life trying to *get over it*. But this wasn't about me. This was about the wellbeing and future success of my daughters. There was no way I could back down. My daughters' lives weren't some line in a red or black column. Every time an administrator put pressure to drop my daughters from receiving a service they still needed, I pushed back. The more I spoke up, the more confidence I gained in speaking out.

By the end of the year, as my daughters were finishing first grade and preparing for second, I was asked to lead the school district's Special Education Parent Advisory Committee (PAC), helping support parents of students with learning differences. So many parents contacted us to discuss their struggles to get the services their kids desperately needed and were legally entitled to. Story after story came in of administrators trying to weasel out of their special education duties, trying to slough off kids any time they thought they could get away with it. The more I learned, the angrier I became. In collaboration with a few other committed and talented parents I'd become friends with, we drafted a lengthy and scathing letter to the school committee, enumerating the extensive program deficits at multiple school settings. We demanded change.

Our plan was to submit and read the letter at an upcoming school committee meeting, open to the public, held in the high school library, and televised on local TV. Despite the necessity of public speaking at various times in my previous jobs, I absolutely hated having to do it. I hated being the center of attention. I was filled with anxiety whenever all eyes were on me and felt best suited to a strong supporting role. That's why I was thrilled when my PAC vice president, the father of my daughter's classmate, volunteered to be the front person during the meeting. He'd do the speaking and, if necessary, I could add supplemental information or provide facts to back up his points.

Another reason I was relieved to not be speaking that night—I was finally having my appointment at Mass General's weight loss clinic, and I'd spent months on the wait list. This was all within a year after my initial discovery about myself and having spoken mostly with my AIS-DSD Support Group about my condition. After battling with my weight—partly because of my hormones and partly due to my tendency toward emotional eating (food is my drug)—I was hopeful that I could explain my unique condition and my history of estrogen therapy and have these medical specialists finally provide me with solutions for losing weight and maintaining my weight loss more effectively.

I met with the endocrinologist at Mass General, referred to me by Dr. Bingley, and I explained to him everything I knew about my medical history, my XY chromosomes, the removal of my internal testes as a teenager, and my prescription hormone replacement therapy since that point. The doctor's interest was piqued. He told me how fascinating my case was. His questions became probing, then invasive.

"Do you know if you have a clit? Why don't you undress so I can give you a genital exam."

Was he a doctor or a freaking tourist? It was like being 15, 16, and paraded in front of the medical residents.

This shook me. The numbness crept up, right there in the doctor's office, but then something else ignited in me. A type of anger, but not just rage, not just a temper flare.

"Not only is that inappropriate, but that is incredibly insensitive," I said. I didn't yell, but there was a force in me that I'd used only to help my daughters. "We're done and I'm leaving," I said. I grabbed my purse and walked out, not even checking out at the front desk. I had to hold myself together—there were emotions churning through me that I was not yet fully processing. I fought back tears until I reached my car in the parking garage. Once my door closed, I lost it. Completely bawling. All of my appointments from my early teenage years flooded back. The probing examinations, feeling vulnerable, feeling like a freak.

I had never before spoken up to a medical professional. I had never spoken up for myself at all. This time, I hadn't blacked out. I didn't retreat into myself. I stood up to this unprofessional and insensitive doctor and told him no. Now, I was allowing myself to feel all the uncomfortable and harmful feelings that flooded in. And I felt everything. Years of hurts, shame, despairs, guilt, weakness. I wanted to reach out to the young girl of my past and be the person to advocate for her. To fight the doctors on her behalf.

Though I hadn't stopped crying, I collected myself as much as possible and turned on my car and headed out for the twenty-five-minute drive home. Somewhere along the route, I realized there was a lightness around me. It had felt good to speak up and be empowered enough to refuse the exam and decide to leave. I had reclaimed my power over my own body. I finally had taken control.

What would have been great was to have nothing else to do for the rest of the day but bask in the glow of my newfound empowerment. Also, I could have used an evening to recoup after a few decades' worth of emotional flashbacks. But that was not to be.

The school meeting was scheduled for 7pm, but at 6 the PAC VP called to tell me he couldn't make it. I would be left to face the entire school committee and superintendent and drop the proverbial bomb all on my own. After my emotional medical experience, now I had to get myself together to present the PAC letter of critique to the school committee? Okay, well—I had to do it. This was for all of our kids with special needs.

They called my name to come up before the committee, including the superintendent and all the elected school committee members sitting in a row at a long table. I walked up to the podium and microphone set up to face them. Behind me were the three rows of chairs where attendees sat and listened, some waiting for their turn to be called up to the mic to speak. I read our letter of complaint. I was clear and forceful.

A jolt went through the room. I had dared to criticize the Superintendent and Head of Special Education in our district. I had shared stories of students suffering as a direct result of the district's attempts to cut costs, the district ignoring its legal obligations to the students. After fielding a few questions, I walked away from the microphone and out the back of the room, noting a mixture of knowing smiles and nodding heads, along with several sets of pursed lips and judging eyes. My heart pounded, and I could have felt doubt, but this was something that needed to be done. That night, it had fallen upon me to be the advocate for our kids and fight the district. For our little suburb, this was big news. The next day our local town paper, *The Milton Times*, recapped the meeting—the letter, and my address, made headlines.

The community of special education parents gave me so much positive feedback. But that community was small. No one else outside of our group seemed to care.

Still, that night was a turning point for me. Perhaps I only could have done it because I had finally stood up to a doctor. And I only could have stood up to the doctor because I had been learning how to fight for my daughters. Advocacy had turned inward and then outward. I had faced my demons twice that day, and I realized that I was good at it. The advocacy led to one-to-one meetings with the Superintendent and the Director of Special Education, which led to the first-ever production of a real parent handbook exclusively for special education services. Viable steps would be taken to improve services offered by the district. It had happened—I had been of real-world service to vulnerable children who were being neglected. I liked being able to speak out, the small power of affecting some type of change, and even more, I liked myself more for being able to speak out. This was a taste of a more aggressive kind of advocacy, one that could ignite results. Dare I say it? I was getting my first taste of being an activist.

CHAPTER 10

NO LONGER SILENT

In late spring of 2010, Steven was recruited for a new job in Manhattan, which would require us to relocate from the Boston suburb where we'd lived for the last ten years.

"What do you think?" he asked. "Do we move? Leave the house? Uproot the girls from school?"

Three years earlier, we had gutted and painstakingly renovated our house. I loved it so much. I'd fought for our daughters to get the services they needed at their school district. Still, I barely hesitated to say *Yes, absolutely*. An opportunity for a fresh start? We'd be going somewhere nobody knew me. Our community had, in many ways, become so conservative in its social expectations that I was suffocating. Since my discovery of my CAIS and meeting my community of Orchids, my world had finally opened up, and now I wanted more. Steven was of the same mind. A change would do us all a little good, and going to a large city, exposed to a diversity of cultures and mindsets, felt liberating. We'd be leaving at the end of the school year, as my girls were making the transition to 3rd grade. I'm sure the school was beyond delighted when I announced I would be stepping down from the PAC and my daughters would be leaving, despite the cursory *Oh, so sorry to see you go.*

We spent one day exploring some homes in a few Connecticut neighborhoods within commuting distance of Manhattan. These seemed eerily similar to the community in Boston we were leaving— none of them felt right. With that, we headed back to Manhattan and, within 24 hours, we found an apartment and put down our deposit. That summer, a few months after our girls turned nine, we moved into our Upper West Side rental.

The move marked the end to my portrait business. You can't swing your camera by its strap in New York City without hitting an excellent photographer. I had been working on word-of-mouth from a small-town network of moms. Plus, it would be difficult to hustle a client list while spending so much time getting us all settled and the girls into a new school. We would be starting from near-scratch in having to advocate to get Alex into a special education school for kids with language-based learning disabilities. I thought the problem had just been in a smaller district—no, the problems were the systemic issues involving shunting students with special needs in the most cost-effective manner for the schools and requiring the least amount of effort on their part. It went so far that we had to sue the school district.

After researching every school in the area, I lobbied hard to get the girls into PS 333, a very good public school for grades 1 to 8 on the Upper West Side. They had a solid special education program, an indicator (I thought) that the instructors and administration would be on the ball. I was thrilled to learn, days before our move, that the girls had been admitted.

In August, two weeks before the start of the school year, I went up to my assigned special education registration office at 125th Street, in the heart of Harlem, to complete the process. I knew with the move, the disruption in their lives, that they would need some continuity of programs, no matter how excited they had been for the new adventure. Armed with my girls' IEPs, I advocated for the continuation of services they had been receiving in our Boston suburb: speech and language therapy for Charlotte, while Alex would need that therapy plus a smaller classroom co-taught with a regular and special ed teacher. PS 333 had such a class format for grades 1 to 5 and, after reviewing Alex's IEP and most recent testing, my assigned caseworker agreed that she should be placed in such a class.

On the first day of school, the girls and I walked the seven blocks up Columbus Ave, over to West 93rd Street, and up the steps of PS 333. We dropped off Charlotte at her new 3rd grade classroom, with one teacher and 30 students. The teacher looked confident and in charge, so I took a deep breath, hugged Charlotte goodbye, and walked Alex to the other end of the hall at what I thought would be her new classroom. When we got there, the principal stood in front of the door and refused to let us enter.

"I'm afraid there's been a mistake. Alexandra will be in another class, down the hall."

"Is it a supported class?"

"No."

"How many students?"

"I believe 32, with your daughter."

"What? 32 students and one teacher? But I have her IEP and the paperwork from the district office."

"I'm sorry, but there is no more room in this class. Now, if you want to find another co-taught special ed classroom for Alex, you will need to take it up with the district office and seek another placement."

Alex had approval and I was holding the forms—I couldn't believe this was happening. I tried not to let the principal or Alex see the tears of anger boiling up as I grabbed Alex's hand and walked her to the newly assigned classroom. Inside, the young teacher struggled to get control of his students, unsuccessful at his attempts to wrangle them into the desks and settle down so class could begin. *Oh no no no no.* This was not going to work.

Over the following days, I spun into action, researching on the internet, making calls, determining possible options. Meanwhile, Alex came home every day, exhausted and upset, until finally at the end of the week, she broke down in tears. "I'm just trying to learn, but it's impossible in that crazy, wild zoo of a classroom."

Later, I learned that a child had been bullying Alex, telling her she was stupid and ripping up her papers and tossing them into the trash. Okay, what was this? The teacher couldn't even notice this much, or think to watch out for the girl who was supposed to be in a supported classroom? As soon as I found that out, I pulled Alex out of that class, and we met with a private school consultant, telling her our story and begging her for help. She told us there was a really perfect school for Alex's learning profile on the Upper West Side, called the Gateway School, but the classes were extremely small and totally filled for the year. "But there's another possibility, in Brooklyn." We went to check it out but, on the long commute there, I realized how impossible it would be to make that every morning, while also having to get Charlotte to school, despite how lovely and what a good fit the school appeared to be when we got there. We rode home in a cab, and I was feeling dejected until a call came in from the consultant's number. "You're not going to believe it, but the Gateway School just called. A student in their 3rd grade classroom of nine didn't show, and they are willing to meet with you and Alex tomorrow. Can you make it?"

She was enrolled at Gateway that week, sitting around a table with eight other kids and two full-time special education teachers, in a school that was known for helping students like Alex. I breathed a huge sigh of relief for her, but there was a further hurdle: the tuition fee, which rivaled that of a fancy college. We paid it, and then I was referred to a well-known special education lawyer downtown. He was gruff, sloppy-looking, but was a straight shooter who didn't mince words. "You have a case," he said. "I'll sue the school district and make them reimburse you to pay for Alex's tuition as an out-of-district placement moving forward, since they were not able to meet her needs." Wow, I thought. This guy knew his stuff. And his plan worked.

That Alex ended up in a private school, with a class of nine kids and two teachers, was a luxury and a privilege, but it should be the *norm* for any child with learning differences. It shouldn't take parents like me to fight for this.

* * *

Though I had few friends in the area, I met some moms through my girls' schools. I was excited to make new friends, as if I was the one starting school. A topic that came up early on was the need for a new dentist now that we'd relocated. One of the moms at Alex's fancy private school had *the best* dentist, according to her, located near Columbus Circle. "He's got amazing patients—celebrities, and even the newscasters from the morning shows. And CNN. We just love him."

Well, that was a high recommendation. I booked my first appointment and I understood why the mom seemed to fawn over him, and I'm pretty sure it didn't have to do with his prowess with a Cavitron. The dentist had a chiseled face, perfectly manicured hands, and a cadre of young women dental assistants who swooned in his presence. It was quite something. I had a simple filling done, but I went back for a second appointment a week later because I was having continued pain after the filling, which I'd never experienced before.

"Well, I'm sure that's not from anything to do with the filling," the dentist said. "Honestly, I'm the best around. If you're having pain, it must be from something you're doing. Are you sure there's nothing you can trace it to, maybe from home?" His tone was defensive, incredulous that I would dare critique his performance. It hadn't even been a critique—I was having pain in the spot he'd filled the week before and wanted him to fix it. Instead, I got the "Who the hell are *you*?" act, catching me completely off guard. The tears were already welling. This would have been about the time the old Kimberly would have checked out, mentally. But I wasn't that Kimberly anymore. Once again, something clicked inside me.

My face hot, voice shaky, I sat up in the chair, and before I even realized what was happening, I said, "That was not an appropriate reaction to me telling you I had pain. You should not be getting defensive with a patient, trying to make me ashamed and uncomfortable."

By the look on the hygienists' faces, you'd have thought I'd bitten off his fingers and spat them at him. Not one of them tried to calm me down or help me. Meanwhile, the dentist continued to say that he'd never had a patient experience this kind of pain after a procedure he'd done, and that his record spoke for itself.

I had not attacked him. I deserved respect and was in pain, and I had wanted him to fix it. But I was tired of not being taken seriously by doctors. I got up and walked out the door. I pushed past the receptionist and patient at the front desk, who had heard what went on. Everyone in the waiting area stared at me as I pressed the elevator button and waited for it to open and whisk me away from this degrading experience. I wasn't reading into his tone, and I wasn't looking for a fight. I wasn't looking for some ax to grind. Once alone in the elevator, I burst into tears. I thought of intersex children and the fact that pediatric surgeons often defensively refer to their patients collectively as a "happy silent majority" who grow up, move on, and never complain to them about the treatment they received. If we don't speak up, the assumption is we have not been harmed, and most patients simply don't complain. On the subway ride home, my epiphany was the same as it was when I'd left the endocrinologist at the weight loss clinic. I had taken control and had spoken up for myself against an inappropriate medical provider, and it had felt good. All the years I'd spent letting men in white coats with degrees tell me how things were going to be, never questioning my own comfort or wants, even treating me like shit, all of it fought to break out of me at once. I wanted to take back all those years. I couldn't, but going forward, I promised myself in that subway car that from here on out, I would always fight for myself.

Now, how to channel that energy?

* * *

I had signed up for Facebook on New Year's Day, 2009, having learned about it through a few of my Orchid sisters. Of course, now there are plenty of opinions of the efficacy of Facebook and the Zuckerberg empire, but this resource was a tremendous boon to the intersex community. Special groups on this site have been fundamental in reaching out to individuals and other intersex groups, creating an immense, international meeting space. Right away, I joined a private, secret group run by the AIS-DSD Support Group. Within a month, I had over 100 "friends" from within the intersex community. It replaced communication via the email list almost immediately. Despite the later problems with Facebook, I still call it a necessary evil and am thankful it exists because it is an easy, private way for a marginalized and disparate community to connect and feel less alone. People who had been on Facebook and had "come out" on social media suddenly found that "friends" had stopped following them or unfriended them soon after their disclosures. Many shared their heartbreaking stories. Many more shared the stories of love and support they got from family and friends when they did come out. There might be moments of feeling down, but with the community at your back, more often than not, there was a strong sense of empowerment on those group pages.

Many more private intersex pages popped up. I made it a point to join most of them—it was important to me to keep my finger on the pulse of the ever-growing, ever-changing community I was now a part of. As I became online friends with many more people, I watched them post their coming out stories, many of which were met with love and support, albeit with a dose of curiosity and the occasional stupid question asked, most often involving invasive biological questions. Of course, there are always the private messages we don't see, though in our groups we sometimes hear about them after the fact, especially if they have been cruel or crushing.

I still wasn't "out" as having CAIS to people beyond my immediate family and Ellen, with the exception of this group. When I moved to Manhattan the following year, I relied on the group page to connect with other members of the intersex community in New York. As soon as we had moved, I reached out to a couple of the Orchids I knew who lived in the city, and we got together for dinner. Having them nearby made me feel connected in a way I hadn't in Boston, especially after learning I was intersex. Because New York is so big, there were many other Orchids around. So being new to the area, and with plenty of time and motivation to connect with people, I reached out to more of my fellow Orchids that I'd known online and in person from the conferences and arranged meetups, usually weeknight dinners. Three people responded right away, and we connected within a week. I organized more dinners, more social gatherings, for anywhere between three and twenty people at a time. We were not unlike your average group of "ladies who lunch"—we just happened to be bonded by being born with similar traits, which led to a unique and rare shared experience.

I toyed with the idea of making my own coming out post on Facebook, but I didn't seem to get around to it. Instead, I focused my time by joining the board for my AIS-DSD Support Group. Now that we were settled in New York and my girls were doing well, I was beyond ready to do something constructive with my newfound availability. This was my first step in getting involved in the community and giving back in a concrete way—more than just supportive posts and messages and financial donations, all of which are still very important.

The board for the AIS-DSD Support Group wasn't your typical nonprofit board. Because there was no actual staff, board members were active volunteers, doing the work of answering calls and emails from members and prospective members, fundraising, planning and running the annual conference. There was much to learn about navigating the politics and personalities that make up an organization. Not everyone volunteering on the board was equipped to share the workload, and so much of the planning and organizing fell to a small group of the board members. This became a full-time (volunteer) job, one that I didn't talk about much at home, despite it being my entire life outside of my family.

At this point, my daughters were getting old enough to understand their mom was busy at work on *something*, and they were asking questions, wanting to know if I was going back to taking pictures or if I was being a lawyer. They were savvy and I wanted to be honest with them, but also, any minute, they could start menstruating and I wouldn't know how to help them through that process the way other moms could. It was important for me to finally sit them down and, without explaining everything, give them enough to know that Mama was different. The truth was that I'd gotten quite comfortable with not having a period, so much so that the thought of having one grossed me out. Definitely not what my daughters needed from their mom. Suddenly, I was facing the old fears of not being a "real" woman and— worse—not being a "real" mom. Would these old feelings be chasing me down my entire life, resurfacing at each milestone I couldn't share with my daughters? Was this a motherhood test that I would never be able to pass?

Thankfully, there was this juggernaut entity known as American Girl. Soon after moving to Manhattan, we discovered the big flagship American Girl Store near Rockefeller Center and St. Patrick's Cathedral. We took the girls one Saturday afternoon, who were excited to check out the doll clothes and have afternoon tea. What made me happy was discovering the amazing selection of books American Girl produced. Most of them are pre-teen and teen novels, based on their dolls, set in various time periods. Charlotte was especially fascinated by these books. Then, we discovered the puberty books, a series entitled *The Care and Keeping of You*, and I snatched up a few, thinking I needed all the help I could get. The girls and I flipped through parts of the first one together. "You should both read this on your own," I told them. "When you're ready and in the mood, and then feel free to talk to me about any questions you might have."

Internally, I was petrified they would ask me questions I couldn't answer. That evening, I shared with them that I was born a bit different and didn't have female reproductive organs and therefore didn't ever get my period. "It also means I was never able to get pregnant."

"Oooh, you're so lucky you don't have to get a yucky period!" they exclaimed. Then, Charlotte added, "Well, I plan to adopt someday, so I don't need to have a period either."

Oh my darling, wonderful girls.

* * *

That summer, I flew across the country to be with my tribe of Orchid sisters at the annual conference in Seattle. Though I always missed being away from my family, still the conference was a breath of fresh air. Catharsis still happened, bonding as always, but now I was also learning more about such things as queerness, even within my own niche community. Intersex had its own niches, as I grew ever more aware.

At this conference, I crossed paths for the first time with Anne Tamar-Mattis, founder of Advocates for Informed Choice (AIC). Anne was an attorney and an ally of the community by way of her spouse. She was basically a one-woman organization who started AIC in 2006, after graduating law school and using a fellowship to pay her salary, with the goal of developing legal strategies to end the medically unnecessary and harmful surgeries performed on intersex kids' bodies without their consent. AIC had obtained its 501(c)(3) nonprofit status[1] a year before the Seattle conference. She spoke at conferences such as ours, as well as other, smaller organizations, to discuss with people their rights, occasionally giving workshops on navigating the legal system to fight for intersex rights especially regarding within the medical community. Arlene Baratz, mother of Katie, whom I'd first seen on *Oprah* and then met in Dallas, was a founding board member.

We connected right off the bat, and I was eager to pick her brain on the legal issues. She was sharp and incredibly warm-hearted. We exchanged information, and I hoped that we'd be able to work together on some project in the future.

Meanwhile, as luck would have it, 2860 miles away, Charlotte was having a transformative experience of her own. I got the call from Steven. "So…Charlotte got her period this morning," he said.

My first thought? Relief. I wasn't there to screw up anything. The irony was not at all lost on me that it happened while I was at my Orchid Conference.

"What did you do?" I asked.

"I went to the drug store and got her a box of sanitary pads. I showed her where the instructions were, and then I took her to day camp." I immediately hung up with Steven and called the summer camp nurse to make sure she was aware that Charlotte might need assistance.

She chuckled after I finished telling her about my phone call. "Charlotte has already come to see me this morning. Your husband bought her slim panty liners—they were pretty insufficient for what Charlotte needed. The poor thing bled through her shorts. But we've taken care of her and have plenty of spare products and extra clothes she was able to use. And now she knows what to get. Maybe tonight, have your husband run to the store with her and let her grab what she needs."

I was so grateful for how understanding the nurse was and all her wisdom in this issue. No doubt she had plenty of personal experience as well as experience explaining to young girls what was happening with their bodies. Had it been me at home, instead of Steven, I might have picked out the same slim panty liners that he did. I had no clue what a 10-year-old girl would need for her first period. I was no more experienced than my husband.

Once the conference was over and I returned home, I sat down with Charlotte and Alex again in their room. Now that they had a little more experience, I revealed a little more of my story to them. "So what Charlotte is experiencing," I said, looking at Alex and then at Charlotte, "has never happened to me. I was born a certain way that keeps me from menstruating. But even though I have no experience, I will do my best to help you both mange it—we'll be learning together."

CHAPTER 11

ADVOCATING OUT LOUD

The following year, I was assigned to plan the 2013 AIS-DSD annual conference—in Boston. It would be a sort-of homecoming for me, though I hadn't moved too far away. I hadn't seen my dad much. He never came to visit us in New York, though my mom flew up from Florida a few times. Tara came down once or twice, and I saw her several times when we went back to Massachusetts to visit. My parents had not seen each other in almost a decade. Still, I wanted to take advantage of the opportunity not only to see my parents but to have them see what I was a part of now, the results of the work I'd been doing. I flagged mentioning the conference to them for later.

Instead, I reached out to Anne Tamar-Mattis to offer my services to her in any way that I could be of help. Though I had never done any fundraising or grant writing before, after working on the board of AIS-DSD and seeing what was necessary, I felt sure that I had the skill set for that kind of work, especially something part-time that I could do from home—I was still very busy with the support group work. I sent off an email asking if she needed any help fundraising on a volunteer basis so I could get some experience. She jumped at the offer, giving me a couple of leads to research, and soon, I was drafting my first grant proposal.

Meanwhile, with plans to remain in New York for several more years, Steven and I found a new apartment in Manhattan, one that would accommodate our girls who were now almost teenagers. But we also decided it needed a complete renovation before we could move in. So this down-to-studs reno was happening while I was planning for the Boston AIS-DSD conference for the following July, but our contractor promised us work would be completed by January, leaving me close to six months of solid focus and preparation for the Boston conference between January and July. However, the project got delayed because of Hurricane Sandy that October. Construction, like many things in Manhattan during that time, came to a halt. Building didn't get going for another two months, and didn't resume until January, right when I was supposed to be diving headfirst into preparing for the Boston conference. Then, just as things were getting underway with both the renovation and the conference planning, I got a call, out of the blue, from Anne. She had a position for me at AIC, a full-time position doing fundraising, strategy, and some communications work. "Mostly your role would be to raise money to help grow the organization." I'd be Director of Advancement. Though I had only been looking for part-time work, this offer was too good to pass up: a job where I could still work from home on a personal subject I cared deeply about. I signed on March 1st.

This was an exciting time at AIC, as the organization was about to launch its first impact litigation case on behalf of an intersex child. In December of that year, I would be making my first big trip for the organization: a conference in Berlin, where I would give a presentation on intersex medical violence to a large group of potential funding organizations and foundations.

The work at AIC pulled me in, despite being in the middle of moving an entire household into our new apartment. Over this time, I talked more openly with Alex and Charlotte about being intersex and what it meant. They quickly became well versed and comfortable with the knowledge. As both had started menstruating, sometimes they admitted to me they were jealous that I didn't have to deal with cramps, PMS, and sanitary pads. "While I can't say that I wish those things," I told them, on more than one occasion, "I'm happy that being intersex led me to adoption—that's how I became *your* mom, and I wouldn't want it any other way." Then, I reminded them that what their bodies were doing, despite the pains and inconveniences, was a healthy and positive thing. "Your bodies are doing what your bodies are supposed to be doing. Someday, it might not seem like such a pain."

The following January, I represented AIC at a medical conference in Baltimore. I gave a talk to a room filled with medical professionals, and for the first time, I told my personal story, out loud, to a group of people who did not have CAIS. This was not the intimate venue of the Orchid Conference. All the while, I was getting ready for the big Boston conference, staying overnight at the conference site near Logan Airport, then meeting with the planner. Over the entire first half of the year, I had bi-weekly planning calls with board members deciding the program, the speakers, the meals, and additional activities. Offering some of the biggest assistance was Amy, a parent member of our support group who had a young daughter with CAIS. She took on administrative tasks involving the computer, such as designing the programs. The process was overwhelming at times and exhausting always. Steven asked more than once why I was doing so much volunteer work, and his questions were tinged with growing frustration over my aggravated moods that he had to hear about or experience. When I'd volunteered to take on this planning, I did not have a full-time job, nor did I plan on getting one before the July conference, and I hadn't planned on still being up to my eyeballs in renovation. There were nights I nearly fell apart. However, I couldn't quit.

Conference planning also entailed work with potential attendees and new members. A new member reached out to me on the group's Facebook page. He was from Japan and was desperate to attend, though he wasn't sure he could afford to make the trip. This was going to be the second conference since AIS-DSD began admitting male-identifying intersex people into the group. Over the last two years, the group had expanded and it became more diverse. In large part, this was driven by demand, but also by a few of the parent members who joined when their children were babies or toddlers; over the course of time, the children they'd called their daughters started to identify as boys. AIS-DSD certainly wasn't going to kick out these members so, as a result, they slowly started accepting men and non-binary-identifying intersex members. This was a good thing; our community was growing. Not without growing pains—some of the intimacy was lost because of the expansion, but it was a necessary growth. The word was getting out, people were finding us, and the group was thus fulfilling its purpose.

I helped the young man in Japan get a partial scholarship to afford attending, which some years we could do better than others. He was so grateful and said he couldn't wait to meet me.

Through our conversations, he also let me know I was the first intersex person he had interacted with on the Facebook page. That made me think back to my earliest interactions with Mandy, the president of the AIS-DSD when I joined and the first intersex person I'd (knowingly) spoken with. Over the last decade, I have been that "first person" for a dozen or so intersex people, and it's been one of the most satisfying experiences of my life. That first person is so critically important. Mandy moved to Texas with her partner and daughter, but we kept in touch on major holidays and via text updates. She was the beginning of me finding my tribe.

* * *

One of the requirements of being the conference organizer was to make the short welcome speech at the Saturday morning opening session, which I dreaded. But I was an advocate now—if I could speak up in front of the school board with a message none of them wanted to hear, then I could certainly give a few welcome words to my Orchid sisters and brothers.

On email with my mom one evening, I finally mentioned the conference, that I was organizing, arranging speakers, that it would be in Boston, that I was giving the speech. I tested the receptiveness of the maternal waters. "You know," I said, "you could even come up if you wanted. Come to a couple of sessions, see some of my work."

She wasn't opposed, but she didn't give a concrete answer until a few days later. "I'd love to come, sweetie. It will be a perfect time to come up, plus I can help take care of the girls when you have to do conference work. It would give Steven a chance to go to some of the events, too."

A couple weeks later, I floated the notion of coming to the conference to my dad. "Mom is coming up from Florida to take part, but then she's going to watch the girls for a bit. I'm going to be speaking."

"That's so great, Zimmo. It sounds like a lot of work."

"You could come too, maybe a couple of sessions. I'm sure you'd find some of the talks informative."

"I probably would," was all he said. He didn't commit, but I didn't want to push him. Then, a week before the conference, my dad asked where Steven and the girls and I were staying.

"At the conference hotel, with the girls. Mom's coming up to help out and watch them so Steven and I can both participate." This was going to be Steven's first time at the conference. My gratitude wasn't only for the extra pair of hands; having his support, knowing he was there if I needed him to be, and knowing he'd have my back kept me from panicking about the small stuff because I knew it would get done.

Then my dad said, "So what time should I be there for your speech?" I was floored. There was no indication he'd been planning to come, and maybe it was a last-minute decision for him. I was so grateful and told him I was looking forward to seeing him. Then I hung up and called my mom, so she could be mentally prepared. As is her definitive mode, my mother did what she always has done—acted like it was no big deal, said she was over it, but I knew that inside it was a really big deal, that she was nervous and dreaded having to deal with him. But she wouldn't want me to worry about her.

* * *

Amid all the chaos of the year, the conference date came, and when we drove up to Boston, I was excited and ready. During registration, I made sure to be by the table to greet attendees and offer any assistance I could. Then, I heard my name. It was the young man who'd come from Japan. He ran over to me and gave me a hug. Then, he got down on his knees and thanked me for helping him to get there. I was shocked, and of course uncomfortable as all the eyes in the room turned toward us, and my first instinct was to retreat inward. But the whole point of the conference was this exposure, this much-needed interaction that he had been desperate to have. The moment was all about this young man, so happy to have found his tribe, finally, among us. His very Japanese display showed how much respect he had for the help I'd been able to offer him. This weekend was all about connecting, feeling all our feelings, and finally being our full selves. How long ago the five years since Dallas seemed to me now. It hadn't been that long at all.

This, I understood, is what had kept me going through the days of deepest stress and self-doubt. Now, it was time for my welcome address.

I walked to the front of the room, toward the podium for my short speech, and when I was a few rows from the front, I saw them: my parents in the second row—sitting next to each other. *Holy shit*. I turned around and left the ballroom, making a beeline for the closest restroom, where I went into the stall and fought back the deluge of tears that threatened. The sadness at seeing them together at the same time for the first time in years was overpowering. And suddenly I was a child again, mourning the loss of my family unit. Mixed with this was the understanding that they were both there for me, trying their best so many years after my diagnosis and surgery. I could have stayed in that bathroom stall for another hour or two, but I was already five minutes late opening the conference. Time to pull it together and head back in. I blotted my eyes, careful not to smear my makeup, cleared my throat a couple of times, and then I somehow moved my body back into the ballroom and was at the podium again.

Leaning close to the mic, I made sure my speech was in order, that I could turn the pages without too much flurry of paperwork, and that my hands, which were already shaky, would be hidden. I took an extra breath before beginning.

"Welcome to the 17th annual AIS-DSD Support Group Conference." I cleared my throat away from the mic. "My name is Kimberly Zieselman, this year's conference host and organizer." I thanked the volunteers who put their heart and soul into making the weekend a success, as well as Anne, who supported me by allowing me to juggle my new full-time position with Advocates for Informed Choice. Then, I told my story, to the entire room of people.

I told them how I had learned that I had CAIS only five years earlier, when I was 41 years old. That I had been lucky to find the support group online, then came to Dallas to be face-to-face with dozens and dozens of other people just like me, who understood and shared similar experiences and had knowledge about my "condition." I told how doctors told my family and me that my reproductive organs were not fully formed and that they would likely become cancerous if not removed immediately. How I had never been told I had XY chromosomes or internal testes, or the dreaded words "male pseudo-hermaphrodite" and "testicular feminization" that I had later discovered written all over my medical records. How at age 15 I began my life on hormone replacement therapy and was told to carry on—with no information or support.

It was hard to get through my speech without my voice cracking and the tears flowing, but especially when I got to the next part.

"This wasn't just happening to me—this was also happening to my parents. They were lied to as well. Remember, this was before we carried the internet around on our smart phones. This was back when most of us didn't challenge a doctor's recommendation. Most of us just complied and moved on. Both my mother and father are here today; and for the first time, after 30 years, they will finally meet other parents who get it. Mom, Dad, thank you so much for being here." The room erupted in applause for them. The emotions were acutely intense, but I did not black out. I lived through it. I remembered it immediately after. To this day, I remember exactly how I felt looking into the room and seeing my parents, not only in the same room for the first time in ten years, but sitting together. There for me.

"Fortunately, today more and more parents are getting information and support soon after their child is diagnosed. Many are finding their way to our website, Facebook, and email groups, as well as our annual conferences. The families, young children, and teens present at these conferences each year give me so much hope. Hope that things are indeed changing for the better. Hope that word is getting out, and hope that someday, no parent or individual will face a diagnosis alone ever again."

Here we were, in Boston, where I'd grown up and lived most of my adult life, and where I had met Steven, where we started our family.

"Many of you have traveled a long distance to be here. As you will note from the map displayed at registration, we have individuals and families from across the US and Canada as well as Brazil, Italy, Japan, South Africa, and Australia. I think this underscores the importance and need for face-to-face support. We have over 180 people here today, far surpassing our expectations. Our largest past conference totaled about 140 people." That was the most incredible part. Though space was going to be a bit tight at times, we did our best to accommodate everyone—we all got a little cozier that weekend.

What was most impressive were the 80 first-time attendees to the conference, either who had intersex traits or had intersex family members.

I ended the speech by thanking everyone for coming and reminding them to take care of themselves and each other as they experienced both the joys and the emotions that often accompany the first visit to the conference. Finally, I welcomed the brave and wonderful men who were with us this year for the first time. "Our support group has grown in so many ways even in the last five years, and having you with us this weekend, our brothers and friends in the community, is a wonderful step in the right direction."

My dad attended a plenary session that day, but he didn't stay for too long. Being near my mom made him uncomfortable, and he was among strangers in an unfamiliar environment. But this had been a huge step for him, and what he was able to give me that day made me feel very loved.

Tara also came for the afternoon sessions, and we were able to have a drink and chat for a while. "I'm so proud of you, Sissy," she said, and hugged me. I was so happy to see her and have her there to support me. Until Steven and the girls came along, no person had been closer to me than my sister. Though we were different in many ways, we shared the same odd sense of humor. We had been through so many emotional ups and downs, especially our parents' divorce. Tara was the only one who could truly understand that part of my experience, just as my Orchid sisters were the only ones who could understand what it was like to be intersex.

Meanwhile, my mom participated in a few sessions geared for parents of intersex people. When I asked how it went and how she felt, she said they were helpful. "I was able to relate to many of the comments made by parents. Especially about feeling a sense of guilt over their children being born intersex in the first place and not being able to do enough for you as you grew up."

"Oh, Mom." We hugged each other. Finally, though, the emotional roller coaster of the conference had gotten even to her.

I was glad for her to be spending quality time with Alexandra and Charlotte, taking them for ice cream or meals, showing them the

Boston they hadn't gotten a chance to see in their young years, the Boston my mom still knew well despite her relocation. By helping watch the girls, she was also actively doing something to help me. Though she wasn't doing it to make up for what she'd been unable to help me with back in my adolescence, I sensed or at least hoped for a catharsis and healing happening for her.

I would still have questions flare up about how much, and when they knew; or flashes of feeling the must have lied to me. But those mattered less and less. Most of the time, it seemed unlikely to me that they knew and withheld my CAIS from me.

Another surprising development was the appearance of Dr. Lydia Bingley, my primary care physician from the time I was 26 to when I left Boston at 43. She'd been liberal in her approach to healthcare and insurance, and her politics in general had aligned with my own. I didn't email her regularly, but every so often I would send her an update on my life or ask her a quick question. Despite being busy with her practice and teaching courses at Harvard Medical, she had usually been available to me. I had emailed her some information on the conference, how planning was going, and telling her if she was interested in learning more that she should stop by for a session to check it out. I hadn't held out any hopes and didn't want to pressure her into attending. I happened to see her coming into the ballroom during a panel of intersex people telling their stories, and I waved her over to sit with me. One woman was speaking on the damage that had been done through secrecy and a lack of information and said, "the truth is always the healthiest option."

Dr. Bingley leaned close to my ear and said, "I'm not sure telling the truth is the best path. Look at your life—had you known the truth at age 16, your life may have been much more difficult."

Wow, I thought, and this took me aback. I had known the harm of not knowing. I imagined my life if I had known. There would have been other difficulties, sure. But I look at the cases of the young advocates such as Katie Baratz, who *did* know and was happy she knew.

Maybe I wouldn't have spent years feeling like a fraud and a phony. Sure, Dr. Bingley's professional experience would give her a different perspective and insight. But maybe this was what she needed, hearing this panel discussion. She'd had no prior experience in dealing with the intersex community, so I didn't challenge her and remained polite. Really, I was grateful she had come at all. It was a sign of how much she cared.

After the panel and between events, my mom stopped by with the girls. I introduced Dr. Bingley to my mom, who had heard so much about Dr. Bingley over the last couple of years. My worlds felt connected, or at least in the process of connecting. The truth and openness felt good.

Steven, meanwhile, couldn't have been more incredible. His help was instrumental to my sanity—he checked with me constantly to see if there was anything he could do to help, and did whatever task I asked of him. He is much more comfortable in new social situations if he has a purpose, a job, and can be actively doing something. But he also got into the community element, and he ended up spending a lot of time at the bar socializing with people he was meeting. The day of my speech, he was part of another session featuring partners and spouses who spoke about their experiences of being in a relationship with someone who was intersex. Steven had agreed to be one of the speakers. For his turn, he talked about our story a little more, and then he went on to say how much this group had helped me, what a tremendous community we were, and how seeing me happy and finally free had meant the world to him. Much of the audience (and me along with them) were wiping tears away by the end. He gave such a great speech, and at the end, I got up and hugged him. Yes, I thought, this is what a partner is. This is love and support. Sure, life had dealt me some curve balls and a couple of proverbial fastballs to the helmet, but to have this family and this life now? Between Steven and Charlotte and Alex, how lucky I had been after all.

Though my girls spent most of the time with my mom touring

Boston (in the middle of a heat wave, no less), they did come to the Saturday night dinner celebration, which featured a talent show and fundraising auction. They were very into the silent auction, especially because Steven bought them each twenty dollars worth of one-dollar raffle tickets so they could race to the different baskets, dropping in their tickets, plotting which they wanted versus which they thought they could win. The show and auction's unofficial emcee was Eden Atwood, one of my Orchid sisters and a fairly well known jazz singer. She kept the crowd going with music and commentary, then between talent show acts, she called up different kiddos who were present and had them pull a number out of the bag and announce the winner of the next basket of goodies. During one break, she called up my girls, who sheepishly giggled their way up to the microphone to pull out a ticket for the prize of a home spa day. When they read off the number, we realized it was one of their tickets. They had put in nearly half their combined tickets for this prize so they could give it to me, to pamper me after working so hard on the conference. They were thrilled that they won me this gift. I was thrilled and touched at my amazing girls. Yes, once again, I got emotional and didn't worry as much about my makeup this time.

CHAPTER 12

RESOLVING TO CHANGE

After the conference, I returned full-throttle to my work at AIC, specifically on the Resolve Project,[1] which aimed to encourage communication between intersex patients and the physicians or medical institutions who had harmed them with unconsented surgeries when they were children.

This was our attempt at reparative justice—to seek apologies from the doctors who had harmed intersex people, helping to create a path toward healing for both the intersex patients and the doctors.

Since I was not simply a staff person or advocate, I was one of those intersex people harmed by the medical community, I needed to participate in this exercise myself before trying to convince other intersex people to do this. So, in November of that year, I wrote a letter to Massachusetts General Hospital.

Empowerment is a radical act. It challenges the status quo, which isn't always malicious, though its side effects can feel the same as the effects of a malicious act. People go with the known, the status quo, because that's easier than reinventing the proverbial wheel, even if that wheel happens to be steamrolling large groups of people. I was taking ownership of my body and my story, and in doing so was attempting to rewrite the narrative that had been written of people like me without our point of view. Why wouldn't the medical community want to pivot its practice away from pediatric surgery, delaying it until patients could consent?

The words were not difficult to write, though reliving the pain was. But I didn't hedge, I didn't have to dig deep or pace myself. This letter poured out of me. This letter was decades in the making.

I addressed the letter to the Office of Patient Advocacy:

To Whom It May Concern,

I'm a 47-year-old women with Androgen Insensitivity Syndrome (AIS), writing to share my personal experience as a patient at your hospital affected by an intersex condition, or "Disorder of Sex Development" (DSD). I know that I appear to be a DSD patient "success story," but in fact, I have suffered and am unsatisfied with the way I was treated at Massachusetts General Hospital (MGH).

Too often I have heard of doctors reference the "silent majority" of DSD patients who have been treated in childhood and then go on to live a happy contented life, when in fact, there is very little evidence that this is so, and follow-up has been extremely limited. Medical professionals would likely include me in that "silent majority," seeing only a woman who identifies as female, graduated college and law school, has been married for over twenty years, with two adopted children and a successful, fulfilling career.

While I have been fortunate in many ways, I no longer want my voice to be buried among that assumed silent majority, Instead, I am speaking out today to tell my story and hopefully make a difference.

My goal is to inform MGH in a manner that results in better care and, more importantly, prevents harm to others.

Thirty-two years ago, I was 15 years old with amenorrhea and referred to Dr. P. Morrow, a reproductive oncology surgeon also at MGH. My parents and I were told that I had a partially developed uterus and ovaries that would likely become cancerous if left inside for much longer. We were told that my vagina was abnormally short and may require future surgery to lengthen it in order to have successful intercourse with male sexual partners.

I was never told that I had complete Androgen Insensitivity Syndrome and XY chromosomes, or that the gonads being removed were actually testes, not ovaries. I was told that I was having a "full hysterectomy" and would need to take hormone replacement therapy for the rest of my life. That summer I spent my 16th birthday recuperating from surgery. I went back to high school in the fall and spent the next 25 years living a lie.

A lie that has had a profound and harmful impact on me.

At some level, I knew I was not being told the whole truth. It was the way both my parents and the doctors acted that signaled to me something more may be going on. But I was afraid to ask questions—it was clear that my parents were in distress, and I didn't want to cause them any more pain. Over the years I have wondered just how much my parents knew but withheld from me (albeit with good intentions).

I lived the next 25 years with the feeling that something awful was being hidden from me and not knowing whom I could trust.

When I asked if I could meet someone else with my condition, I was told that I was different, that there was "nobody" with my medical condition in the world, that my situation was "very rare." I was told to go on with my life and not talk about my surgery because it wasn't important; I was healthy and could adopt children someday if I wanted to become a parent. I was told to be a good girl and take a hormone pill each day for the rest of my life to stay healthy.

But what I heard was, "you are not a real woman, you are a damaged freak, so go out and fake the rest of your life and be sure nobody knows your secret."

So that's what I did. I was a "good girl" and took my pills, didn't ask questions, and did what the men in white coats asked me to do. There was no support provided for either my parents or me.

No social workers, no therapists. Perhaps most shockingly, **there was no true informed consent**.

A few years ago, I was diagnosed with post-traumatic stress disorder caused by anxiety I had been harboring for over two decades about my past surgery and the possibility of getting cancer. This led me to obtain my medical records from MGH and discover the truth.

Covering several pages of handwritten records were words like "testicular feminization," "Male pseudo-hermaphroditism," and "Androgen Insensitivity Syndrome."

But the most disturbing thing I read was not even those stigmatizing words that had been sealed up and hidden from me for so many years, but something else. There, handwritten in cursive on a piece of lined paper, was a statement dated 6/27/83 that read, "The procedures, risks, benefits, and alternatives to it have been discussed. All questions answered; patient and parents have consented." Underneath that scribbled statement was Dr. Morrow's signature, my father's signature, and my 15-year-old signature. There was absolutely no reference anywhere on that page or the surrounding pages about what "it" was. That was our "informed consent."

Some may say what you don't know doesn't hurt you, but I strongly disagree.

And this is what I want your medical providers today to understand—withholding information from young patients, lying to patients, is harmful.

In my case, my parents were also lied to. They were never told the whole truth about my XY chromosomes or testes. But in other cases, parents are told the real facts but specifically instructed not to tell their child the truth for fear that they will be devastated, psychologically traumatized, or worse. That sets up a terribly unhealthy dynamic for a parent-child relationship. It leaves the children with issues of trust that have long-lasting implications well into adulthood.

For me, **the lies were harmful in an invisible way**—they set up a damaging dialogue in my head that perpetuated a sense of being "fake," not being "real," and never being "good enough."

I had a sense that there was more to the story and I was being lied to. Being told not to talk about my condition with others, having to pretend to be like all the other girls, wanting to fit in, and being told that there was nobody like me in the world all contributed to my feelings of being isolated, different, and ultimately, detached emotionally.

Although one may think that being told I had typically male chromosomes and testes might have made me feel even less real and more like I was faking life as a female, it in fact did just the opposite. When I finally learned this truth, it was very affirming and anxiety-releasing. I finally had the whole story, I finally knew who I really was, and I had no more fear of "cancer." Before, when I didn't know the truth, I intuitively knew "something" was wrong and that I had been lied to. I imagined things much worse than the actual truth and felt I was a real freak of nature—damaged and alone. ("I must be such a freak of nature that they found it necessary to lie to me!")

While I have no doubt that the medical providers involved thought they were protecting me (and my parents) by hiding a "shameful" truth about my body and medical condition, it was wrong to replace that truth with lies that perpetuated my fear of cancer and forced me to imagine much more radical versions of "my truth." It was wrong to set up a situation that left me not knowing whether I could trust either my parents or my doctors.

It caused me to shut down emotionally and put up walls. With the help of a caring therapist, I now realize that I didn't really experience or feel true happiness or sadness. I placed a great deal of pressure on myself to succeed and prove myself, whether in my personal life or my work. I "blacked out" when situations got overly emotional. I have no recollection of my husband proposing to me. After adopting my beautiful twin daughters, it took me years and years to accept that I was a "real" mother. And despite my unconditional love for them, I struggled to feel worthy of theirs. Whenever I found myself in heated arguments or controversial discussions with friends or family, I would "black out" and forget what had occurred. My mind had found a way to cope by burying all extreme feelings, by retreating.

In turn, I missed out on the real human emotions of joy and even sadness of my life experience.

Those are the hidden costs of the lie.

Being told a lie about my condition and being told I was alone, with nobody else like me in the world, was devastating. Thankfully, in 2009, I discovered an online support group and now personally know hundreds of people "like me." Connecting with others and getting information and support has been nothing less than life changing. Now I have the joy of seeing kids as young as eight or nine meeting at the AIS-DSD Support Group annual conferences around the country and connecting with others online who are just like them. They are embracing their differences in age-appropriate ways with the support of their parents and a large loving community. These kids are learning the truth about who they are and are being told they are not alone and, in fact, they have an expanded community that includes others who "get it." This is the way it should be.

Please be sure to let children with DSD and their families know that there is amazing peer support out there and help them connect with groups like AIS-DSD and others.

I want you to understand that these feelings and experiences I describe are not unique to me—I have talked to many others who share extremely similar feelings and have experienced strikingly similar emotions and have suffered in much of the same way.

Please know that **withholding information and lying ultimately harms a child.** Children and adolescents with DSD need to be given age-appropriate, honest information in stages, ideally combined with peer and psychosocial support.

Physicians can't do this on their own—they need to function as part of a team of caregivers that looks at the whole child and their family and collaborates to meet his/her/their psychosocial needs, and the needs of his/her/their family and caregivers.

Finally, **surgeries on children with DSD are often medically unnecessary and ultimately harmful.** In hindsight, I wish I had been given the choice to keep my testes and been monitored regularly instead of rushing to surgery. Hormone replacement therapy is a poor substitute for the real thing—especially at age 15 with a long life ahead.

Luckily, I escaped surgery to lengthen my shorter-than-average vagina. It turns out the body I was born with worked a lot better than the doctors seemed to think it would. But many of my "sisters" with AIS have not been so fortunate. The physical and emotional pain they continue to endure as a result is heartbreaking. There are cases all over the country and indeed the world of young children with DSD being operated on solely for cosmetic reasons and before they are old enough to have any say in the matter.

Please understand that just because a child is born with genitals that look different from the norm, or have chromosomes that don't match their outward appearance, this does not automatically mean that they will be unhappy with their bodies or struggle with their sexual identity when they get older. Do not make assumptions about sex or gender, and do not make decisions about a child's body based on the parents' concerns or needs. It is the child's body, not theirs.

Please understand that children with intersex conditions or DSD quickly grow into adolescents and young adults who form individual identities and preferences and deserve the freedom to make decisions for themselves.

Please carefully consider my experience, understand that I am just the voice of one in many thousands, and recognize the importance of thoughtful and appropriate care for children and adults with intersex conditions or "DSD." **Please ensure that unnecessary surgeries on children or young adults with DSD are never done at MGH.**

Please promise that children and their parents will receive true informed consent along with crucial psychosocial support.

If your physicians have considered me one of the "silent majority" of DSD patients who is satisfied with their care, please take me off that list. I am not satisfied, and I am no longer silent. Although I am sure many things have changed over the last thirty years at MGH,

I have spoken to enough young people and their parents to know that there is still much room for improved DSD care at medical institutions everywhere.

As healers who are committed to caring for your patients, I am asking MGH now to take responsibility for past actions and take what steps you can toward healing old wounds. **I would like the hospital to respond to me in writing within the next two weeks and provide answers to the following questions:**

If a child or adolescent patient presents at MGH with a previously undiagnosed DSD, what do you do?

If a baby is born at MGH with evidence or suspicion of an intersex condition, what steps do you take with the parents? The child?

If an adult patient presents at MGH with a previously undiagnosed DSD, what do you do?

What is your practice for informed consent when a child receives surgery or other "treatment" for their DSD?

Do you refer patients and families to a support group such as AIS-DSD or others?

Do you offer psychological support or counselling on-site to patients or families affected by DSD?

All I am seeking from MGH is an acknowledgement of my experience and recognition of harmful decisions made in the past and, most importantly, evidence of improved care and practices. Please give me hope that I can share with thousands of others like me that leaders in medicine such as MGH are indeed now willingly doing the right thing, listening to their patients, and respecting people and families affected by intersex conditions.

I very much look forward to your reply and will follow up in two weeks if have not heard from you before then.

Sincerely,
Kimberly Zieselman

* * *

I emailed my letter and bcc'd Dr. Bingley. She had come to the conference, after all, and I thought of her as a progressive patient advocate, so I imagined her replying with a supportive *you go girl!* kind of response.

I was a little thrown off when she replied with the one line, *Hey Kim, Don't you think you should mention my role in disclosing this to you?*

Though I had included her name in the first draft, I had ultimately left her name out of this, as I didn't want to put her in the middle of anything uncomfortable. However, I wrote back that if she was supportive of my sharing that information, I would happily reveal that part of my story when I spoke with MGH, as she was indeed the best part of my MGH experience. Otherwise, I asked her, what did she think?

I forwarded her response to Anne, asking her if she thought Dr. Bingley's tone was off, even annoyed, or if I was reading too much into it. The email was certainly abrupt. Doctors can be busy and not have time for long emails, but this had a different tone from any of her previous emails.

In the meantime, Dr. Bingley replied:

Yes, you should tell them. Plus I apologized to you for my ignorance.

Whoa, what? Her apology happened when I told her that my community suggested that my hormones were too low of a dose for what my body needed. I try not to project my feelings onto an email, knowing how hard it is to gauge tone, but it was difficult to not interpret this as defensive. Did she think I was directly attacking her? She hadn't even worked at MGH when I had my surgery, so I wasn't thinking of her at all when I wrote my letter.

I conceded to Anne that I probably should have predicted that Dr. Bingley might take this letter as an attack on her and that I may have made a mistake in not including her in my story. That she helped me get my records and did indeed later apologize to me for not knowing how to care for me regarding hormone replacement therapy was not something I forgot about, but I was focusing on my treatment during adolescence. Of course, it was foolish of me not to realize that she is indeed part of MGH, though she hadn't been until many years after I was already under her care. I wrote to Anne:

> In my defense, she and I have talked briefly about the Resolve project, and I assumed she would just get it—and I actually would have expected encouragement from her. She has been the one "good guy" doc I have had...and I think down deep, I have been even questioning that lately. I didn't want to face it, but this letter has forced it...and she's become unexpectedly emotional. I still think it's my fault—in some ways, I am still that damn "good girl," not wanting to disappoint anyone, including the effing docs!

How telling my email was, looking over it much later. Despite my moment of empowerment, at the first display of someone I perceived as an ally showing resistance, my inclination was to backtrack and accommodate their feelings. That is how these old systems become so entrenched. The marginalized have been conditioned to silence and retreat.

Yes, I sent an apologetic email to Dr. Bingley.

I told her I'd be happy to highlight her helpful role and ultimate apology to the Patient Advocate, and that I thought of her separately from MGH so, in my mind, when I sent the letter, I was thinking only of my experience as an adolescent, which hadn't involved her. I said my mistake was probably not in giving her a heads up first and explaining what I was doing, but that writing this letter was a difficult process, and that I suspected it had not been easy for her either, and could we perhaps set up a time to talk on the phone?

Her reply:

> Don't apologize. I will likely be called in to be involved so might as well tell them about my role in this.

Had I been wrong to expect her to have been more nurturing? She was my primary care physician and had diagnosed my PTSD. We had been through so much together, but I wondered if maybe now I was asking too much from her.

Six days later, my response from MGH came:

> On behalf of MGH, I would like to apologize for your dissatisfying experience back in 1983 with Dr. P. Morrow.

There was additional boilerplate language about so much time passing, there being nothing they could do, then a statement on what a great institution MGH was.

To say I was disappointed by the response would be an understatement. It was a dismissive and even belittling email. I wasn't sure what to do, how to process this. Anne was comforting and disappointed for me as my friend. "As an attorney, though, I'm not surprised by their response." They would want to cover their asses.

I had a hard time accepting their reply as the end of the story. Alright, I would simultaneously push back while still attempting the patented Kimberly damage control. I wrote directly to the Patient Advocate:

> Thank you for responding to my email and apologizing on behalf of MGH for my "dissatisfying experience back in 1993 with Dr. P. Morrow."
>
> However, that response oversimplifies the situation and dismisses my attempt to begin a conversation with the hospital about DSD care, seeking evidence of improved practices. You stated that the hospital is unable to do any sort of "clinical review" of care due to the amount of time elapsed, and since Dr. Morrow is no longer at MGH. But I am not seeking a clinical review of care. I am not interested in digging up the past, but, as I pointed out in my previous email, instead aim to engage in collaborative dialogue with the hospital about current practices for DSD care.

Perhaps MGH would be more willing to dialogue knowing that I have absolutely no intention or desire to take legal action against MGH or any of its employees.

In fact, have your attorneys send me something to sign if that is what it will take for the hospital to engage in honest dialogue about DSD care.

Additionally, I'd like to share with you something I neglected to include in my original letter. Dr. Lydia Bingley was my primary care doctor from approximately 1994 to 2010 (I have since moved out of state; otherwise, she would still be my doctor). Although currently at MGH, she was associated with another practice when I began seeing her as a patient as a young adult. Dr. Bingley was always a wonderful and caring doctor to me and in fact, she was the one who helped me to finally know my true diagnosis by obtaining and explaining my medical records about six years ago.

Since that time, Dr. Bingley and I have had many conversations about my condition, my experience, and the implications of the truth being hidden from me all those years. She has always treated me with respect and clearly has had my best interest at heart. In fact, a few years ago she apologized to me for not doing a better job at treating my condition. I want to express how much it meant to me to have Dr. Bingley acknowledge that she isn't perfect but that she cares for me as her patient.

Today, I not only serve on the volunteer board of the largest United States patient and family support group for those affected by DSD, the AIS-DSD Support Group for Women and Families; but I also work for Advocates for Informed Choice (AIC), a non-profit organization dedicated to protecting the rights of children born with intersex conditions or DSD. I feel passionately about these issues and am currently dedicating most of my time to trying to make a difference for the approximately 1 in 2000 children born each day with a DSD.

AIC believes that apology in medicine can be very healing for both patients and doctors.

Although Dr. Bingley, for example, was not involved in my

diagnosis or surgery or care as an adolescent, she became my primary care doctor in my young adulthood and had little to no training or knowledge about DSDs or appropriate hormone replacement therapies for someone with AIS, but I know she did the best she could at the time. And after I learned my diagnosis and sought information and support from the AIS-DSD Support Group and others, Dr. Bingley was very willing to listen to the information I had gathered and work with me to improve my care/hormone replacement therapy. And although I never asked her for an apology, she gave me one. And that goes a long way toward cementing a doctor-patient relationship. I am grateful to Dr. Bingley for her care.

Please understand I am not reaching out to MGH in anger or "dissatisfaction" (although it is very emotional for me to do so), but instead my communications are an attempt to begin a conversation and raise some awareness to the crucial need for improved DSD patient care across the country. MGH is an internationally respected leader in medicine and as such has both an opportunity and a responsibility to do the right thing.

Your "apology" on behalf of MGH was extremely empty. There was no reference to any details in my letter or even my diagnosis. That may be enough to shut down most patients from thirty years, but I didn't write that emotionally draining and difficult letter to MGH just to be shut down. I hope MGH will do the right thing and bring this communication up a notch to the appropriate level and take this opportunity demonstrate exceptional compassion and leadership by engaging in meaningful dialogue, and setting an example for the rest of the medical profession.

Email reply from Patient Advocate dated 11/11/13:

Dear. Ms. Zieselman,

I am so sorry to hear that you were disappointed with my response. I recommend that you continue to speak to your healthcare providers to ask them for recommendations about who you might engage in a collaborative dialogue about DSD care for patients. Best wishes for a wonderful holiday season.

Burn. In. Hell.

I reached out to Dr. Bingley, asking what she thought and suggesting we talk by phone, since things could be misunderstood over email, but she never replied. Her emails stopped. I suspect the hospital attorneys advised her to cease communications with me. From a legal standpoint, I could see the noncommittal language of the correspondence and the closing-off of discussion was a tool in case of litigation, though I hadn't threatened any, specifically mentioning I was not interested in litigation. I was at a dead end, for the time being.

I felt sad and abandoned. The woman I imagined to be my first ally was gone. Our entire history came to an abrupt, bad end, and I realized she would never be my doctor again.

It took a year for me to have the epiphany that Dr. Bingley might have been guilty. I was in the shower, thinking again about the efficacy (or lack thereof) of my emails to MGH, almost as if it had resurfaced spontaneously from the back of my head. Of course she had copies of my medical records in her office all along—since my first appointment with her when I was 26. Sure, she wasn't practicing at MGH at the time, but my surgeon had referred me to her office. What I had blacked out in all the tumult of my discovery: Dr. Bingley told me she tried to tell me about CAIS earlier, but I wasn't ready to hear it. That I "had my hands on my ears, repeating unicorns and rainbows" over and over was how she put it. How patronizing is that to a patient? She did not ever try to show me my medical records before. That I know. And when she finally did, she left me in the room by myself, as if she didn't want to really be around for the fallout. So—even if I had dissociated, what, was hinting enough? I know she never said, "Kimberly, I have news to break to you—you had testes removed." That would have stuck in my consciousness. What if I had been diagnosed with something like cancer and didn't want to hear it—what, she'd just keep that from me too? And then it also hit me—she recognized that I had PTSD right off the bat. She knew the harm that had likely been done to me psychologically. I clung so much to her being my ally that I never realized that she had not treated me with full care and authenticity. When Dr. Bingley gave me those records for the first time, I had it so much in my head she had dug them out of the archives, it hadn't registered that she was in possession of them the entire time. That she could have (and should have) made sure that I knew and then treated me right away—for 15 years!—for the PTSD she knew I was suffering. I rinsed the conditioner out of my hair and got out of the shower, wrapping myself in the towel, and sitting down at the edge of my bed. How had I never put this together? That was why she was so defensive and cut all communication with me. She was in fact part of the harm. She was in fact part of the accusations I was making in my letter about physician non-disclosure. She was a guilty party and I hadn't allowed myself to contemplate it because she'd been nice to me and I had needed a doctor on my side. But that now felt like a lie. Holy shit. Looking back now, it seemed she was covering her own ass. She must have known that I wasn't told, and she had repeatedly not told me. Oh, she tried but I was busy thinking about unicorns and rainbows? Bullshit. Maybe having known the truth upfront would have given me the tools to cope from the get-go and I wouldn't have retreated and dissociated.

I didn't mention this to Steven. Like always, I ate my feelings and went straight for a bagel with extra cream cheese when I went to the kitchen for my morning coffee.

CHAPTER 13

INTERSEX BUZZ

While Steven and I were out on a Saturday morning in Manhattan, my iPhone started vibrating in my purse with multiple Facebook notifications. One of the hosts on *Fox & Friends* reported on Facebook's new policy that allowed users more identity descriptors on their profiles, "intersex" being among them. Co-host Elizabeth Hasselbeck emphasized that there were "over fifty additional gender options, including 'transgender,' 'intersex,' and 'neither,'" holding onto each word as if it were a bomb about to detonate. Then, she tossed to Clayton Morris by saying, "Heading over to the '*male*' Clayton," who replied, "No, I changed mine to 'intersex.'" In another broadcast, Tucker Carlson reported on the same story, and as he listed a few of the 56 new options, he said, "and 'intersex,' whatever that is."

The buzz of messages I was receiving was from several of our InterACT Youth[1] members who had heard about the show and watched the posted clips. Within a few days, some of these burgeoning intersex advocates drafted and sent an open letter to the network to educate the employees about intersex, letting them know that poking fun at intersex, turning it into a joke, was inappropriate and hurtful. A week later, fourteen days after the initial on-air comments, Clayton Morris was discussing a story on graduation gowns, or more specifically, on the discomfort some students graduating from high school had because the gowns were color-coded for gender, though the story was frontloaded with a discussion on students being overly sensitive. As soon as it was brought up that a "pro-gay group" had been the first to "complain," saying that some students were having difficulty choosing their gown color if they didn't identify with their imposed gender, Clayton Morris stepped in, saying it wasn't a matter if they just thought they were a different gender, because maybe they were born that way. He went on to say that "there are millions of Americans and children who are born with sexual organs which are not there or are not fully developed and therefore don't define themselves by a particular gender. I mean, that's a fact. It's not as black and white as we would like to make it. Just pick whatever color gown you want. Imagine being a parent and your daughter is born a specific way where sexual organs are not developed. Then as a parent you have to be sensitive to the fact that your daughter doesn't identify with a particular gender."

Co-host Anna Kooiman brought up intersex and transgender bathrooms, adding the fear of going through puberty and having to be a girl in the bathroom with a boy. Mike Jerrick broke in, annoyed that everyone was overthinking graduation gowns, but Clayton Morris pressed on. "Just put yourself in the shoes of those children, though, who have to deal with that," he said. "Look, I made a pretty ignorant statement a few weeks ago. We were talking about the Facebook story where they added the bunch of different gender-identifying things. And I made sort of an offhanded comment and I regretted it later because, now wait a second. There are people who are actually dealing with this, and I'm an idiot for saying something stupid like that. So before you open your mouth, just think about it a little bit."

This was a huge moment for the community. LGBTQ+ advocacy groups and outlets and journals, not to mention broader-reaching outlets such as *Huffington Post*, reported on what it meant for the usually derisive and demeaning network to issue such an inclusive and apologetic statement.

The moment was so empowering for the young advocates who sent the letter. A small group of intersex youth had written a simple letter to Fox and caused them to make an on-air apology? This was an "a-ha moment" for me. I had always believed in our young people's voices—young advocates these days are armed with so much knowledge, passion, and empathy. It was AIC's mission to give them a voice and control over their own bodies. But the light bulb suddenly went off—AIC and its interACT Youth group needed to intentionally put more time and energy into raising awareness through the media, and importantly, we needed to empower and support young voices in the process.

We had many options on deck—we would no longer be silent or hidden.

* * *

At the same time I had been working on the Resolve project, another project was working its way down the pipes. At the AIS-DSD conference in Boston, I'd asked Ross Murray from GLAAD[2] if he would run an advocacy and media workshop at the end of the weekend. When he showed up in a bright pink blazer, I knew I was going to love him.

Four months later, Ross emailed me to say that someone at MTV was thinking of adding an intersex character to their show, and Ross wanted to know if he could refer the producers to me. I rolled my eyes—wasn't MTV either music videos and "reality" TV designed to provoke audience reaction or humiliate participants? Defensiveness kicked in—would they want to sensationalize the show by adding a "hermaphrodite" into the *Real World*, or some other atrocious setup? However, with some reluctance, I agreed to be connected. Within days, I was on the phone with Hollywood executive producer Carter

Covington and several writers for the pilot of a program called *Faking It.*

Carter assured me it would not be a reality show; it was a "dramedy" set in a fictitious high school in Texas. He explained that the school was going to be the opposite of most conservative high schools in the state—a place where football players and cheerleaders weren't the most popular kids. Instead, the LGBTQI (the I for intersex) kids would be the cool kids. Carter explained that he identifies as gay and that he wanted to make one of the five main characters, Lauren Cooper, intersex. After a conference call with him and his writing team, I was convinced not only that their intentions were genuine but also that it was time that an intersex person was depicted in a meaningful and respectful manner. Sure, intersex people had popped up on a few TV shows here and there, but they were always sensationalized, portrayed as an abnormality or a medical curiosity at best, or even offensively, as is the case with a 2006 episode of *House* titled "Skin Deep," in which the Sherlockian medical detective discovers a model, over sexualized by everyone on the show (and who has also been sexually abused by her father), actually has AIS, and her medical problem is that her internal testes are malignant. House proceeds to misgender her, calling her a dude while she's crying that she's a girl, then quips, "I'm going to cut your balls off. Then you'll be fine." All the viewers waiting for a character to identify with instead saw a medical freak show for a final shock reveal.

Six months later, I had a brunch date to meet with Carter, Wendy Goldman (the head writer of *Faking It*) and Bailey De Young (the actress playing Lauren Cooper). Accompanying me on this meeting would be Christa, one of my dearest Orchid sisters and one of the interACT Youth members. She was in her 20s, and closer to the age of the character on the show. Before leaving for Hollywood, Pidgeon Pagonis, interACT Youth Program Coordinator, told me to get in touch with one of our new members, Emily. Emily lived in Los Angeles and worked at Cartoon Network. The Boston conference had been her first AIS-DSD conference, and I had remembered her long jet-black hair and megawatt smile as she Irish step-danced across the stage during the talent show.

I was so busy playing hostess the weekend of the Boston conference that I hadn't gotten a chance to connect with Emily. So I invited her to join Christa and me for our breakfast meeting with Carter, Wendy, and Bailey. We were three women with CAIS, talking with Hollywood players over scrambled eggs and fruit. As we shared our individual CAIS stories, the scene became emotional, and both Carter and Bailey were clearly touched. Bailey is a beautiful, petite blonde with big blue eyes and a sweet personality, and it was important to her to get her performance right and do us justice.

When breakfast was over, we drove to the show's writers' room—a large office space filled with big tables and chairs, a couple of couches, and several large whiteboards lining the walls, which featured a draft outline of Season 1. Christa, Emily, and I sat together on one of the couches, sharing our stories again with the writers, who were eager to understand how to incorporate intersex into Lauren Cooper's narrative. While I sat on the couch, relating a story I had told multiple times, sharing my experience, it hit me that I was in Hollywood, advising on the creation of a show, with a character with CAIS, just like me. I did actually pinch myself. What a difference six years had made.

That evening, the three of us sprawled across the beds of my Burbank hotel room, recapping the day. "Can you imagine," I said, "if we did a PSA with Bailey and an interACT Youth member to talk about what it's like to be intersex?" We laid out what we would say, how it would work in conjunction with the show, and fantasized over the potential impact it could make.

A month later, the producers and writers sent us episode scripts. Emily was now serving as an intern with us, helping me coordinate this project and sharing the scripts with our interACT Youth members to review. We occasionally tweaked a word or two, but we were grateful for how hard the writers were working to honestly and authentically incorporate an intersex narrative into Lauren's character. I was grateful for how seriously the *Faking It* team took this responsibility. They even invited Emily to come to the set and give an "Intersex 101" presentation to the entire cast and crew. It was important to Carter that everyone understood what intersex was and was not—awareness raising and education for all.

Because of the nature of the show, Lauren wouldn't be disclosed as intersex until the premier of Season 2, though the first season would establish clues and concepts that would lay the groundwork for her character's reveal. And, as it turned out, MTV was interested in working with AIC and interACT Youth to produce a PSA called "9 Things You Need to Know about Intersex," which featured Bailey De Young and Emily. It aired directly after the premier in September of 2014 and was shared widely on social media. The dream born on a couple of Burbank hotel beds came true. Then, when the episode premiered, BuzzFeed wrote a column highlighting the revelation, offering an explainer of intersex and why having an intersex character on television was so groundbreaking. The column even quoted me a couple of times. It was pretty exciting.

Some of my favorite moments from the show included Lauren saying, "I was born with XY chromosomes, but I developed as a female, okay? The pills I take are estrogen because my body doesn't make any. There, now you know." It was an honest explainer without being a content-heavy info-dump. Then, she says, "I didn't get to pick my label. I'm stuck with it, and I'm doing the best I can, okay?" And later, Lauren says, "If we're going to have a real relationship, you need to know the real me because I don't want to hide who I am anymore from anybody."[3]

After the episode, I received so many emails and Facebook messages from intersex kids, adults, and parents from around the country, as did the show runners and our AIC and interACT Youth members. One intersex adult wrote:

OMG, this is AMAZING! What I would have given when I was young and still watched MTV to see something like this!

Even more touching messages came from parents of intersex kids. One wrote:

I'm so amazed, I lay on my bed on my belly, head close to the TV, and soaked in every moment. Wow, what a scary moment. What an amazing moment. The world has officially changed tonight.

And from another:

Thank you, thank you for educating people in order to create a better place for my daughter. To hear the character Shane tell Lauren that "Nothing is humiliating about what you just told us" brought me to tears. That is all I want for my child: compassion, love, and understanding. Ignorance is such a hurtful thing, and by opening people's eyes and educating them, you are eliminating the ignorance that has bound me in fear for my daughter. I could hug you for doing this, for the lives you are changing, and for reaching out and educating yourself!

In the fall right around Halloween, our family was hanging out at our house with family friends—a couple who had also adopted twins from China, who were a year older than our girls, and whom we had met during the adoption process. The grownups were chatting in the family room, and the four girls were talking over pizza in the adjacent dining room. Suddenly, I caught snatches of their conversation, which was focused on their favorite TV shows. One of our young guests then said, "I love *Faking It*—did you know they have an intersex character on that show? So cool!"

These girls had no idea I was intersex or that I was consulting on the show. My girls quickly let them know I was, of course, and then they continued on to discuss episodes and then their other favorite shows. It was matter-of-fact. Intersex was going mainstream. Steven looked at me and said, "See? This is why you do what you do." In that moment, I felt awe, pride, relief, and most importantly, hope.

This was a big deal in my house, as I was doing something that not only made my girls proud but that they thought was immensely cool. Because of my consulting work on the show, a major perk was when Steven and I got to fly Alex and Charlotte out to Hollywood for their 14th birthday, taking them to the *Faking It* set to watch the filming of an episode. They got to meet the cast and pose for pics with them, including with Gregg Sulkin, one of the five main stars and whom they had known from his appearances on shows such as *Wizards of Waverly Place*. They also thought he was pretty cute.

Faking It ran for three seasons total and had a small niche following. It will forever be the first TV show with an intersex person as one of the main characters. It will also be the first show to have an out intersex person play an intersex person on television. In season three, Episode 304, one of our interACT Youth advocates, Amanda Saenz, played Raven, an interACT Youth member who is invited over to Lauren's house by her step-sister Amy in the hopes that Lauren would allow herself to connect with another intersex person and start taking down some of her emotional walls. The final episode of the series ends with Lauren coming to terms with being intersex, finally announcing to her entire school at a school committee meeting as a way to help save the school. It's a victorious and uplifting moment, and if the series had to end, at least it was nice to end on that note.

Carter and I had had great plans for Lauren, such as exploring her medical history and finally tapping the issue of medically unnecessary surgeries, but alas, that was not to be. Carter told me countless times and he's been publicly quoted as saying that one of things he's most proud of about *Faking It* is the introduction of an intersex character on mainstream television. That made me feel so good. So visible, for the right ways.

A column in the *Advocate* that was part review, part chronicle of the watershed moment wrote that the show "is advocacy, activism, and education all rolled up in a veneer of entertainment, and for intersex young people, it's changed everything."

* * *

Everything was changing.

"There were probably even intersex dinosaurs…if you think about it." Pidgeon Pagonis, former inter/ACT Youth program coordinator and current intersex activist, met up with Emily, and two other intersex people, Alice and Saifa, to shoot a three-and-a-half-minute video entitled *What It's Like to be Intersex*. This wasn't some small-time operation; the video was produced by BuzzFeed.[4] It went viral almost as soon as it first aired on March 28, 2015. The video turned out so well because of Emily's access in the entertainment industry and her experience in video production. BuzzFeed was helpful in following Emily's lead, sitting with Emily for hours after filming and letting her assist in the editing process. Having an experienced intersex person advising on the editing and final production were key to the success of the video.

Each person in the video had a compelling story, sometimes heart-rending. Saifa, who identifies as a black intersex man, tells how he was forced to conform, living as female until he was 25, feeling wrong about it the entire time. Later, he went on to confront the doctor who performed his harmful genital surgery at age 13 and who had told him if the surgery wasn't performed, he would get cancer. Saifa reports that the doctor was condescending and told him, "You intersex activists don't know what you're talking about." As if Saifa, and the rest of us, haven't been living with the experience and understanding it better than any outsider could.

Pidgeon explains that intersex is nothing new and has been around since the beginning of human existence. Probably even with dinosaurs, yes.

The impact was immediate and monumental. We were contacted by Irene, a young woman who stumbled across the video one night in her room at home in Russia and realized she was intersex. It prompted her to ask her parents more questions and to get copies of her medical records. She no longer felt alone, for the first time in her life. She retold her story on the interACT blog,[5] and then BuzzFeed wrote a follow-up story[6] to show how the video was helping people.

I met up with Irene for the first time at University of Surrey in England, in September of 2016. We were both there to speak at an academic conference on intersex[7] organized by psychologist and professor Peter Hegarty,[8] an intersex ally, particularly in the realm of mental health issues. I had organized an international intersex panel, working closely with Holly Greenberry, an intersex woman and the founder of Intersex UK. Meanwhile, Irene presented research she had been doing since discovering her intersex story, and she shared with me that it was the BuzzFeed video that had changed her life. She became an interACT Youth member and now travels the world advocating, after finding a family in the queer and intersex communities and starting the first intersex group in Russia—despite the anti-LGBTQ environment of her home country. It was a powerful moment to meet her and hear yet another story of secrets and harmful medical intervention, all taking place under a very different social and political system.

I had a difficult time keeping up with my flight itinerary. I would have loved to stay longer in Surrey, but it was only a turnaround trip for the conference. It was not lost on me that I was getting to see great swaths of the world, but mostly from airports and conferences.

* * *

One place I never dreamed activism would take me was the White House.

In the summer of 2015, while searching for something online late one night, I stumbled across a site seeking nominations for LGBT artists who were "Champions for Change." The site was sharing a post from the Obama White House, which was looking to award LGBT artists who were empowering their communities across the country. While the call for nominations didn't expressly include the I for intersex, I knew that when President Obama named Randy W. Berry to be the first Special Envoy for the Human Rights of LGBTI Persons in the State Department, Berry had been responsible for specifically adding the intersex I to his title. Thus, the administration might be open and even eager to have an intersex candidate for its Champions for Change award. I didn't even think twice—Pidgeon Pagonis would be perfect for such an award. I had known Pidge since we met at an AIS-DSD conference back when they were just entering their twenties. They had made a big impression on me from our very first meeting. They had been on staff, though they had since left AIC to focus on their individual advocacy and artistic ventures, including the making of the short documentary called *The Son I Never Had*. Pidge was so incredibly smart, creative, and endearing on top of being a courageous intersex activist identifying as a queer gender non-conforming intersex person, still riding the momentum of being in the viral BuzzFeed video.

Without having to think or plan, I filled out the online nomination form, explaining why I thought Pidgeon deserved a Champion for Change award. Several weeks later, I received an email with the good news that Pidge had indeed been selected as one of the nine awardees, and we were invited to the White House for a special ceremony.[9]

Pidge and their dad flew in from Chicago, and we all met in line at the White House security gate to be cleared. We were buzzing with excitement about what was ahead. In line we spotted Jill Soloway, the director and writer of the new Amazon Prime series *Transparent*, as well as several of the show's stars, including Jeffrey Tambor. Soon after we noticed Jill, she came over to us, recognizing Pidgeon from social media. We talked with Jill about the importance of representation in the media, including intersex representation, and also how groundbreaking *Transparent* was in centering a show around a transgender person. Our day was made, and we hadn't even gotten inside the

White House yet. Except after twenty-five minutes in line on that chilly late-November in DC, Pidge realized they forgot their ID necessary for security screening—without it, they wouldn't be admitted to their own award ceremony! They jumped into an Uber back to the hotel, and I anxiously kept checking my text message updates as I inched forward in the security line, then was admitted. Fortunately, Pidge made it back and through security in the nick of time.

Now that the drama was over, we could sink into the positive, inspiring event. Each of the nine awardees shared their stories and discussed their work. The whole mood was one of immense possibility for queer folks in America.

I look back to that night with love but also a pit in my heart. Within a year, Donald Trump's election would usher in an opening for hate, for taking away the rights of so many LGBTQ+ but especially trans people. So much of the hope would turn to fear for safety and a place in our world. Even Randy Berry would be shifted from Special Envoy for the Human Rights of LGBTI Persons to Ambassador to Nepal—a wonderful position, of course, but the position he departed would remain unfilled.

CHAPTER 14

CIRCLING BACK, MOVING FORWARD

I sometimes have to laugh at how my life was—and remains—divided by normal mom advocacy and intersex advocacy. I'm a totally normal mom, with mom worries. I'm an intersex woman, with a complicated history. I've experienced privilege and hardship. I had the privileges of parents who were well off enough to send me to good schools, and I've been able to become successful enough as an adult to do the same for my daughters, which I know so many parents are unable to do. I use my education and experiences to advocate for my girls and for me, but also to amplify the voices that keep getting suppressed by various systems of power or bureaucracy. I had horrible things happen to me, but the damage fortunately wasn't enough to stifle my voice forever.

Back at the beginning of my work with Carter and *Faking It*, after only about nine months of being settled into our newly refurbished co-op apartment on the Upper West Side, Steven and I started talking about maybe moving back to Massachusetts. The rat race of Manhattan was getting to Steven and, to be honest, while I loved living in New York for the first few years, now that we were closing in on our fourth, the intense frenzy and push-and-pulse of the city was wearing thin for me as well. Everything was harder than it should be, more expensive. Getting the kids to their two different schools each morning was a crush of city buses and cabs, blasting horns, a trample of pedestrians, and an overall sensory overload. After the first two years, Charlotte had been moved to The Calhoun School, a small progressive private school on the Upper West Side. Though Alex's tuition was still covered by the NYC school district thanks to our lawsuit, Charlotte's annual tuition for 5th and 6th grade cost as much as a new car. It was ridiculous, and we were exhausted.

That being said, I would not trade our four years in Manhattan for anything, and I'm so glad we did it as a family. During their tween years, the girls grew up with so much diversity of people and ideas all around them, all while growing comfortable living within a big city. We exposed them to Broadway musicals, foods that we never could have gotten in Boston, and people from every country in the world.

What pushed me over the edge of wanting to leave happened that winter. I had a late afternoon, mid-week appointment in Harlem for Alex's requisite IEP meeting at the district office on 125th Street. She didn't have to come, so it was just me. That winter, there was so much snow that the snow banks were shoulder-height at least. I left my apartment on 107th and Riverside Drive and headed up to Broadway. As I'd done countless times in those almost four years, I hailed a yellow cab, and, as the cab pulled up to me on the sidewalk, I reached over to open the back door and duck inside when out of nowhere, a young woman pushed me right into the snow bank and hustled herself into the back seat while screaming profanities at me. I heard the phrase "entitled bitch" and "I was there first" out of the maelstrom of obscenities blasted in my direction. The cabbie didn't blink, kept both hands on the wheel, looking straight ahead until the young woman finished her fit and closed the door so he could drive off. I pulled myself out of the snow and caught the eye of an elderly woman making her way up the street who had witnessed the whole thing. I made a "can you believe what she did?" face at this woman, and she quickly put her finger to her mouth, making the "shh" gesture, and shaking her head. I understood what she, a seasoned New Yorker, was telling me: don't make a fuss. Let it go so as not to put myself in further danger. The cab pulled away, and I looked all around me before raising up my hand again to hail another cab, which eventually came. As soon as I got in for the short ride up to Harlem, I called Steven, tears streaming down my cheeks, and said, "I'm done. Time to go home."

Steven secured a new position at the company he'd left four years earlier, but he was required to start work back in Boston immediately. While I prepared to put our newly renovated apartment on the market and make plans for our move back to Boston, Steven spent the weeks living in a company-rented hotel room and then commuting to be with us on the weekends. This routine lasted for five months.

Now, my big worry was to get the girls into the right schools for them, and to make sure we could find a house in an area that would allow us to get the girls to their respective schools, and Steven to work, without spending hours of our lives in the car or on the train. Before we had kids, Steven and I lived on the North Shore of Boston. We loved it and decided on that area instead of moving back to our old town, where we had some friends, but also had a history with the school district and were leery about putting our kids there again. We knew a great public school system would work well for Charlotte, but Alex was coming from a private school specializing in language-based learning disabilities (LBLDs), and we were focused on getting her a similar placement in are new area. Landmark School, in Beverly, MA, is world-renowned for its success in language-based learning disability education, so we started the application process the minute we knew we were moving back.

By late March, we found a great house in Hamilton, fifteen minutes from Landmark, and signed the purchase and sale agreement. Landmark invited us to a family open house for potential students. Over the phone, we were told that Alex was basically admitted, but there was a "final step" during this visit, which would be an informal interview with the admissions counselor after sitting in on some classes. As soon as we got the invitation, we were relieved, believing she was in, and in our confidence, we could allow the 30-day deadline after signing the purchase and sale agreement on the house to lapse—the deadline for backing out of the deal without penalty.

The day before the interview, I drove the girls the four hours up to Boston where we met Steven in his hotel room near his office in the financial district. The next morning, we drove north for the big day. After the open house visit and interview, we told the kids we'd be taking them over to the new house to see it for the first time—we were all excited. All morning, we had tours and presentations. Then, the admissions counselor called Steven and me into her office and closed the door. We were sitting in a living room loveseat, while she sat in a cozy chair opposite us, then opened up a file.

"On paper," she began, "Alex looks like a great candidate. All her testing and teacher recommendations are in order, and it seemed like a slam-dunk. Until we met her."

My heart sank.

"Your daughter seems to have quite a bit of anxiety, and we have decided that, socially, she would not be a good fit here at Landmark."

I couldn't believe what I was hearing. My eyes welled up, and my cheeks burned. "Of course she has anxiety," I blurted, "she was nervous about interviewing. And this whole move is a big change for her. For all of us."

"I'm sorry, but this is my decision. I see a lot of children—this is what I do."

There was no way we could convince her otherwise, though I tried. I started to speak again, feeling the familiar wellspring that I used when writing my letter to MGH, when I stood up to the stupid dentist, the list goes on, but I felt the force bubbling up, and then Steven's hand was on my knee, giving it a squeeze. He gave me his sidewise glance of *I know you are about to say something that there's a good chance of you regretting, but fuck her, let's get out of here now.* We knew each other so well by now. We stood up together, giving a curt goodbye, and got the girls, who were reading as they patiently waited for us in the lobby. We rushed them out to the car, and I slid on my sunglasses to hide my tears from them, looking straight ahead through the windshield as Steven drove away. It was all I could do to say, without my voice cracking, "Alex, we decided this might not be just the right school for you, honey. What do you think?"

Without missing a beat, she said, "Yeah, I got that feeling too." That was that.

We never went to visit that house in Hamilton. Despite our lawyer trying to get our seller to refund our deposit based on the circumstances, the seller refused, and now we were out thousands of dollars and no home, and we *still* had to figure out where Alex would go to school. That afternoon, I Googled a special education advocate[1] and attorney in the Boston area and explained our situation, and she agreed to meet with me the next morning at a bagel shop. That afternoon, she arranged for us to meet with the head of another special education school, in Newton, just west of the city. It would be an unreasonable commute each day from the house on the North Shore, and we now needed to figure out another town with a decent commute that *also* had an excellent public school for Charlotte. A month later, I brought Alex back up from New York to spend a day at the new private school, to test it out before making our decision. Things seemed to go well, but I had a little pit in my stomach. The school didn't seem like a perfect match, but we needed something, and so we agreed to move forward with enrollment. I'd grown up in this area, so I was familiar with the towns, and within a few weeks, we'd narrowed our home search to Sudbury, where we searched online for available houses.

We found one that worked and, in June, we moved again. However, within a few weeks, Alex broke down in tears one night. "I don't want to go to that private school," she said, feeling the weight of the world on her shoulders. She gave us three very specific reasons why, related to her experience visiting that day. "I didn't want to tell you because I didn't want you to be upset after having to switch towns once already. Everything's been so hard—I didn't want to make it harder."

My heart almost broke. I hugged her and thanked her for telling us.

"It's okay," I said. "And being too busy finally paid off—I haven't gotten a chance to sign the papers and send in our deposit check. No harm done!"

She looked up at me. "I—I want to try public school with Charlotte. I think I'm ready."

Turns out, she was right. She fully mainstreamed into regular classes, and since entering high school, she's maintained As and Bs. She knew.

Yes, we probably could have kept the North Shore house and had her do public school up there, but our current school system was great for both girls. No use in looking back to wonder *what if* on that account.

PART IV

FULFILLMENT

Out and Out Front

My greatest joy—my girls—were happy and excelling and able to follow their own interests and passions. Meanwhile, I was doing the same.

In September of 2014, Anne called me up for one of our weekly check-in meetings. "Arlene and I have been scheming—we want to offer you the position of Executive Director," she said. "I'll be staying on as Legal Director. I want to focus full-time on the impact litigation. And Arlene and I have always said it was our goal to have an intersex person lead this organization. It's the right thing to do."

"We've been grooming you since Day One," Arlene told me later. "Hiring you as Director of Advancement was just the first step."

"So you're saying I was tricked into this job," I joked, but I was so happy and flattered that they both thought so highly of me. It helped that I had won the organization a big grant to do a strategic planning process, enabling us to hire consultants and collectively find ways of growing and moving forward.

As much as I had valued my work on the board of AIS-DSD, I couldn't do both any longer. My time on the AIS-DSD board had run its course, and I decided to step down at the end of December, which would mark four full years.

During the course of our strategic planning process at AIC, one of the main things we addressed was the ongoing debate within the global community over the use of "DSD" language. Referring to being intersex as a *disorder* of sex development had been divisive as far back as 2006.[1] The term was pathologizing, leading to stigma from the medical community as well as the larger population. If people hear they have a "disorder," they often become reluctant to come out, get the help they need, or advocate for themselves or their peers.

The term "Disorder of Sex Development" (DSD) had been officially coined in 2006 when the American Academy of Pediatrics (AAP) published a new consensus statement written by a group of special interest doctors.[2] Intersex was a term that came from within the community and was already in use before 2006. However, the term given by the doctors became part of the lexicon.

AIC had taken the position of using both *DSD* and *intersex* but often fell back on *DSD* because it was what the medical community used, and parents could relate to that more easily. We were trying to work with and within those communities, despite our agreement that *disorder* was pathologizing. Looking back at the times I've used the term DSD, I can't help but wince. When I first made my discovery, I preferred the medical-sounding terminology. I thought *intersex* was more of an identity term that seemed most popular outside the United States. The people who were identifying as intersex were also predominantly identifying as queer. I hadn't liked the term because it sounded like "inbetween sex"—or maybe it was more my strait-laced upbringing that made me afraid of a term that seemed to put so much focus on the word "sex." I had to break down my own squeamishness—really, my own pathologizing.

For up to a full decade after the publication of the consensus statement and launch of the term *DSD*, there remained rampant controversy in the intersex community over its use. Intersex activists throughout (much of) the rest of the world were extremely concerned about the medicalized nature of the new term, which had been coined by doctors who clearly benefitted from pathologizing our intersex bodies. The term DSD helped to justify medical interventions such as surgery to "fix our disorders."

After 18 months at AIC, and getting my feet on the ground, as well as having a broader yet still-developing understanding of the community politics, I understood how important it was to move away from DSD language as much as we could. I listened to AIC's Youth program members, who had named their program interACT, and I began using intersex almost exclusively. It was what most of our young interACT advocates wanted—after all, our entire mission was focused on respecting young intersex voices. This is what gave me the idea to rebrand our organization using the name that our youth advocates had created. After all, they had been instrumental in generating a rare and precious unicorn of an apology from Fox News, and they had been the best advocates and instructors in the process of developing the intersex character for *Faking It*. They weren't our "future leaders"—they were already leaders.

I pitched the concept to the board and, by the end of 2015, we were well on our way toward rebranding as interACT: Advocates for Intersex Youth, in honor of those youth voices, making a conscious effort to center them in our work. Also, something I'd run up against frequently in my work: "Advocates for Informed Choice" often confused people into thinking we were an advocacy group for abortion rights, which I knew was something that did not help us, though I was politically pro-choice. This association wasn't clear on our outdated website, either—our mission needed to be immediately clear and accessible to those who needed to know what we did. After the board were convinced of the new branding, the new website was developed at the end of a very busy 2015, with the official launch in mid-January of 2016.

* * *

On Facebook, I'd been sharing different articles on intersex rights, facts, and updates about the work I was doing. At some point, my friends I'd never told I was intersex started to catch on. They sent private messages of support, a few *Wow, I had no idea!* comments.

Then, in the fall of 2016, interACT was contacted by a writer from *Good Housekeeping*, who was looking to do a story about the intersex community. They ended up interviewing me as well as two others, including Emily, who still did work for me at interACT, coordinating our youth program and

assisting me with communications projects. *Good Housekeeping* also interviewed Lynnell, one of the pioneer intersex activists in the country, whom
I respected greatly. Lynell had begun speaking out in the 1990s—and was
one of the guests on Oprah's show that I had watched right after my own
discovery. Lynnell also served on interACT's Board of Directors.

I told the journalist about my path to discovering I was intersex, but
I mostly talked about my husband and my kids—it felt significant to me
personally. The publication of the article on October 21st coincided with
International Intersex Awareness Day, October 26th. This was the first time
I had publicly, to such a large group outside the intersex community, told
my story. The article was shared mostly on social media—Facebook—and
I had a few positive responses from Facebook friends, some surprised but
said they suspected I was intersex based on my recent social media activity.
Otherwise, it wasn't that big of a deal.

That all changed in August of 2017.

I wrote and then pitched an opinion piece to *USA Today* entitled, "I was
an intersex child who had surgery. Don't put other kids through this." My
goal was to target the practice of medically unnecessary surgeries performed on children too young to understand and consent to the permanent
and life-altering procedures. *USA Today* accepted the pitch and published
my piece both in print and online (80% of their readers are now online)
on August 9th.[3] The piece included links to other resources and featured
a video interACT had produced with Human Rights Watch (HRW) earlier
that summer to coincide with the release of a new research report. There
was a photo of me in my high school cheerleading uniform, taken a few short
weeks after my surgery was performed.

Seeing my work in print, though, was a huge deal. It made the process
feel more legitimate somehow (an indication I grew up in the '70s and '80s,
pre-internet). I was thrilled to see my opinion piece as one of the front-page
teasers.

The response to my piece was a personal triumph. What was even more
interesting to me was who I heard from—including people who knew me
from my distant past.

For example, I received an email the same day the piece was published from a guy who knew me from high school, although not well. He wanted to commend me for the article and my "courage." He then wrote how I was helping out young people today, and that he too had kept a secret about his life until after he'd graduated college—he had been sexually abused as a small child. It took him years to divulge this to anyone, and now he was speaking on a national circuit to help high school students to cope with abuse. He wrote that he'd been sitting on a plane and recognized me on the hill—this was in reference to the photo, published with the story, of me in my cheerleading uniform on a hill at our high school. He wrote:

You are a beautiful person inside and out. Best of luck with your mission.

I teared up, for him and what he went through, for the acknowledgment, the recognition. Being seen was a big deal. So many people I had known in high school were going through things, but no one talked about it. Was everyone experiencing pain told to suck it up and get over it? How many people felt like they were alone?

Another woman from high school, whom I'd known a little but had completely lost track of after graduation, wrote:

You are doing amazing things! It can't be easy, but it's so important. I feel like our parents just listened blindly to doctors on so many levels. My mom took diethylstilbestrol (DES), and as a result, doctors said I could never have kids. I anguished over it and then without warning had two of them back to back without medical intervention. But, Lord, the time I wasted feeling bad for being different... Nothing compared to your world. I can't imagine your fight. You are such a total, smart, brave inspiration! Your girls are beautiful and I'm so glad we reconnected... You go and go and go, girl!

About a month later, I received a highly unexpected Facebook message from a man who was a coach and gym teacher at my high school, hoping I remembered him.

My first year was your freshman year. Just read your story. Wow! I think back to our "gym" curriculum and it didn't involve "health" then. Slowly we came of age and became a "health and fitness department." What you went through is why education is so important. On top of that, it's the "health ed." that can actually make a difference—as long as the correct information is given in a correct forum and manner. I can only imagine what you must have felt when you heard this from your parents. Actually, no, I can't imagine. I'm very happy to hear and see that you are making a difference. I retired from teaching a few years ago but keep in touch with my department. Does your organization have a speaker bureau? Would it be okay for me to share your story with my former colleagues in the health and fitness department? Great to hear you are doing well—keep in touch!

So many people from my past were reaching out, from the group I was most afraid to tell. What never occurred to me was that this was no longer just my story. Shortly after the evening the story was in print, Steven's cell phone rang—it was his boss. I heard Steven say, "Thank you, I appreciate that," before hanging up. His boss had been sitting in an airport, waiting for a flight back to Boston after a business trip, and had picked up *USA Today*. He happened to read my story and called my husband to let him know. His reaction was supportive and positive, but that was the first time it dawned on me that my being public did impact Steven.

"Don't worry about me," Steven said, "you have my full support. And apparently my boss's as well!"

Of course I worried about the potential effect on my girls, although not too much, as Alex and Charlotte were becoming strong and opinionated young women. One evening, Charlotte had left a pile of her 8th grade papers on the kitchen table, which wasn't a rare occurrence. But that night, I noticed a yellow worksheet on top, which she had filled out by hand. It was an in-class assignment asking students to write about someone they admired and why. She had written about me, that I was intersex and so brave because I was talking about it, and working to help other children and families to not have to suffer in the future. That I was helping other people to be proud of being intersex. Her words meant so much to me (more tears), not only after hearing she was proud of me, but also because she was empowered to talk about me and intersex openly. I sought out Charlotte in the house and gave her a big hug.

The following year, as the girls were finishing 9th grade, I received an email from one of the health and sex education teachers, reporting that during class that day, she was covering LGBTQ+ issues and briefly touched on intersex. The teacher told me that Alexandra's hand shot up after her definition, and that Alex politely told her that her definition was not really accurate, and that she should "talk to my mom because she is intersex and an advocate." The teacher invited me the following September to talk to the health and biology departments to train them on intersex.

The family that advocates together...

All the years of advocating for my daughters and myself had not turned them into shrinking violets who couldn't do anything without their mother clearing the way for them. Instead, my daughters had become confident in speaking up and not embarrassed about their intersex mom but proud of her. That was another moment as a parent that I will cherish forever. Even better? Alex's classmates were all cool about learning her mom was intersex and what it meant. Progress is slow, but it does happen. At least in our area of the northeast, and elsewhere in the country, the younger generation is so much more open-minded and accepting of difference and diversity of all types. It gives me hope.

A while later, Steven and the girls gave me an action figure, dressed as a warrior. On her, they attached a red shield, with "XOXY" emblazoned across the front, and a smaller "Courage" printed below that. They said it was because I am an intersex human rights defender. Steven and my girls love Marvel comics and all things fantasy. Me, not so much. But this was their way of including me in a world they shared with each other, while telling me they are proud of me for my activism work. It was one of my best gifts ever and sits, on watch, on my office desk; a reminder that I was given the strength and ability to do the necessary activism work and a reminder of the awesome responsibility that I have been given.

CHAPTER 15

SO QUEER

"That's so *queer*," kids in the '80s said. "Queer" was used as an insult when they didn't approve of the way a classmate acted or dressed. When someone was weird or different from the others. It was common to say, and then later it was understood to be a harmful insult if said. I had a couple of friends in high school who were gay, but they were not out, and we never talked about it. We all just assumed they were gay and left it at that. Beyond that, my experiences in school and the first couple of decades of work life didn't expose me to many LGBTQ folks. I was, I admit, clueless. So when I started working at interACT (at the time, still AIC), diving head-first into the intersex social justice movement, the first time I heard colleagues use the term queer, I immediately bristled, both surprised and uncomfortable. I finally asked Anne, who was still my boss at the time, why she and others sometimes used the term.

"It's been reclaimed by some gay people who can get away with using it exclusively with one another," Anne said, "and recently it's becoming a more generally accepted umbrella term for people identifying as LGB or T."

The "queer rights" movement is diverse and complicated, and right away I realized there was much to learn from past and current LGBTQ advocates and organizations, some of whom were the first to step up and become intersex allies.

I would be lying if I said it wasn't at times a bumpy path for me during the early months. I was now working with colleagues in different capacities who were all much more experienced working in social justice movements. Most of them also identified as queer. I was someone who had "passed" as a cisgender[1], heterosexual, XX woman for her entire life. That I was not just *passing* but *identifying* as a cis heterosexual woman in every way. I had lived a privileged and also sheltered life.

Because of my inexperience, I made unintentional gaffes. One time, when talking to the former president of our board, an intersex and queer-identified man, I mistakenly referred to a person—with whom I had only spoken once on the phone—by using she/her pronouns. The person had a feminine sounding voice and their name was one typically associated with a person identifying as female. However, the person was a transgender man, and I had misgendered him. My mistake might have been innocent, but it was important for me to understand the harm that was done in making wrong assumptions. I had much to learn about pronouns, identities, and my own privilege of being able to exist in this world, identifying my gender in the same way the world perceives me—as female. This is a privilege not all intersex people have.

Though I now identify as intersex, and more specifically as an intersex woman, that wasn't always the case. When I first discovered the truth about my body, I only identified with having a medical condition, and even worse, a *syndrome*. That was the harm of pathologizing intersex as a disorder of sex development. So for the first few years, I didn't question the terminology much, accepting CAIS as a medical *problem* that caused my body to deviate from *the norm*. In connecting with other women with CAIS who could relate to my own feelings of shame and inadequacy for being born differently, I felt no longer alone, no longer freakish, no longer a syndrome.

That progress was highlighted for me when Dr. Georgiann Davis, now the current president of interACT, published *Contesting Intersex: The Dubious Diagnosis* in 2015. I met her at my very first AIS-DSD conference in Dallas, at the same time she was commencing her research for the book. Georgiann, who identified as female, was born with XY chromosomes and testes, information that was withheld from her until she discovered the truth in her medical records years later, when she was an adult—just like me. After we were introduced at the conference, I agreed later that year to be interviewed for her project, mostly because I was excited to have an opportunity to be with another Orchid sister again many months after returning from my first conference and feeling more alone than ever. She flew from her hometown of Chicago, and we met up for lunch at a Mexican restaurant near where I was living at the time. After ordering our burritos and digging into the chips and salsa, she turned on her recording device and began with her questions. My answers revealed I was hovering around the medicalized terminology—the dreaded DSD—to describe myself.

By the time the book came out, however, my preference and opinion had completely changed. I was now comfortable with describing myself as an intersex woman, and with being a part of the LGBTQIA+ alphabet soup. I was relieved I'd used a pseudonym for the project.

* * *

About two years after joining what became interACT, I was accepted into the Arcus Foundation's fellowship program for executive directors who were early in their roles or careers directing an LGBT-focused nonprofit organization—despite the fact that my organization was not technically an LBGT organization, and despite the fact that I didn't identify as LBG or T. It was a bit of a stretch to include me in this fellowship program, but I am still so grateful that I got to be one of two straight fellows in a class of 13 from across the United States, and the only intersex person. While Arcus doesn't expressly use the "I" when describing their social justice funding focus, they did and still do fund intersex advocacy and organizations, including interACT. They were one of the first United States LGBTQ-based and -focused foundations to recognize the relationship between intersex and LGBTQ oppression and to invest in us as a nascent social justice movement.

Our first in-person gathering as a fellowship class took place in Portland, Oregon, in late June of 2015. The weekend was an abnormally hot one, with temperatures reaching into the hundreds. I was already uncomfortable and nervous about participating in this group where I would be an obvious minority. I was older than most if not all the other fellows, only one of two heterosexuals, to my knowledge, the only one who was a parent, and the only fellow who was intersex. The "I" was on none of the Arcus materials. I feared being rejected by a group of people made up of those who were supposed to be my peers. Would they think I was a tourist or interloper? Would they wonder how the heck I ended up there?

But I'm so glad I did. Each of the fellows was so impressive, and they were very welcoming and accepting of me, the white cis straight privileged middle-aged woman who had somehow landed alongside them! Without being naïve—I'm sure there were raised eyebrows or even a few eye rolls at first—the other fellows at least hid any annoyance or dismissiveness from me and, by the end of the 18 months, I developed friendships with some of these amazing young queer leaders.

During that 18-month period, I also attended my first Creating Change conference. With more than 3500 in attendance, it must be one of the largest annual LGBTQ+ conferences in the country. Together with my interACT staff, we went to raise awareness about intersex issues. We had an exhibit booth and hosted workshops and receptions, and I moderated a panel. I was able to connect with some of my Arcus fellows but, otherwise, I felt out of place. Many attendees were expressing their gender identities and sexual orientations with

flamboyance, as this was a conference where people came to let loose.
Though I respected and admired the festivities as a casual observer,
I wasn't comfortable in the scene, being the odd fairly straight-laced
(cis-hetero-normative middle-aged white) woman out—which is how
much of society makes the LGBTQ+ communities feel on a daily basis.

* * *

I do think it is important for people who present as I do to seriously
consider being a proud intersex member of the LGBTQ+ communities. But it's also okay if they don't. Today, there are still a number of
people who are, by definition, intersex—*born with one or more physical sex
characteristics that don't match what is typically described as either a male or
female body*—but who refuse to use the term intersex, preferring DSD
or another alternative.

Through my work at interACT, my world and perspective expanded
rapidly, and I loved it. Very often, I was one of the only people (if not
the only person) in the room who didn't identify as queer or LGBT.
Intersex, being an umbrella term, brought me together with so many
types of intersex people who were identifying in countless ways. What
I learned right away was that the binary of male or female that I
had learned as absolute fact was anything but. This wasn't opinion
or whim; there are too many of us proving that sex (let alone gender)
doesn't fall in one of two binaries. I had embraced intersex, the less
pathologizing term that described my own experience as a person
born with a non-binary body, a body that includes physical sex characteristics that don't align with what medicine and society expect for
either a "male" or "female" body. I no longer believe I have a *disorder*
of sex development but a *difference* of sex development that gave me
an intersex body.

Therein lies what I think is the core reason why it makes perfect
sense for intersex to become part of the broader LGBTQ+ movement.
While many, if not most, intersex people, me included, identify as

straight and cisgender, most of us experience shame, stigma, discrimination, and harm simply because our bodies are deemed different or unacceptable by mainstream society. This fear of bodily difference and non-binary bodies is similar to the fear of people's sexual orientations and non-binary gender identities.

In fact, I believe that it is this fear of bodily difference, akin to homophobia, *intersexphobia* if you will, that drives some doctors to recommend, and parents to agree to, medically unnecessary surgery on intersex children and infants. I am convinced that such doctors want to erase the intersex parts of us to fit us into strictly binary-looking "male" or "female" bodies. In some cases, when I've spoken with members of the medical community, with parents, and with children who were operated on, it was the unfounded fear that a non-binary intersex body would increase the chances of the child "becoming" gay that has been fueling the harmful interventions on intersex children and babies without their consent.

Therefore, it makes sense for people born with diverse sex characteristics, even if they identify as straight or cis, to align with the broader LGBTQ+ movement and fight for the broader human rights. We can be LGBTQI+. That being said, it is imperative that the LGBTQ+ community not simply "tack on the I" to the acronym in the spirit of inclusion as just another identity.

In the spirit of "not about us without us," LGBTQ+ advocates need to include intersex people and perspectives in the intersex-focused work and should be knowledgeable about intersex narratives and the community's key issues, at the top of which are harmful nonconsensual medical interventions on children.

CHAPTER 16

DO NO HARM

The Hippocratic oath "Do No Harm" is an ethical code attributed to the ancient Greek physician Hippocrates. Over the ages, this oath has become a guide to conduct by doctors. The original, classical version of the oath includes the phrase, "I will keep them from harm and injustice."[1]

In the modern version, the oath reads, in part:

I will apply, for the benefit of the sick, all measures [that] are required, avoiding those twin traps of overtreatment and therapeutic nihilism.

I will remember that there is art to medicine as well as science, and that warmth, sympathy, and understanding may outweigh the surgeon's knife or the chemist's drug.

I will not be ashamed to say "I know not," nor will I fail to call in my colleagues when the skills of another are needed for a patient's recovery.

Above all, I must not play at God.

I will remember that I do not treat a fever chart, a cancerous growth, but a sick human being, whose illness may affect the person's family and economic stability. My responsibility includes these related problems, if I am to care adequately for the sick.

I will remember that I remain a member of society, with special obligations to all my fellow human beings, those sound of mind and body as well as the infirm.[2]

Many medical schools have a special ceremony in which students take the Hippocratic oath[3] as well as other modernizations.[4]

However, people born with intersex traits have been telling the medical profession for nearly three decades that the medical field has been harming and continues to harm us, both physically and emotionally. Still, the harm continues.

Everyone needs competent and compassionate healthcare and medical treatment during their lives. In many countries, it is in fact a right for its citizens to have access to care. The intersex community is no different. We need doctors for all the same reasons the rest of the population does. We also need medical providers who understand the wide range of intersex variations and how our *differences* of sex development may require unique care throughout our lifetimes.

One example of this is the difference in the role that hormones play in our bodies. Many of us have unique needs regarding our hormones. In my case, my healthy testes were removed—without my consent—as a child, and therefore, I lost a crucial source of hormone production that my body desperately needed. Since age 16, I have been on a hormone replacement therapy regime similar to what doctors give menopausal women—all because there has been no meaningful research and there remains no well-informed protocol for treating a person like me. (And, frankly, there hasn't been enough research done on the impact of hormone replacement therapy on menopausal women either!) I have struggled with my weight on and off my whole life but particularly in my adult life since turning 40 and since adding higher levels of estrogen therapy to my regime, which I only did after finding out the truth and getting information from the AIS-DSD Support Group.

My group—not my doctor—helped me realize that I was on a very low dose that wasn't giving me the benefits of adequate bone strength, vaginal lubrication, and some even said increased clarity.

As a 52-year-old intersex person and a leader in the global intersex movement, and as someone with access to medical care and resources, I do not know where to go. Imagine the thousands of people who don't even have access to the money and information that I have. Thus, thousands upon thousands of intersex adults like me go without competent care.

Sometimes, those of us who go to doctors are treated by the white coats as curiosities, sometimes as freaks. We are humiliated or even shamed.

One of the reasons we have not made as much progress is due to the lack of quantitative data documenting the harmful impact of nonconsensual, unnecessary medical intervention on intersex babies and children. In debating these medically unnecessary interventions performed without patient consent, doctors maintain that only a few intersex people who have had genital surgeries performed on them without consent are actually unhappy; most are part of the "silent happy majority" who are treated in childhood and go on to live (seemingly) contented lives. However, when asked, most doctors appear to have drawn this conclusion from the fact that most of their patients have not returned to complain about this treatment. While there is little evidence to support the success that doctors claim, there is quite a bit of evidence to suggest that my suffering is the norm rather than the exception.

In 2014, a group of intersex advocates seized the opportunity to document our intersex narratives in the *Narrative Inquiry in Bioethics Journal*, published by Johns Hopkins University Press—which, ironically, is the very institution where the practice of intersex surgeries was born. I answered the call for submissions to tell my story in an essay I titled "Invisible Harm." I laid out my full story and the harmful impact, how medical professionals would likely include me in the "silent happy majority" of surgically treated patients, as they would see now only a woman who identifies as typically female, who graduated law school, had been married for over twenty years, had two adopted children, and had a successful career. I wrote that yes, I had been fortunate in many ways, but I no longer wanted my voice to be presumed buried within that silent majority, and that was why I was now speaking out to tell my story. My essay, published in Volume 5, No. 2, Summer 2015, also detailed my attempt to communicate with Mass General Hospital and the disappointing response from my trusted primary care doctor. Again, the act of putting my story on paper was both empowering and also freeing.

Getting my and other intersex narratives published in an esteemed journal was a wonderful and huge step. However, soon after publication, we realized that only people who paid to subscribe to the journal could read these stories. How was this going to be helpful if there wasn't free and open access to our stories? How could we share the data of our harms?

There was a new "Voices" project of Johns Hopkins University press, so we would capitalize on that option. I fundraised the $10,000 needed to purchase open access and also package, through "Voices," the intersex portions of the journal separately as a stand-alone publication entitled *Normalizing Intersex*.[5] I made sure the publication truly reflected our community all the way to the cover art, which was a sketch drawn by a young intersex person. This was a good first step, but it wasn't enough.

I continued to believe, foolishly, that if only the doctors read our stories in a published journal that intersex narratives of harm would be perceived as more credible. The medical community would not be able to ignore the evidence, and so they would finally be a part of the movement to help end the harm.

I was wrong.

* * *

For over a decade, there were earnest efforts on the part of multiple intersex activists and allies in the United States to work with doctors to improve patient care and put an end to harmful practices. I joined other activists and allies to become part of the Advocacy Advisory Network (AAN) of the Translational Research Network (TRN), which was funded by a National Institutes of Health (NIH) grant. The AAN was formed as an NIH grant requirement that stipulated the need for community input. However, to the lead doctors and researchers on this project, our inclusion was nothing more than an annoying grant requirement. Our expertise (from intersex people, a lawyer, ally bioethicists, and other ally physicians) was dismissed several times.

What made things even worse was the TRN project entirely funded an organization called Accord Alliance, which had been previously funded by community donations, founded in 2006 by intersex people and allies including physicians to improve medical care by replacing an old, then-defunct organization (the ISNA) with a fresh collaborative approach involving multiple stakeholders. This major conflict of interest was evidenced over and over again. One instance was when the TRN proposed a genital photography project. Members of the AAN expressed our serious concerns for the project, because we did not believe that the potential harm to the pediatric research subjects had been conveyed accurately. Despite knowing our concerns, the leaders of the TRN went ahead and circumvented the NIH's submission requirement to have an AAN support letter to accompany the genital photography project, and instead penned a letter from "Accord Alliance" without the whole group's approval. This circumvention—and the project—was an embarrassment to all of us. An even greater embarrassment occurred when we had to protest to NIH, informing them of the deceptive letter. However, the proposal for the project was withdrawn.

This was the last straw. As a result, the crashing halt to the collaboration came in November of 2015, when the vast majority, including me, of the AAN resigned after several years of trying to work formally with practitioners. We wrote an official letter of resignation to the NIH Translational Research Network and NIH Research Coordinating Committee, outlining how, because of ongoing miscommunication and lack of meaningful inclusion (despite our wide-ranging expertise), having our names associated with TRN was doing more harm than good, because chronic issues with TRN prevented meaningful advocacy input. How, despite our efforts, TRN failed to include advocates in the design and goals of the projects. How, having been denied a presence at initial meetings of investigators, we hoped that subsequently close involvement in projects could influence the direction of research—yet, most were already IRB-approved[6] by the time we saw them. Instead of an opportunity to contribute, we had experienced a pattern of misrepresentation in which our involvement and concurrence had been falsely implied. We did want to make it clear that our resignation had nothing to do with the TRN clinicians and researchers who were devoting their lives to caring for and about us and appreciated the presence of those members at our support meetings, and their availability to listen to members and their ability to change their views based on new input and data. One of the ironies was that we had discovered that we could be extremely effective in supporting the development of research that met the needs of our communities when we were involved from the beginning of the design and research goals, when we could give input into sensitive language, and when we were engaged to ensure that the specific concerns of this community regarding human research ethics and informed choice were addressed.

Alice Dreger, a well-known bioethicist and founding member of the AAN, had already written her own letter of resignation, stating how she couldn't continue to engage in conversations around "shared decision making" that allowed certain decisions to be made that she believed violated the most basic rights of children. She had been hoping to work from within the medical community, to change it from within, but unfortunately, the truth was that medicine had not let in our most basic criticism and insight and it didn't look like the medical community was interested in doing so any time soon.[7]

Eight other members of the AAN board left our positions with heavy hearts. I was disheartened about the turn of events, and though confident in my decision to resign as an AAN member, I was a bit uneasy about where this would lead my activism—which was inevitably moving in a more confrontational direction. Having been a lifelong conflict avoider, I felt a little anxious.

* * *

Flash ahead a year and a half later, and I was more confident in my voice and in the confrontation (though it was exhausting to me physically and emotionally).

Human Rights Watch collaborated with interACT for a groundbreaking research report, "*I Want to Be Like Nature Made Me*": *Medically Unnecessary Surgeries on Intersex Children in the U.S.*[8] In July of 2017, I was in Chicago for the release of the report. We had spent a year interviewing intersex people of all ages, their parents, and some doctors. I had gone into the New York office of Human Rights Watch over the previous two years to meet with people and give presentations on intersex rights, hoping to get their attention and an offer of help. In early summer of 2016, I got a call from an HRW staff member, saying they were ready to help and had gotten approval to dedicate a full-time researcher, Kyle Knight, to the project for a year. They would also employ part-time an intersex person as consultant on the project. Once interACT joined HRW, they hired an intersex person who is a practicing physician, Suegee Tamar-Mattis (the partner of AIC's founder, Anne), to conduct interviews with intersex people as well as doctors and families of intersex people. The result is a 180-page report filled with anonymous quotes and strong recommendations for change. The report revealed some indications of changes in the medical field that were moving in the right direction, but it also underscored continuing medically unnecessary surgeries throughout the country[9] and, perhaps most striking, a pro-parents' rights and pathology-driven attitude that remains pervasively harmful to intersex kids.

The same day as our press conference, I also met with key medical professionals at the Lurie Children's Hospital's DSD team. I was joined by our two attorneys from interACT, Al lttelson and Sylvan Fraser, together with members of the HRW team. We sat together on one side of the table, opposite Dr. Earl Cheng, urologist and head of the DSD clinic, along with two doctors on his team, who both happened to be women.

The meeting began with the usual requisite pleasantries and show of appreciation for taking the time to get together. Our goal of that meeting, piggy-backing on the release of our report outlining these human rights abuses against vulnerable children, was to request that Dr. Cheng and his team at Lurie stop performing clitoral reductions on infants under the age of two years old. We at interACT and HRW hoped that if we offered to work with them and hold them up publicly as leaders for taking a big step toward protecting a large number of intersex patients that they would agree to stop doing a highly controversial procedure. They could at least delay offering this procedure until a child is older and can meaningfully consent to the procedure if they so wish.

Once Al offered this proposal to the group, Dr. Cheng was quick to respond, saying there was no way he could do that. "And we aren't doing that many clitoral reductions anymore."

My thought was then—why do them at all? There was some back and forth, including the Director of the LGBT Project at HRW, Graeme Reid, explaining that we couldn't exempt intersex children from the protections we offer all other youth. After Dr. Cheng continued to argue, I chimed in and spoke about my experience hearing the tragic stories of intersex people I knew who had suffered as a result of those exact surgeries. As I was explaining that we could avoid these harms by postponing clitoral reductions, he cut me off, quipping, "We need to take the emotion out of this."

He dismissed my offered evidence of harm as nothing more than a nuisance, not even worthy of discussion. I felt silenced once again, and my eyes warmed with tears as I fought back the mixture of frustration and anger. Sylvan jumped in to speak about the fact that an existing Illinois criminal statute aimed at preventing female genital mutilation probably already made the practice illegal, and that it was probably just a matter of time the hospital faced legal action.

Dr. Cheng's response? "Let's set the law aside."

Um, what? So, we were there to talk about the harm done by these potentially illegal surgeries, yet we were not going to talk about actual harm or legality? Did he not feel accountable, answerable, to anyone?

Needless to say, we left that day with nothing more than further proof of how deep Dr. Cheng had dug in his heels, as well as with a confirmation that the two doctors, both women, were silenced when they tried to influence the discussion. For over an hour, I witnessed the power dynamic between them, with neither of the doctors speaking up unless first acknowledging Dr. Cheng and deferring to him repeatedly during our meeting.

I would go on to learn just how much the mostly male urologist surgeons are the ones calling the shots and refusing to admit to causing harm.

Though I was disappointed in the meeting, I was also perhaps more fired up than ever. These urologists and other medical professionals could not continue to dismiss me or the thousands and thousands of intersex patients beginning to speak out. It might take more time, but Dr. Cheng and the others like him would one day be forced to listen and finally start doing the right thing.

* * *

Another of the strange twists came three years after being dismissed by Mass General and my former primary care physician, Dr. Bingley: I came across an article in an MGH publication[10] that debated the practice of genital "normalizing" procedures on intersex children during their first year to bring their bodies cosmetically in line with one sex or the other. The article then highlighted findings in our interACT and HRW report, finding adults who had such surgeries as infants had a "mixed satisfaction with the results," acknowledging the sometimes harrowing experiences, "particularly when they did not grow up to identify as the sex that their surgery assigned them. It may be time to rethink the treatment of intersex children..." Yeah, no kidding.

The article also quoted pediatric specialists discrediting the data, saying, "the report is spearheaded by activist groups, which makes it problematic." The very hospital where I had been harmed and then had dismissed me when I had tried to communicate with them was now publishing an article specifically talking about the advocacy work I had been behind while also at least obliquely dismissing the work of activists who had gone through these surgeries. Yes, I was pleased to see them writing about the issue in one of their blogs, but I had never been given an apology nor had they ever reached out to me or interACT. Why couldn't they have just responded to the letter? Though I was worked up, I was too busy to direct my frustrations toward any action or op-ed writing. I don't know what good it would have done, but it might have made me feel better.

CHAPTER 17

A GLOBAL MOVEMENT

When I came onto the intersex activism scene in 2013, I had peers both in the United States and in other countries who had been doing this work for a while and whom I could look to for guidance. I knew they (especially those abroad) were skeptical of me, the new American, especially since intersex activism's main cause is to end unconsented genital surgeries on minors and these surgeries had originated in the United States at Johns Hopkins, who then exported this harm around the globe. Furthermore, it was a small group of American intersex people who worked with the medical community in 2006 and had agreed to the use of the new "DSD" terminology that most of the activists around the globe hated. That language had gone on to divide the community for many years and was still active when I began at AIC in 2013. Most of the recent debate played out on social media and private Facebook groups and discussions. To make progress, the global community would have to work together, and to do that, I was going to need to gain the trust and respect of my international peers. It would take time, especially when our communication took place mostly through social media.

But then, starting in March of 2015, the same month as the airing of the BuzzFeed video, I had the opportunity to meet several intersex activist peers from around the world at a convening in Geneva, which was arranged and funded by a couple of progressive foundations interested in backing our still-nascent movement. I was among about a dozen other intersex leaders invited for a couple of days to this convening. This was a wonderful opportunity to meet in person those I'd only "met" on Facebook, such as Morgan Carpenter from what was then OII Australia and is now Intersex Human Rights Australia (IHRA);[1] Mauro Cabral Grinspan, Director of GATE,[2] an important group working globally on gender identity, gender expression, and bodily diversity; Dan Christian Ghattas from Germany, the now-Executive Director of Oii Europe;[3] Daniela Truffler from Switzerland and StopIGM;[4] Miriam van der Have, the Executive Director of NNID[5] in the Netherlands and Co-Founder of Oii Europe; Julius Kagawa, Executive Director of SIPID[6] in Uganda; Hiker Chiu of Taiwan, the Founder of Oii-Chinese;[7] Kristian Randjelovic from Siberia, Co-Founder of XY Spectrum;[8] Pol Naidenov from Bulgaria, Co-Founder of Trans & Intersex Allies;[9] and finally, a true intersex pioneer, Mani Bruce Mitchell from New Zealand, Executive Director of ITANZ.[10] Mani was also one of the founding board members of AIC (now interACT), all the way through 2017, and currently listed as Emeritus on our website.

While I was there, I was alerted to a great article published by the online site Everyday Feminism entitled "9 Ways Intersex Youth Want You to Support Them."[11] I read it on my iPhone during a coffee break while sitting around our meeting conference table at the Geneva hotel, excited to share it with the group and say how pleased I was. It was one of the best things I had seen written in the media to date, truly lifting up young intersex voices. The author had interviewed several interACT Youth members for the story.

A couple of my colleagues then looked at each other sheepishly. "What?" I asked them. "Did you read it? Didn't you like it?"

"Well," they began, "the article says InterAct is a youth-led advocacy group for young people with intersex conditions or DSD. And they're spearheading a change in the way youth relate to and take ownership of their bodies. But your organization's use of *DSD*, even when also using *intersex conditions*, is too pathologizing. It's playing off the medical community's aim to 'fix' us." At that time, I was floored they could get so hung up on language that they could just disregard the positive aspects of the article, which was in fact lifting up young intersex voices and further raising awareness.

The next morning at breakfast, I sat with one of them and we talked more about the topic. That may have been the beginnings of me understanding more where they were coming from, while they understood more about my happiness in seeing the stories get told, utilizing the language that was in use by the medical community we still needed to work with. Being together, in person, was the opportunity necessary to build a real relationship and trust among one another. That convening started the change of my entire outlook and of course I learned to reject the label of *disorder*.

* * *

Another result of the wide-ranging impact of the BuzzFeed video, I was invited by the UN Office of the High Commissioner Zeid Ra'ad Al Hussein to participate at an intersex expert meeting in Geneva in September of 2015,[12] which included about 30 invited experts from various UN bodies, the World Health Organization, International Human Rights Law experts, and so on. Seven participants were intersex people representing Argentina, Australia, Germany and Switzerland, Taiwan, and Uganda. I was the only representative from the United States. The privilege and honor were not lost on me, and I was both excited and nervous, hoping I would represent well. I had learned so much already from my previous trip to Geneva, but now, the stakes seemed even greater.

The High Commissioner opened with the following statement:[13]

This is a historic meeting: the first time that the United Nations has convened a discussion specifically to address the human rights situation of intersex persons.

I am happy to see among us UN and regional mandate holders, intersex experts, colleagues from other UN agencies, experts from national institutions and academia, civil society activists and health professionals. I thank all of you for joining us to contribute to our common goal of ending human rights violations against intersex people.

When I started as High Commissioner a year ago, I knew little about intersex people. I don't think I was alone in this: it reflects a general lack of awareness. Too many people assume, without really thinking about it, that everyone can be fitted into two distinct and mutually exclusive categories: male or female.

But in fact, human beings—like most living beings—are more diverse and complex than that. Our diversity—the differences between our experiences and perspectives, as well as the shapes of our bodies—is something that we should celebrate and protect, in all its forms.

All human beings are born equal in dignity and rights. Those foundational, bedrock principles of universality and equality mean that all of us, without exception, and regardless of our sex characteristics, are equally entitled to the protections of international human rights law.

Unfortunately, the myth that all human beings belong to one of two distinct and separate sexes is deep-rooted, and it contributes to the stigma, and even taboo, attached to being intersex.

This is linked to the very serious human rights violations that you are here today to discuss. They include medically unnecessary surgeries and other invasive treatment of intersex babies and children; infanticides of intersex babies; and widespread and life-long discrimination, including in education, employment, health, sports, accessing public services, birth registration and obtaining identity documents.

Such violations are rarely discussed and even more rarely investigated or prosecuted. The result is impunity for the perpetrators; lack of remedy for victims; and a perpetuating cycle of ignorance and abuse.

But there are signs that the tide may at last be turning, thanks to the tireless work of intersex organizations and human rights defenders, over many decades.

There have been clear recommendations by several human rights mechanisms urging States to take steps to address these violations. In a few States, there have been important court judgments and recently, new laws have begun to protect the rights of intersex people.

But much more must be done—both to raise awareness, and to document and prevent violations. Even in those countries that have taken positive steps, we need to bridge the gap between legislation and the lived realities of intersex people.

My Office is committed to this work. In addition to convening this meeting, we released, earlier this month, a factsheet on the human rights of intersex people, as part of our ongoing Free & Equal public information campaign. We are also giving increased attention to the specific situation of intersex people in our work and reports. While our recent report to the Human Rights Council focused—as mandated—on violations based on sexual orientation and gender identity, it also highlighted specific violations faced by intersex people, and made a number of specific recommendations to States.

You have important work ahead of you in the next two days—taking stock of progress and challenges, reviewing lessons learned, and identifying opportunities and priorities for change in the years ahead.

After his statement to our assembled group, he played a video to kick off the meeting: it was interACT's BuzzFeed video! I looked up and there was Pidgeon, Emily, Saifa, and Alice on the big screen at the back of the room. All of us present sat around a huge U-shaped table, and the open end faced the back of the (windowless) room, and the screen. Our video, now playing at the United Nations. I was proud and awestruck. In that moment, and over the two full days there, despite my nervousness about being there with academic and human rights experts from around the globe, my own personal experience as well as the experiences of the other intersex people in the room were not only valid but arguably the most important expertise in the room. In just over a year, I had gone from Hollywood to the UN. All of this activism was starting to make an impact.

Not everything was empowerment and global unity, however. On the second day of this meeting, I had one of my most difficult interactions with an intersex person ever. I was speaking into the microphone, sitting around that U, fighting against all my past insecurities over speaking out, saying something about the importance of intersex visibility:

"It is especially important to have our young people showing the world that being intersex is something to be celebrated and not fixed."

Suddenly, one of the other intersex activists spoke loudly into her mic:

"You are wrong. We shouldn't be celebrating being intersex—that is what has caused us to be mutilated as babies. How can you say this?"

I was startled. Already under stress from being in that forum, her attack triggered a very emotional reaction from me. Though I fought back tears, I could barely speak into my mic to say that I disagreed, though I hadn't meant to upset her. I sat there for another few minutes, trying to regain my composure, but it was useless. The tears started to flow, and even with my years of experience at keeping my emotions at bay, I couldn't do it. Sure, in the grand scheme of things, I had learned to let my emotions show, and I was feeling instead of dissociating, but for the sake of all that is good in the world, why did that have to happen at this moment? Of all places, in front of all these important people at the UN, I needed to keep it together and I couldn't.

A couple of my colleagues—the same two who had argued with me about using DSD language just six months earlier at our meeting in Geneva—were now shooting me knowing looks and mouthing *Are you okay?* Their concern and kindness were much appreciated, but that only made me cry harder. It was inevitable—I stood up from my seat and made my way out of the room and found a restroom where I could pull myself together. Not long after, during a planned meeting break, I had calmed and was able to speak with my colleagues who had been so concerned.

"Just so you know, this is not the first time something like this has happened with her."

"Yes, we've seen similar moments before."

It was clearly an issue of her getting triggered by what I had said and perhaps already by what some others had said that afternoon. She, like so many of us, had a history of trauma. And as the adage goes, hurt people hurt people. I recognized this intersex woman was in some ways reliving trauma and that it wasn't about me. It was a lesson I've had to put to use a number of times since then—a necessary lesson in order to do this work in our community.

* * *

The convening in Geneva wasn't just paying lip service. That same month, the UN's Free & Equal campaign published a wonderful two-page "Intersex Fact Sheet"[14] that I and other intersex experts consulted on before finalization.

Then, the following year, on October 20, 2016, the annual Intersex Awareness Day, the UN Free & Equal campaign published a wonderful new website about intersex human rights, featuring a brand-new video, and at the bottom of the page, highlighting quotes from several intersex people around the world, including me, Katie and her mom Arlene, and Pidgeon.[15] What I wanted to say was on the myth of the "silent happy majority" of intersex people so often held up by doctors. "I used to be part of this 'silent majority'—but was certainly not happy…It's time to end the silence and invisibility of what is actually a traumatized and violated majority."

I had changed my views on language, but I knew that I could not be silent. We had been silent for too long. The harms still came despite our silence. We needed as much visibility as possible.

That year marked the 20th anniversary of the ISNA protests,[16] which involved a small group of brave intersex pioneer activists including Morgan Holmes[17] and the late Max Beck who stood outside the annual conference of the American Academy of Pediatrics, after not being allowed to speak at the conference, holding a banner that read "Hermaphrodites with Attitude," based on the title of INSA's newsletter. They spent hours handing out leaflets and speaking with conference attendees, including surgeons, clinicians, nurses, and social workers.

For 2016, interACT obtained over 70 signatures from individuals and organizations on a new resolution[18] to reaffirm the importance of intersex human rights. Additionally, as a follow-up to the 2015 UN expert meeting, a number of UN treaty bodies, special procedures, and regional human rights bodies adopted a joint statement publicly calling for states to urgently adopt measures to end violence and harmful practices against intersex people.[19] And finally, the US State Department issued a statement in support of intersex human rights. I and other interACT staff had met with State Department staff, encouraging them to recognize intersex human rights and help us fight against harmful medically unnecessary surgeries in the United States and abroad. On Intersex Awareness Day, they published a statement[20] via John Kirby, Assistant Secretary and Department Spokesperson, Bureau of Public Affairs:

> On the occasion of Intersex Awareness Day, the United States stands in solidarity with intersex persons around the world.
>
> We recognize that intersex persons face violence, discrimination,

stigma, harassment, and persecution on account of their sex characteristics, which do not fit binary notions of typical male or female bodies.

Intersex persons routinely face forced medical surgeries that are conducted at a young age without free or informed consent. These interventions jeopardize their physical integrity and ability to live free.

The United States is a proud and founding member of the Equal Rights Coalition, a recently established Coalition of 31 governments that aims to "strengthen cooperation to advance the human rights of, and support inclusive development for all persons regardless of sexual orientation, gender identity or expression, and sex characteristics." We hope this Coalition will work to share best practices and to jointly address challenges in support of the human rights of intersex persons.

Through the Global Equality Fund, the United States, together with the Fund's 25 government, foundation, and business partners, are supporting new efforts of the intersex community to mobilize and organize, with the goals of increasing awareness of and support for intersex persons and their human rights. The Fund was launched in 2011 to support civil society in their efforts to advance human rights and uphold dignity for all.

On Intersex Awareness Day, we are reminded that all people everywhere are created equal and should be afforded equal dignity and respect, regardless of sex characteristics. We look forward to continued cooperation with civil society, like-minded governments, and others to advance the human rights of intersex persons.

Going so far to say that intersex people routinely face nonconsensual medical surgeries at a young age, which jeopardize our physical integrity and ability to live free, was beyond amazing to see. The United States government had made a powerful statement of support for our cause. I was thrilled, emotional, and filled with incredible hope that we were nearing the end of the long fight, or at least, that the end wasn't as far off as it had seemed.

But then, on November 8, 2016, an entirely different type of person was elected to be the next President of the United States. I woke up the morning after in disbelief. Then, fear set in, and finally the harsh reality of what was ahead not only for the intersex community but also for the rest of the LGBTQ+ community, and frankly, just about every social justice organization and program. The rest of the year was a blur.

My father, of course, loved Trump. The day after the election, he posted to his Facebook page, "Great day for America, great day for my grandchildren." I couldn't have disagreed more.

We wouldn't be able to look to the federal government for support. The only thing that kept me holding onto a shred of hope in these days was that I knew we had found a powerful new voice in the intersex rights movement who, in the beginning of 2017, would be coming forward as a new champion for the bodily integrity of intersex babies and youth.

CHAPTER 18

INTERSEX *EN VOGUE*

Statistically, there has to be at least a few intersex celebrities. I would love for us to live in a world in which they feel it is safe to come out. It took a lot of courage from the early LGBTQ+ celebrities to come out to the public, and especially for the early trailblazers, it was not easy (and remains difficult in many ways, with only a few exceptions). But I believe the only way to change society is to sway public opinion: once people know and understand a different community, they lose the fear or stigma of that community and begin acceptance.

Our intersex community definitely needs a big platform. Unfortunately, in our culture and the age of Instagram, we desperately need celebrities to disclose they are intersex and help in the fight for bodily autonomy. Unfortunately, the world hasn't been accepting of people born with bodily differences.

Hopefully, that is changing.

The change began one day back in September of 2015, when I received an email introducing me to a famous fashion model, Hanne Gaby Odiele.

Hanne is a huge celebrity in the fashion world. Discovered in

Belgium at a rock concert at age 17, she came to NYC and in a short time grew to be an internationally renowned fashion model. In 2015, she was already at the top of her career. Her look is unique—an eclectic kind of urban chic with attitude. Hanne is also intersex.

She wrote to me that she wanted to come out as intersex and help fight for intersex rights in order to protect kids from harmful medical interventions like what she experienced as a kid, suffering from the results even today.

A few weeks later, in October, the two of us met midday in a small café not far from her modeling agency in Soho. I was struck with how unassuming this supermodel seemed, dressed in old jeans, sneakers, and an oversized white button-down shirt. No makeup, her hair natural and casual—not styled at all. She was a complete natural beauty.

She speaks multiple languages, English not her first, so sometimes she needed to pause a bit to find the right word she was looking for. It was a new situation for her. She told me some of her story growing up in Belgium and being aware of two surgeries as a kid. Her experiences were not new to me—what she described were stories I'd heard hundreds of times from intersex people over the last few years. However, something about the way she talked about her experiences in examining rooms at the hands of callous doctors left me shivering. There was a raw emotion and pain underlying Hanne's story, as if she was still that child reflecting on the traumatic experiences and still trying to reconcile them. She was clear with me that she wanted to help stop the kind of treatment she had received from happening to more intersex kids, and that she was ready to come out publicly. She said she was done pretending and hiding this part of herself—it was exhausting. I could *so* relate.

I'd like to think we all can relate, that anyone can who has felt they have had to hide a part of themselves away. When that happens, we are denied the feeling of authenticity and true self-acceptance.

Not only was Hanne ready for that, she also recognized that she was at a time in her career where she could take a risk like this and come out. She was at the top of her career—now she wanted to be in control of her narrative and start living her authentic self. Also, she recognized that being a top model gave her a platform that most people will never have. Her story would be of immediate interest to the global media.

What she needed was interACT's help in refining her message, not only with English as a second or third language to her, but she also needed education and coaching on the history and evolution of intersex rights. She wanted to be a champion for us, for future intersex children, and she knew that she couldn't afford missteps or being off message from not knowing enough. My stumbling was all done behind the scenes—a celebrity couldn't afford to make those gaffes. Thus, a partnership was born. A few weeks later, I was back in Manhattan to meet with Hanne again for lunch, this time with her agent, Michael, joining us. He seemed genuinely thrilled that Hanne wanted to come out as intersex, and he remained a supportive partner throughout the process of moving forward over the next 15 months.

* * *

Finally, in January of 2017, Hanne got to tell her story, carefully and intentionally, to the world, first in the United States in *USA Today*,[1] and later that week, in an interview with *Vogue*[2] detailing her intersex history that went viral. I was hopeful that with her narrative of the real pain caused to her the new platform would take us from raising awareness to raising outrage over the way intersex children have been treated.

A week earlier, Hanne recorded a short video that was shared worldwide, telling everyone that she was intersex while wearing a purple interACT T-shirt. She was proud and didn't want the harms she had suffered to happen to future intersex kids. Soon, interACT was hit with more media requests and inquiries than we could handle. The following days were a blur—our inbox was barraged with email requests, and Hanne was swamped with multiple interviews each day for outlets in the United States and Europe. I don't think I slept much those first couple of days, as I was trying to keep up with everything.

That week, "Intersex" was trending on Merriam-Webster and almost became the word of the year on Dictionary.com.[3]

Soon after, in early February, National Geographic released their film *Gender Revolution*, hosted by Katie Couric, someone I had admired and watched on television for years. A few days after Hanne's coming out media blitz, I found myself in New York at the invitation-only launch event for *Gender Revolution*. The previous year, I had been contacted by a producer for the film who was seeking information about intersex and possible contacts to be interviewed. They ended up featuring our board member and parent of an intersex child, Eric Lohman, as well as Brian Douglas, an intersex man who had been raised as a girl, and Georgiann Davis, sociology professor and author. I was also able to get National Geographic to include an intersex educational supplement written by interACT in the rollout efforts. Again, intersex was going mainstream. It was a celebratory night with other members of the interACT staff—and I got to meet and pose for photos with Katie Couric.

* * *

The day after the Nat Geo film launch, I was in the elevator to the 26th floor of the Condé Nast Building right next to the new Freedom Tower and Memorial in Manhattan, riding up to the headquarters of *Teen Vogue*. Over the previous year, *Teen Vogue* had become a leading voice in progressive politics and current events and a source of thoughtful, researched information in the Trumpian fake news era. Their health editor reached out to interACT and Hanne to do a story with a photo and video shoot. Along with Hanne, they interviewed two other young intersex activists—our very own Emily and Pidgeon. I went with them to the filming, but they were the stars. I was only there to offer support and cheer them on while ensuring everything went smoothly and respectfully. And with *Teen Vogue* being the great organization it is, everything did go smoothly and respectfully.

We spent several hours in a mostly empty but huge studio space. At one end, the cameras and lights were set up in front of a plain white background, and at the other end were the makeup tables, clothes racks, and more tables with endless accessory options, with shoes lined underneath on the floor. Hanne, Emily, and Pidgeon each had makeup and hair done and then were dressed by staff after picking through racks and racks of the latest fashions for young people. I watched out the floor-to-ceiling window as the sky grew dark that afternoon, the city skyline in front of me, and thought, wow—we were doing it. We were bringing the issue of intersex mainstream. Even more people would soon know what the word means and what the experience is. The world was learning that we exist. Invisible no more.

They shot for hours, taking turns talking about their experiences, at times light and cheerful, at other times, somber and emotional, reflecting on the harm done to them. There was a beautiful connection between the three of them that shows up on camera. And I was filled with admiration at what these three people already had achieved in such a short time.

Over the course of the summer, *Teen Vogue* released the videos in a four-part series[4] on intersex.

* * *

Unfortunately, not every organization or film studio that reached out to us was as sensitive and thoughtful as *Teen Vogue*. Immediately after Hanne's coming out, I started receiving a barrage of emails from filmmakers who were ready to capitalize on the "whole intersex thing." Directors, producers, writers, they wanted to make documentaries about the intersex experience, preferably with Hanne, but maybe just the topic in general, they said. I could tell almost immediately that most of them were only interested in a topic they could sensationalize. They were summarily dismissed. There were a few that did seem genuine, particularly from Starfish Media Group, Soledad O'Brien's media company. I'd long been an admirer of O'Brien and her work, and met with Patrick, in charge of development, during one of my trips to New York. Soon we began putting together a pitch to shop to various filmmakers and media channels, specifically geared toward telling the stories of young intersex people, the very current story of their activism, and the fight for bodily autonomy. After Skyping with a couple dozen people in the community, Patrick developed a moving "sizzle reel" video that brought me completely to tears when he invited me to watch it in his office a few months later. He'd managed to capture the essence of the current movement in the United States, driven by young intersex people who, despite suffering deep trauma, were stepping up to fight back. We aimed to do a multi-part series that would go deep into various intersex people's narratives, but to date, it remains on the shelf that we take down and consider from time to time, hopeful someone will agree to finance the project for us.

CHAPTER 19

THE RIGHT
TO TRUTH

2017 continued to be a big year. Much of the next few months are still a complete blur, and not because I dissociated. In March, I testified at an Inter-American Human Rights Commission hearing in DC about intersex human rights abuses in the United States. There was a formal hearing[1] at the Organization of American States before a Human Rights Commission made up of representatives from both North and South America. I joined other intersex people from South American countries to tell our stories before a panel. The experience was humbling, especially stories shared by my fellow presenters, which were excruciating to hear in terms of abuses they suffered. In one case, a presenter was so fearful they would be killed should their testimony be discovered by officials in their home country that they used a screen to block their face from the cameras as they told their story live to the dignified panel. That moment was a stark reminder to me that while visibility and acceptance was gaining ground in my home country, in some parts of the world not that far away from us, intersex people continued to live in the terrifying shadow of persecution, simply for being born with bodies that didn't line up with societal norms of what is typical for either a male or a female.

Then in April, I was in Amsterdam attending the 4th International Intersex Forum (IIF)[2] and convening with over two dozen other intersex people from around the globe. I had met several of them in person at various conferences over the last few years but relied mostly on social media and Skype to communicate and share information. As always, it was so much more meaningful to meet my intersex activist peers in person. There is a much-needed sense of connection and community that can only be achieved by in-person encounters. Though I was only one of two attending from the United States, intersex people were present from every continent except Antarctica. This three-day forum, consisting of informal and formal meetings to share information, educate one another, and develop further strategies for the growing movement, was notable for its size and diversity compared with the three previous fora, including new activists coming from previously underrepresented countries in both Africa and Asia. This was a hopeful and beautiful sign that our voices were growing—but it also presented more of a challenge regarding how to effectively organize, given the larger number of participants and the varying degrees of experience. Regardless of experience and logistical concerns, everyone had something valuable to share, and we all learned so much from each other. Most of all, we were empowered by the strength of the members of our community, knowing we were not alone in this global fight for justice.

One of the points of discussion centered on something set up from the previous IIF in Malta, where the assembled intersex activists not only reaffirmed the principles founded during the first two fora, aiming to end discrimination against intersex people and to ensure the right of bodily integrity, physical autonomy, and self-determination, but they crafted what is now known as the Malta Declaration,[3] an agreed-upon list of demands by the global intersex community, including ending nonconsensual surgeries on intersex children and ensuring intersex people have the right to full information and access to their own medical records and history. While I was not present at the Malta meeting, several attendees in Amsterdam had been, and we talked about the

Malta Declaration in detail and our continuing plan for reaching our community's goals and demands.

* * *

Progress seemed to turn off and on like a faucet. I'd been feeling the early signs of burnout, disheartened by politics, and frustrated with so much of the medical community. In June, Hanne Gaby Odiele and I were invited to speak, along with an attorney from Lambda Legal, about intersex rights hosted by the European Union at the United Nations in New York. A couple of hours before our event, Hanne and I met up and ducked into a Capitol Grill for a drink and to decompress. The last six months had been a whirlwind, and she seemed as tired as I was. We were both proud of the visibility raising we had helped happen, and we chatted about the reality of burnout. Hanne especially had put herself out there in a big way, and the last several months had been intense and a little overwhelming. I had been working mostly behind the scenes but tirelessly, and I wasn't sure if I could keep up that pace. "It's important to find a balance," Hanne said, and I agreed. It was easy to say, and a lot harder to put into practice, as we both knew.

However, every time I felt so fatigued that I wasn't sure if I'd be able to go on, something would come along that would inspire and reenergize me. That day's event was one of those moments. Sponsored by the UN LGBT Core Group, an informal cross-regional group established in 2008, one UN ambassador announced to the relatively large group attending that the Core Group, made up of member mission countries, had officially voted to include intersex in its name and mission, becoming the LGBTI Core Group. This was a surprise, but a totally welcome surprise. Gaining acceptance in another LGBT group was such a meaningful (and crucial) step in building awareness, gaining allies, becoming visible, and maybe finally getting our voices not only heard but *listened to.*

Another surprise that day was seeing my mother-in-law in the front row. She had seen the event announced via an interACT e-newsletter, so she and her friend had driven up to show her support. Only a few years earlier, I was still keeping my intersex status a secret from her and others in the family, and now here she was, listening to me talk about it at the United Nations.

Then in June, a statement by doctors that actually boosted me: three former Surgeons General published an article by Palm Center that criticized early intersex surgeries and called for an end to the harmful practices being perpetrated on intersex bodies.[4]

They acknowledged that many doctors who supported and performed such surgeries had the best interests of patients and their parents at heart, but their review of available evidence, including a reference to the 2016 State Department statement in recognition of Intersex Awareness Day, persuaded them that cosmetic infant genitoplasty is not justified absent a need to ensure physical functioning. They hoped that professionals and parents would heed the growing consensus that the practice should end.

Surely this had to make a difference. This was coming from three previous Surgeons General, for crying out loud.

I would keep waiting for that to happen.

But that didn't mean I was standing idle while I waited.

In September, I was invited to participate as an intersex expert at a series of meetings in Geneva with human rights experts and others from around the world to finalize an important addendum to the Yogyakarta Principles[5] developed a decade earlier and which served as a cornerstone in international human rights law on issues of sexual orientation and gender identity. The original document only briefly mentioned intersex. Two intersex activists from other countries had been working on the project for months and invited me to contribute in the final discussions as a supportive intersex expert. I had so much respect for their work, and it humbled me to be included and trusted in this collaboration. These were the same two activists who, two years earlier in Geneva, had been suspicious of me and somewhat confrontational regarding my acceptance of DSD language as opposed to intersex language. How much I had learned in that time, and how meaningful it was to gain their trust.

It was certainly an honor to become one of the final signatories on the Yogyakarta Principles plus 10 (YP +10) as a supplement of the Principles, formally called the "Additional Principles and State Obligation on the Application of International Human Rights Law in Relation to Sexual Orientation, Gender Expression and Sex Characteristics to Complement the Yogyakarta Principles." The "plus 10" was a reference to the 10 years between the original and the addendum. And now the document explicitly added the "Sexual Expression and Sex Characteristics" to the nomenclature of what the Principles covered, more complete from the universally used SOGI (Sexual Orientation and Gender Identity) human rights language. That in itself was a huge human rights milestone. It explicitly recognized intersex people and the human rights violations we have suffered, including not only medically unnecessary and nonconsensual surgeries but also our common experiences of being denied the right to truth about ourselves and our own bodies.

The document we finalized created two new principles directly recognizing the harms suffered by intersex people:

Principle 32: The Right to Bodily & Mental Integrity.[6]

Principle 37: The Right to Truth.[7]

Principle 37 was the most meaningful to me personally, as the theme of secrets and truth had been weaving throughout my life for so long that to have a formal recognition of the importance of this right and an acknowledgment of the impact it can have when it has been denied was actually healing. The fact that I could play some small role in contributing to its publication was a bonus. This was a historic and important human rights document—once again, I marveled at my path to getting to this point, knowing that the work was still far from over.

* * *

By October, not much had changed among the medical community, but *The Washington Post Magazine* released a cover story entitled "Their Time: After generations in the shadows, the intersex right movement has a message for the world: We aren't disordered and we aren't ashamed."[8] I (along with others) had been working with a journalist for weeks on the story about our movement, particularly the young people our organization was nurturing to raise awareness and advocate for change. As the piece further developed, we learned that her editor at *The Washington Post Magazine* wanted to make it a cover story, and therefore, they wanted photographs and more interviews. In collaboration with that year's organizers of the AIS-DSD conference in Phoenix that July, the journalist and photographer set up in the hotel ballroom for one evening. Several interACT Youth members in their teens and twenties volunteered to tell their stores and be photographed. I commented to a friend at the time, as we watched these bright young people posing and talking, being themselves and wonderful, how far we'd come, how only two years earlier, we would not have had enough young people confident and ready to be so public to make this story possible. Empowering our intersex youth was working, and the lengthy cover story speaks to this, detailing the group's arrival at the conference and how I had arranged a shoot in a vacant lecture hall from 8 to 10pm. In the end, it stretched until well after midnight, with a dozen members of the interACT crew lining up for first and second chances to see themselves glow under professional lights. "Slay, slay, slay," they chanted, as the next day rolled in, and one of their friends worked it for the camera in bright red lipstick and a purple interACT t-shirt.

The next generation of advocates and activists indeed gives me so much hope beyond our immediate uncertainties.

CHAPTER 20

UNTIL EVERY DAY IS INTERSEX AWARENESS DAY

October of 2017 also saw the publication of my opinion piece in *STAT*,[1] a journal dedicated to life sciences and the business of medicines, about the need for adult intersex care in medicine. Apart from our mission to protect children from nonconsensual harmful medical intervention, the other major issue impacting the intersex community is the lack of competent compassionate mental and physical healthcare for us as consenting adults. The longer I do this work, the more I am struck by the irony of doctors fighting to do surgeries on intersex children in order to fix them, but as soon as we turn into adults, we are left with absolutely no informed medical care to help us. Frankly, many of the health concerns and mental health issues we have as adults are a result of what was done to us as children, not simply due to the fact we were born intersex. The harm is society's reaction to and rejection of us.

I mean—I am arguably one of the most informed and well-connected intersex adults in the United States and yet I don't know of an endocrinologist anywhere in the country with a level of expertise in treating intersex patients with, say, hormone replacement therapy. It's totally unacceptable. We are a very underserved population as adults, while being a very abused population as children.

That was behind my opinion piece published on Intersex Awareness Day, entitled, "In the intersex community, we're desperate for quality care. Doctors aren't listening." It was important to communicate the very common phenomenon of intersex people to avoid medical care because of a lack of understanding physicians who are competent to our needs, and the negative health outcomes occurring as a result of this avoidance. Many intersex people don't trust the medical community largely due to past trauma committed by the medical community. For up to two percent of the population, this is a real health problem. I am no exception. For the most part, I avoid doctors and medical care as much as I can. I have gone several years in a row without getting an annual physical exam. It's hard to trust, and I have been burned before, like so many intersex people.

I ended by urging healthcare providers to reach out to intersex advocacy and support groups because we were always looking for intersex-aware referrals. I further called for medical and public health educators to advocate for better inclusion in the curriculum because intersex deserves more than just a paragraph or two in a textbook. An even better option would be to bring intersex people to medical or public health schools so students could learn from us firsthand. Above all, I asked that the medical community acknowledge the trust gap and the reason it exists—the first step toward making sure we're not afraid to seek the care we need and deserve.

* * *

Because of Intersex Awareness Day on the 26th, October will always be a busy month anyway. It's more than just a single day of awareness; the increased media and education and advocacy activity really starts early-to-mid-October and runs through at least the first week of November, often winding down by November 8th—Intersex Day of Remembrance[2] —which marks the birthday of Herculine Barbin, a now-famous French intersex person. This October, though, seemed to be busier than I had ever experienced, and I was already facing exhaustion by this point.

But first, I had an appointment to make with Christa. Christa had been the one to come with me to Hollywood to meet with the *Faking It* team. And now, she was coming with me to get my first—and only—tattoo.

I'd been thinking about getting it for a year but had been so nervous about something so permanent. In the back of my head, even at age 51, I heard my mom's voice saying how tacky she thought tattoos were and all the reasons why she disliked them. I mentioned to Christa that I was thinking about getting it, and as soon as she heard what I was getting, she said she was in and wanted the same one. "I'll go with you," she said.

Christa lived in New York, and so when I went down for Intersex Awareness Day, I made an appointment for the two of us with a tattoo artist I'd found online who specialized in small text and lines. When it was time for our appointment, we met up at the tattoo studio, deciding once there that we both wanted white ink. "It's different," I said, "and a little more subtle." I wanted the tattoo but I didn't want it to be too obvious. It was going to be on my finger, after all.

Christa chose her index finger, so that when she held it to her lips to make a "shh" sign, it would face out, like her little secret. I liked that idea a lot—but I was going to put mine on my middle finger, so it would show when I gave someone the finger—doctors who infuriated me or wouldn't listen or acknowledge the harm they're doing. Christa went first. It only took five minutes, tops, and she smiled and stayed still through hers. Next, it was my turn. I was nervous. I fidgeted in the chair. "Here," Christa said, holding out her hand—the one that hadn't been tattooed. I clasped onto her hand while the tattoo artist held the needle up to my finger, and—oh my god, it hurt like hell. It was the worst pain I'd ever felt. I squirmed enough to annoy the artist.

Though it only took five minutes, it was the longest five minutes I'd been through in a while. I squeezed Christa's hand. Then, when it was finished, I turned my hand to look at the result—*XOXY*. My little mark of celebration and defiance.

"You must have a higher threshold for pain, I guess," I told her.

"Actually, white ink can hurt more," the tattoo artist said. "You have to go over it more times to make it to stand out. Plus, the area on the middle figure is particularly sensitive." Okay, maybe I wasn't such a wimp. Hey, I had a tattoo. Me. I was proud of myself, for doing something that was my own, for doing something regardless of what my mother thought about it, for sharing this with Christa—my dear orchid sister, and for having something to remind myself to stay strong, love myself, and know that I have a big intersex family and am not alone.

I texted a picture to Steven and the girls—they thought it was pretty cool.

Something so small, tiny, really, but a huge step for me. The whole thing was exhilarating, and though I'd been tired lately from all my activism and preparation for Intersex Awareness Day, this was a little boost that was a perfect way to rejuvenate my spirits for the work ahead.

An exciting breakthrough was a concurrent public statement made by the organization Physicians for Human Rights (PHR), titled "Unnecessary Surgery on Intersex Children Must Stop."[3] The physicians behind this statement fight against torture and help people in war-torn and impoverished countries. Now, they were turning inward to medical providers in the United States and asking them to stop physically and psychologically harming intersex children. Of course, PHR has no binding authority over the medical profession, but the statement was highly symbolic, and I believed this added moral pressure would weigh heavily on the doctors and institutions participating across the country. On the contrary, time has shown that the impact has been minimal or non-existent.

But then there was another statement made, this time by the AAP, the very organization that was protested back in 1996 on the day that now marks Intersex Awareness Day. They released this statement[4] exactly 21 years later:

> On Oct. 26, Intersex Awareness Day, the American Academy of Pediatrics joins in supporting families of children born with differences of sex development. The AAP and its 66,000 member pediatricians, pediatric medical subspecialists, and pediatric surgical specialists are committed to the health and dignity of all children, including children who do not easily fit into binary gender categories.
>
> "We all share the same goal of healthy, happy children," said American Academy of Pediatrics President Fernando Stein, MD, FAAP. "When a child is born with any type of congenital difference, parents will have many questions for the medical team, including what caused it and what will happen to their child. Pediatricians have the responsibility to offer useful and reliable information, to help the parents access specialists, and to coordinate the child's care. Above all, it's important to support the child and family."
>
> The care of children with differences of sex development is an evolving field, and the AAP looks forward to additional research regarding treatment outcomes. Meanwhile, the AAP is committed to continued dialogue regarding the best ways to support these children and their families.

Naturally, we had been hoping for a much more direct official policy statement from the AAP, one that would strongly encourage delay of medically unnecessary intersex surgeries until the patient could meaningfully participate in the decision. The report on human rights violations in United States hospitals published by Human Rights Watch and interACT[5] explicitly recommended that the AAP:

> Retract the support of the AAP for the 2006 Consensus Statement as an official position statement of the AAP, and replace it with a

statement that is consistent with international human rights standards and with the AAP statements on Assent, Informed Permission and Consent, and on FGM.

In our ideal version, the statement would:

- Advocate to end to surgical procedures on children with atypical sex characteristics too young to participate in the decision, when those procedures both carry a meaningful risk of harm and can be safely deferred;
- Advise that parents be given complete information about their intersex child's condition and the risks, benefits, and alternatives to any recommended procedures;
- Advise that children and youth with atypical sex characteristics be given complete information about their conditions in an age-appropriate way;
- Recommend that doctors routinely give parents of children with atypical sex characteristics information about available peer support groups; and
- Recommend that parents routinely have access to mental health support and information from mental health experts about their child's condition before making irreversible decisions about their child's health.

I was tired of baby steps, tired of organizations throwing us bones but not doing the real work of change and advocate for open change.

Meanwhile also in Chicago, a peaceful protest outside Lurie Children's Hospital was held by a group of intersex advocates and allies led by the Intersex Justice Project,[6] a group seeking to end medically invasive and unnecessary surgeries in the United States that target intersex children and adolescents by empowering intersex people of color to advance that change. Lurie was one of the hospitals where many harmful intersex surgeries were still occurring, under the leadership of Dr. Cheng, the man who wanted to keep emotions and law out of the discussion on surgical harm. This was the exact kind of direct action that was necessary, and it raised media attention and awareness as well as education. The first coordinator of interACT's Youth program and a co-founder of IJP, Pidgeon Pagonis, had been working in Chicago to get Dr. Cheng to address this issue for years but he had dismissed Pigeon just as he had dismissed us.

I was in New York for Intersex Awareness Day that year, hosting a celebration of intersex people, their families, and activists, though we were horribly understaffed. All communications and media tasks fell to me, on top of all the other coordinating, and I was pushed beyond what I thought I could take. I tried to forge on and take each task at a time to get everything done.

I monitored social media and found a surprising ally on that day. Despite the new administration's ongoing dismantling of LGBTQ+ rights, the State Department again issued a public statement[7] in support of Intersex Awareness Day, recognizing "that intersex persons face violence, discrimination, harassment, and persecution on account of their sex characteristics. At a young age, intersex persons routinely face forced medical surgeries without free or informed consent. These interventions jeopardize their physical integrity and ability to live freely." I was sure a day like this flew way under the administration's radar, but I was grateful for the State Department making a statement. Clearly there were still some like-minded holdovers from the previous administration at State.

I was thrilled to have this small bone thrown in our direction because I knew it meant something to somebody at the State Department, and that acknowledgement in these times meant a lot to the rest of us. I shared and celebrated the State Department's statement on interACT's social media, but almost immediately, I was reprimanded for doing so by another intersex activist.

"Do you realize," they said, "at this same time, the State Department is being sued[8] for denying a military vet and intersex person a passport with their preferred 'non-binary' gender marker? This statement is totally meaningless because they're not backing it up with actions."

It was true and I was aware of the lawsuit. The activist had a point. But still, that point did not fall easy on my ears that day. I was so overworked and stressed that I ended up blocking this person on my social media accounts—something I rarely did. My patience had all but run out, and yes, the State Department was doing shitty things, but I don't know, maybe there were different ways to look at the situation, and maybe highlighting when they did support the community could draw further discrepancies between their public statements and their actions. Thanking them for their statement in support of Intersex Awareness Day didn't have to preclude calling them out for their policy of denying the proper gender marker on the passport.

What I really needed, though, was to nap for about a week and not have anyone call me or ask for anything.

* * *

At the end of the year, I was invited to participate in OutRight Action International's Advocacy Week at the United Nations in NYC. Out-Right is a United States-based advocacy organization focused on the human rights of LGBTIQ people[9] around the globe, and its Advocacy Week, held each year to coincide with Human Rights Day on December 10th, brought in more than 40 international LGBTIQ activists for training and advocacy at the UN. I was one of three intersex folks and I'm pretty sure the only heterosexual in the group. I was honored to speak as the intersex advocate at OutSummit, the one-day conference culminating the week dedicated to giving activists in the United States and around the world the opportunity to meet and discuss critical issues affecting the global LGBTIQ movement. This was a group of very diverse people defending the human rights of various oppressed groups of people by speaking truth to power and bravely speaking out—in some cases risking their health and safety to do so.

After my talk on representation in the media, I was approached by several delightful and enthusiastic young queer people who all thanked me for my presentation, telling me how happy they were to meet me. They knew about my work and treated me like a star. I was humbled and touched. How had a middle-aged cis straight woman from the burbs of Boston become a star in the eyes of these young queer advocates? It turned out they were all part of Voices4,[10] a growing group of queer young people who met weekly and organized non-violent direct actions and political statements. Their slogans include "Queer people anywhere are responsible for queer people everywhere" and "When you mess with one queer, you mess with us all." Adam Werner, the group's leader, invited me to speak at one of their weekly meetings the following autumn. The meeting was in late October, a couple of days before Intersex Awareness Day. I would be in New York for other events as well, and I looked forward to talking about intersex issues with Voices4 in one of the many rooms at the New York LGBT Center.

When I entered the room, though, I had no idea the crowd I'd be walking into—the classroom-style setup was standing-room-only, packed with young people who enthusiastically listened to me for about 30 minutes. Their hands would shoot up, asking really astute, thoughtful questions—it was the best crowd I had ever spoken to. There was only one person in the audience I was aware of being intersex, but all who were present seemed to "get it" right away. They all knew what it was like to be othered and oppressed based on one's natural difference. Their genuine empathy and outrage at the harm done to intersex people was tangible. After I spoke, many of the group came up to thank me and offer kind words of support. It was a level of support I'd never felt before. I had a warm-and-fuzzy high coupled with so much respect and admiration for these queer young activists who were courageous enough to unapologetically be themselves and who still gave so much of themselves so openly. They were proof that the queer community was here to support me and the intersex community and that we desperately needed to support each other. It was also the first time in my life I got to feel like a queen—Queen Z.

However, later on, after speaking at the summit's closing plenary panel held at CUNY Law School, I walked off stage and to the back of the auditorium, where my colleague (and interACT Law and Policy Director) Al was sitting.

"You okay?" he asked, although the question was rhetorical. He was just as tired as I was, I'm sure.

"I'm ready to not be on anymore," I said. "I just want to wrap things up and head home."

"I hear you," he said.

Then a man I didn't know or recognize walked up to me, standing over me. "Excuse me?" he said, "Ms. Zieselman, you are completely off base on your position of surgeries on intersex babies."

"Pardon?"

"These are birth defects. Babies with birth defects need to be able to get surgeries, this is not a human rights issue."

"Well," I said, and I sighed. Here we go. "I think a lot of people, including me, would disagree. One of the reasons we're here is that it is a human rights issue. Being intersex is not a defect. When a surgery is absolutely medically necessary, our position is that they must be done. But for everything else, that should be up to the intersex child to decide if and when to have any other type of surgery."

"You're wrong. It should be up to the parents and doctors to decide."

That was it. I couldn't advocate any longer, and it showed on my face. That was when Al jumped in, heroically, and addressed the man, explaining the issue from a legal standpoint. Also to my good fortune, just at that moment, I was pulled back on stage by other Advocacy Week participants for a group photo. I purposely stood in the back row, fighting to keep the tears from coming. Years of exhausting work had built up, and it was difficult and draining work, and now it was taking a very real toll. I couldn't keep my head down and try to take on twenty different projects at a time or I would lose my mind.

Of course I wasn't actually going to give up. But the holidays were coming up, and I was able to take off a few days. It had been a long year, but a successful and transformative one for our work. I would be able to recognize that…a couple of days later, in a calm and rested moment. Afterward, it was time to gear up for more.

*　*　*

2018 was more of the same, although we didn't have any celebrity coming outs to plan, and there were no big film shoots. In spring, I attended OutRight's annual gala, held at Chelsea Piers in Manhattan. The gala was honoring two advocates, including Lois Whitman,[11] founder of the Children's Rights division of Human Rights Watch. She and her husband were generous donors to a number of important causes, and now she was being recognized for her incredible lifetime of achievements fighting for the human rights of others, especially children.

I had met Lois during the Advocacy Week and Summit the previous December, and we hit it off (despite my exhaustion). She is almost old enough to be my grandmother, and I kept thinking how cool it would be if she were—I was in awe of all she'd achieved, and I wanted to talk with her all day.

This was my first time attending the gala, and I took the train down to the city and went alone. I recognized several attendees I knew through my work, but mostly I circulated the reception on my own, then took a seat in the very back row as the speaking portion was about to get underway. The MC for the event was the delightful Karamo Brown, a new OutRight board member but more famously known for being on *Queer Eye*. When Lois was introduced and then gave her remarks, I sat rapt. And then, from the podium, she mentioned the great work that interACT was doing, and then she mentioned me by name. I was stunned. People clapped, and then Karamo Brown spotted me in the audience. He hurried over to give me a hug. Suddenly, I wasn't so invisible in the back row. But also…I was just hugged by Karamo Brown. *Swoon.*

CHAPTER 21

FIERCE PARENTS, FIERCE ALLIES

Another exciting happening arrived in July with the publication of *Raising Rosie*,[1] a memoir and guidebook for parents written by Eric and Stephani Lohman. The Lohmans are the wonderful parents of a young intersex child named Rosie. It was the first book of its kind, written by parents, and it candidly talks about the immense pressure and sometimes coercion that parents are subjected to immediately following the birth of an unexpected intersex child. Rosie was born with one of the most common intersex conditions—Congenital Adrenal Hyperplasia (CAH).[2] A common trait in babies with CAH is that the genitalia appears as an enlarged clitoris. This is a symptom of an underlying hormone imbalance. Though the larger-than-typical clitoris is not a medical problem, most pediatric urologists (and doctors in other related subspecialties) push parents to let them operate on their baby's tiny genitals to "normalize" them, strictly for cosmetic reasons, despite all the associated risks.

Stephani Lohman, a nurse, and Eric, a major in women's and gender studies, now a university professor of communications and media, were quick to realize the pressure they were under from doctors was unnecessary. They pushed back at several doctors' attempts to convince them there was something wrong with their infant's genitalia.

I had met Eric a few years earlier when he interviewed for a part-time communications job with interACT. Through that process, he told me the story of Rosie. While he didn't end up working on staff, I quickly recommended he join our board of directors—I'm so glad he did. The Lohmans serve as an inspiring example of how parents can advocate for and protect their intersex child, and how crucial their voices are in standing up to doctors who push for these harmful procedures.

CAH also happens to be one of the conditions that remains a flashpoint between intersex rights and resistance from the medical community.

Educating parents of intersex children is paramount. We have to be able to convince them that there is nothing wrong with their child being intersex and direct them to all the resources necessary to help them along the way. The main hurdle is that many parents don't know anything about intersex and have no idea where to look. Because intersex has been stigmatized for so long, they feel shame because of their child's body and want to cover up or erase the fact of their child's non-binary genitalia. This will never benefit the child—that I guarantee.

That's why I am so relieved whenever a parent reaches out to me or another advocate to ask questions or to join the community. One of the more heartening exchanges in recent months came from a father-to-be, who had found out through an early test that their child, due within a few months, had androgen insensitivity. "I really want to get involved in the cause," he wrote, "keep raising awareness, and have the whole scary discovery experience we went through become a normal or accepted practice. We would welcome any thoughts of the best way to get involved and are happy to share further info."

I was blown away. I first off congratulated him on the impending arrival of his child, and then I asked how he'd heard of interACT.

I also asked how the healthcare experience had gone for him. I told him I had AIS and how much it meant to hear there were such parents as him and his wife out there, advocating for their children. I directed him to find peer support from one of the parent communities (in fact, he had already found and connected with another parent) and reassured him that his child was going to be wonderful, healthy, and happy.

He wrote back almost immediately, thanking me, and then detailing how as soon as he and his wife got the karyotype information, they went on a two-week mission to educate themselves. Then he wrote:

> Some doctors have scared us. Candidly, we went to our OB after the anatomy scan, and, within 30 seconds, she asked if we thought we were going to keep the baby. I don't blame her, as her intention was not malicious, but it's reactions and, simply, lack of education like that that I want to help avoid in the future. I want to bring further awareness so that it doesn't have to be a "dire medical emergency" for individuals. With that said, we have also encountered so many caring people, many complete strangers, and also many doctors who have offered amazing time and support to us.
>
> Ultimately, we are now in a place where we are very excited for the soon-to-be arrival of our child, and I am very passionate about helping children, adults, parents like ourselves, whoever, feel supported, no sense of not being "normal" but completely comfortable with who they are.
>
> I would love to connect and certainly also with other parents in similar situations. I purchased the book *Raising Rosie* (and I see Eric is on your board), and that is how I found this organization. Very excited that it exists.

I stayed in touch with this father whose daughter was born healthy, confirmed with CAIS, like me, but with parents who are well informed and ready to advocate for her bodily autonomy. Maybe he too will be a future board member. He's already a perfect ambassador for intersex children and families.

That is why, despite my ongoing frustration with the medical community, I still believe we can chip away at the antiquated (and never acceptable) stigmatized treatment toward intersex people. And even in the medical community, there is a glimmer of light way, way down the tunnel.

Just like the children of my daughters' generation are much more open-minded about diversity and gender expression, similarly the next generation of medical providers have shown up as allies, enough to give me tangible hope for the future. The current crop of medical students seems to get it. They have grown up in a more enlightened and accepting time, and when we are able to speak with them and disclose what has happened to intersex babies and children, they are outraged for us. They will be the ones on the front lines after school and residency, and I am hopeful (cautiously) that they will be instrumental in making permanent changes to how intersex children and adults are treated. Already, they have shown up for us in concrete ways.

Back in 2016, an interACT Youth member was invited to present grand rounds at UC Irvine. She told her narrative and explained the pressures she still faced to remove her testes, and how many other intersex people had it far worse than she did. As a result, a few of the medical students who were in the audience took it upon themselves to introduce a resolution to delay intersex surgeries until the patients themselves were old enough and able to consent. The resolution was introduced and referred to the AMA Board of Trustees (BOT) for review at the annual AMA meeting later in 2016. The BOT issued its report recommending adopting a policy of delay at the interterm in November of 2016.

As soon as I learned about this, I was absolutely ecstatic. This had happened as a result of young intersex voices speaking out and young doctors-in-training taking action. Exactly the way our activism was supposed to work.

So what happened…didn't that fix everything? What happened in the meantime? The report[3] was ultimately referred back for "further study" and then entered the cycle of internal bureaucratic nonsense. The AMA basically punted it for "further study," and then it became a meaningless part of a pediatric decision-making policy they later passed that contained nothing intersex-specific.

However, despite the anticlimactic outcome, I'm still hopeful that before long, those impassioned medical students who took action will be in positions of power and make the changes we so desperately need to see.

Besides, some of our own former young advocates are now becoming doctors themselves. Katie Baratz is now a psychiatrist. Two more I know personally are medical students who hope to revolutionize the medical community from within and provide intelligent, empathetic, and accurate care to intersex people.

And a group of med students separate from the UC Irvine group organized a protest and fundraiser for interACT to raise awareness about intersex rights. How the times are in fact changing.

* * *

Late in 2018, I got a text from Caroline—my dad's Caroline—saying my dad had been admitted to the hospital. I knew he'd had a bad cold, but then he got dehydrated. They ran lots of tests, and because there were other health complications, he ended up in the hospital, followed by rehab, for a month. I stopped by a handful of times, mostly short visits. Fox News was a constant presence on the hospital TV, though I tried to ignore it and avoid politics when talking to my dad. In doing so, we were able to have a few nice conversations. I talked about my girls, about work, things Steven and I were planning for the new year.

On one visit, he was especially down. "It's just so hard to be here like this. I'm not much for hospitals, and I hate being confined."

I saw my opening. Not an opening, as I hadn't been planning to say it, but the question was always there in the back of my mind.

"Yeah," I said, "I don't like hospitals either."

He nodded.

"Dad, what do you remember about my two hernia operations, when I was 6 and 12? Did the doctors ever reveal anything that gave you a clue that something else was going on? Did they not see testes in my abdomen when they opened me up?"

He sat back, and I could tell he was ruminating. "Your mom and I weren't really told anything either time. I think we may have been told it was somewhat rare in females to have hernias like that, but nothing more. And later, when you had what they referred to as a hysterectomy, we did what the doctors advised. When a doctor says, 'potential for cancer,' that's all you hear, all you need to hear. And that was really it. We listened to the doctors and there was no indication that they were hiding anything."

My dad seemed to be speaking from the heart, and I was struck by how good it felt having an honest and open conversation about this. It reminded me that despite everything that had happened, both my parents always had only the best intentions for me at heart. I left feeling a little lighter in the soul. I no longer doubted my dad, that there was the deep secret that he and my mom knew and kept from me. Even when I believed them after our first conversations after my discovery, I didn't know if I was sure I could trust them, though I wanted to. Now, I was going to put it to rest.

* * *

For every step forward a few make, there is still a huge part of the population who dig in their heels and refuse to be pulled out of the darkness.

Still in 2018, I was in Chicago for what was my 10th consecutive AIS-DSD Support Group conference when I ran into a disappointing (gut-rending) display of denial and fear. The day before the conference, the Intersex Justice Project had planned another peaceful protest outside the main entrance of Lurie Children's Hospital. I had never attended a protest in my life, but I knew I wanted to be at this one as a show of support for my intersex siblings. As I approached the crowd of about 40 people assembled, I felt a thrilling charge—a sea of matching yellow and purple T-shirts emblazoned with #EndIntersexSurgery; a diversity of faces, most of them young, all part of a dedicated and empowered community. The Lohmans were there as a family of four with both Rosie and her little brother, all in their intersex t-shirts. The kids held "Intersex is Beautiful" signs. For the first twenty minutes, I stood and watched with a smile on my face, soaking in the solidary, the hope.

And then I felt a sudden wash of anxiety, which quickly turned into numbness, then total exhaustion. I think it was the enormity of the issue and impact of the 5+ years that was overwhelming. My mind and my body were letting me know I needed to step back and protect myself. For the next two days while in Chicago for the conference, I spent most of the time in my room alone or in very small groups for quiet conversation.

But then I went home, unpacked, and not without feelings of dejection and fatigue, dragged myself to my computer. And there, as she always is, my XOXY action figure in red; her defender's shield a reminder that she is protecting herself as well as others, and I said, Okay. I'm ready. Let's get going again. There's still so much work to do.

CHAPTER 22

DEFENDERS ASSEMBLE

The bright young doctors who were becoming allies were a wonderful hope, but they weren't yet able to enact that change we all wanted to see. It would take the work of many allies from all walks of life to insist on intersex rights. One new avenue of hope came from the global corporate world. Now there's a place with plenty of power to change the things it wants to.

Right now, the changes are coming mostly through their individual LGBTQ alliances within many multinational companies, but it's a step. Starting back in the summer of 2017, the UN Office of the High Commissioner for Human Rights (OHCHR) published a new guide,[1] "Standards of Conduct for Tackling Discrimination against LBGTI People,"[2] aimed at multinational employers to improve policies and practices for LGBTI employees. This was a great step, and a much-needed idea, but again, imperfect in the execution. Despite the OHCHR being so supportive of intersex rights in the past, they had very little if any intersex consult in developing this guide, which was disappointing. While the guide refers to "LBGTI" people countless times throughout the booklet, nowhere does the guide mention any specific intersex concerns. I received an invitation to the launch event in the summer of 2018 in New York, and it was the first time I had even heard about the initiative.

However, I had been working with Debbie, a General Electric businesswoman, whom I'd met briefly at the OutRight Summit the previous year, on ways to reach out to and inform the corporate world on intersex rights. She was very involved in a global alliance of corporations that promoted LGBTQ inclusion in corporate policies and practice, and she was interested in learning more about intersex. She was innovative enough to realize that the corporate world was not only behind in its understanding of the intersex community but also recognized the potential strength an alliance could bring. I told her that if her company (or any company) did anything at all to help support or advance intersex rights, they would be true, groundbreaking pioneers. This, of course, also appealed to her sense of business competition as well as her heartfelt interest in helping intersex kids.

I then convinced Debbie to join our board, and together, we have an ongoing project to make further inroads in the corporate space.

One of our first projects was to conduct a webinar[3] on intersex in the workplace for Out & Equal Workplace Advocates,[4] geared to a global audience of staff from many different corporations around the globe. It was a new audience, and they seemed hungry for more information. The webinar was held in conjunction with Intersex Awareness Day. The exchange inspired me to submit an intersex workshop proposal to Out & Equal for their annual summit and to begin work with one of their global directors on a resource guide and a possible new collaborative project.

Again, though, every time I felt like we were gaining new allies, pushing our mission a step forward, inevitably we'd be met with resistance from somewhere.

Five days before Intersex Awareness Day, *The New York Times* reported on a "leaked memo" from the federal Health and Human Services (HHS) revealing plans to change the definitions of sex and gender in their current federal regulations. This was part of the current President's goal to undo every bit of progress made under President Obama; now, the new administration was looking to narrowly define gender as a "biological, immutable condition determined by genitalia at birth."[5] Within hours, the trans community was all over social media, and many in the intersex community were quick to realize such changes could also negatively impact us. For perhaps the first time in a formal way, interACT was invited to the table for urgent conference calls with leaders from a number of major trans and LBGTQ groups to strategize together. I got together with Harper Jean Tobin (Director of Policy at the National Center for Transgender Equality) and Sam Ames (Executive Director of Trans Lifeline) to co-author an editorial in *Advocate* titled "Intersex People #WontBeErased. Support their Trans Friends."[6] We were standing in solidarity with trans advocates but also pointing out the impact on the intersex community. We wrote of the new memo that the planned redefinition "effectively weaponizes the concept of 'biological sex' against transgender, gender-nonconforming, and intersex individuals. The intersex population therefore throws a hefty wrench into the administration's proposed sex classification scheme: not all intersex genitals match what we would typically associate with either binary category, nor do all chromosomes. For example, some intersex people, like coauthor Kimberly Zieselman, develop with XY chromosomes, internal testes, a vagina and vulva, and go through a 'typical' feminization at puberty because of their sensitivity to testosterone."

Now if we could only get politicians to listen.

* * *

We were approached by California State Senator Scott Wiener, a Democrat from San Francisco, about filing legislation to protect intersex kids. I was thrilled. Some lawmakers were taking note, and here one was actually reaching out to help. After much discussion, we decided to try to pass a nonbinding resolution first—this would be easier, and it would garner media attention to raise awareness, laying groundwork for the harder fight when he would file legislation that would restrict medical practice.

Usually state resolutions are not controversial and often sail through the process with other legislators easily supporting it as a favor to the sponsoring legislators. But our bill was different—it was more controversial and complicated and ended up being referred to two separate committees for hearings, then sent for review in both the California Assembly and Senate. Despite some opposition, coming mostly from practicing pediatric urologists, CA SCR-110[7] ultimately passed the legislature at the end of summer 2018, and became the first legislation ever passed anywhere in the United States that recognizes the harmful medical practices done to intersex children *and* gives a direct call for change.[8]

Starting in 2019, the legislative fights began in earnest. State bills popped up in California, Connecticut, Iowa, Texas, and Nevada thanks to the hard work of intersex folks and allies on the ground in these states working with their legislators—many of these lawmakers were hearing about intersex for the first time. Grassroots were growing. Between the recent increased visibility thanks to intersex awareness campaigns and California's passage of the first-ever resolution calling for the protection of intersex kids, the medical community—specifically the pediatric urologists—were on high alert. They could no longer dismiss or even ignore us. We were visible and making progress, and now they were forced to respond. Opinion pieces lashing back against intersex advocacy started popping up online, and they all sounded similar, making misleading statements or outright misstatements (being generous) and lies (more accurate). The pieces had such a similar phrasing and use of language that it was clear there was an organized voice behind the lies the medical community (again, mostly the collective pediatric urologists) were spouting off in the media: they had hired themselves a PR firm. My suspicions were confirmed when an ally doctor shared with me one of the recent email newsletters, seeking donations to pay for their fight "against intersex activists who are trying to regulate our practice."

Okay, game on.

Oh, and which PR firm had the Society of Pediatric Urologists hired? The same K Street PR firm hired by the Catholic Church to manage the abuse scandals.[9]

Then, after filing the first-ever intersex supportive resolution to be passed, California State Senator Scott Wiener had been working with interACT and Equality CA to sponsor SB-201,[10] which would punish doctors who participated in medically unnecessary surgeries on intersex children without their informed consent. The American Civil Liberties Union (ACLU) of California came on board as an official sponsor, and we had public support from AID-DSD Support Group, Amnesty International, GLAAD, GLMA: Health Professionals Advancing LGBTQ Equality, Human Rights Watch, Lambda Legal, The National Center for Lesbian Rights, the Palm Center, PFLAG, Physicians for Human Rights, and the Trevor Project. Momentum was building and we were no longer alone, now joined by a growing list of powerful and credible LGBTQ and human rights organizations.

On February 5, 2019, days after Senator Wiener filed SB-201, I was contacted by the NPR show "Air Talk" in Southern California (89.3 KPCC) and asked to appear as an intersex advocate to talk about the issue for the spot "Should CA ban nonconsensual 'medically unnecessary' surgery on intersex minors?"[11] which also asked if minors should have the final say on surgeries performed on them. Minutes after calling into the station to do the interview from my home office in Sudbury, the producer told me that we would be joined by a urologist. Shit. I had no time to prepare for what was sure to become a debate instead of what I had thought would be a pretty light lift interview. After hearing a few remarks from me, where I shared my personal story, the host introduced Dr. Peter Bretan, a practicing urologist in

Santa Cruz and president of the California Urological Association, and president-elect of the California Medical Association.

One of the questions was what age would I consider to be a blanket age, if there was one, that would mark a minor as able to consent or not consent to surgery. The truth is that there are so many factors going into this that it isn't easy to pick an age and say, "Here, hold off until this time." What is a child's capacity to understand what is being done to them? That ranges for each child. In my case, probably in my late teens, I probably would have been ready—*had I been given all the appropriate information.* That is the key. Sadly, parents today are put in a very difficult position of having to make a decision without being given all the information necessary to make the best possible choice. Parents are trying to make the best decision on behalf of their child. What we advocate for in cases where there is no medical necessity, just to be clear, I said, is that children who are born intersex should have a say in their own bodies, regardless of whether it reflects their gender identity. Of course in those cases it is important that children make a decision. But even in cases where gender is not an issue, which is the vast majority of these cases, people born with intersex traits have a variety of differences and they should be allowed to just be.

I was then asked about my experience with my own parents and whether I had discussed their decision to go through with the surgery, and I said that frankly my parents were not given the full information and did not even know I had XY chromosomes. The thing is that, with the internet, more information is out there than what my parents were given, but what a lot of these doctors don't tell parents these days is that they have the option to delay surgery in most cases.

Then Dr. Bretan, with all his pedigrees, came on and was asked about his main concerns with this bill. His main concerns were that, "we are probably throwing the baby out with the bathwater. The vast majority of patients with intersex are not in Kimberly's category. They are in a different category, which is pretty straightforward. And those patients, as well as their parents, benefit from this operation. Their psychological wellbeing—we have studies that show that."

I'd love to see these studies, personally.

"The problem that I'm alluding to," he continued, in his languid, sleepy monotone, "is called Congenital Adrenal Hyperplasia—" oh here we go, I thought—"and Kimberly is right in everything that she said, and my heart goes out with her, because I think if you can delay surgery up to adolescence then you could delay it after 18 then they could make their own decisions."

I waited for the *but*.

"However…"

There it is.

"…the vast majority of these patients with Congenital Adrenal Hyperplasia present itself at birth, and these patients usually are genetic females, they have identified themselves, and we know this from studies that they identify themselves as females. And what they have is an overactive…they lack an enzyme, so they make too much, they make too much of the male hormone, which is not supposed to be there, obviously, in females, and it hypertrophies, or it enlarges the clitoris to the point that it pretty much looks like a penis. And obviously, if you are the family member of a genetic female and you have this disorder, and by the way, this disorder, they have to take Prednisone the rest of their life or else they'll—they won't survive—so these decisions are made with a multi-disciplinary team: pediatric endocrinologist, pediatric urologist, neonatologist as well as pediatricians. And we have multiple studies, and I hate for this group, I have my own patients that have testified for this and they have…the patients have grown older and have applauded this surgery, and they are quite satisfied with it. But more importantly is that the perception of the family taking care of this patient from the get-go, early childhood, they know—you're changing the diapers of these kids, they know they are dealing, after corrective surgery, with a genetic female as well as a phenotypic…ah…ah…a female completely with the removal of the hypertrophied clitoris. This is not ambiguous. This is defined. Now, in Kimberly's case, I agree 100 percent. But the bill that we are dealing with throws out all surgery, including the majority of patients who suffer from Congenital Adrenal Hyperplasia."

I just about lost my damn mind. His concern is the families who are worried when changing diapers that they might see a longer clitoris? And also, this isn't ambiguous genitalia that would fit the criteria of intersex?

The host then asked if CAH was carved out of this bill, would he then be comfortable with this law being applied to other children. Bretan hedged, then said, "That would solve a major portion of this problem, getting rid of any discussion. But you know what, what we have is, this is not a discussion with urologists—I have never seen this decision in families…it's a multidisciplinary team. Now, if surgery has been delayed, as in Kimberly's…her…her…her own example, I think that could wait. I mean, if you have already become a teenager, and you delayed it that long, then you could delay it all the way until adulthood. You should make the decision yourself. But what I'm discussing is exactly what you're questioning here. I would like to preserve that for Congenital Adrenal Hyperplasia. We have data, strong data, to support that."

I was then asked for my response. Oh, there was so much I wanted to say. I had to stay calm. Sure, he sounded like he was supporting me, but there was plenty underlying his comments, and first and foremost that presenting with a hypertrophied clitoris was a disorder to be ashamed of, that it needed to be eliminated immediately because families would feel weird knowing they had a baby who was supposed to be female but looked different (*What the actual fuck?*), and that urologists and their multidisciplinary team were always right on this.

"I have to disagree with that," I began. "Unfortunately the studies are not that clear, and in fact, at least one in eight children born with Congenital Adrenal Hyperplasia do not identify as female. So talk about throwing out the baby with the bathwater, are we going to sacrifice that one child in eight, call them a genetic female, and reduce the size of their phallus so that it is more 'appropriate' in the doctors' and their parents' eyes, or a quote-unquote genetic female, which I also take issue with. You can't really talk about genetic males or genetic females. My body is a case in point. I also think that we are not talking enough about the harms that are associated with these medical interventions on all children, including children with Congenital Adrenal Hyperplasia." The report we released with Human Rights Watch dealt with this. Dr. Arlene Baratz has written about the mixed responses of an ideal age for surgery, in very limited sampling sizes of CAH patients, who also might not have been told that delayed surgery was even an option.[12]

I was asked about those harms, and so I talked about the risks associated with surgery on the most basic level, and I mentioned that a recent warning issued by the FDA that anesthesia could cause serious damage to the developing brain in children who are under the age of three, and referenced a major study done in Australia that showed long-term effects from anesthesia used on infants. But I wanted to focus on the pervasiveness of the psychological and emotional harms, which are not talked about enough, and I said that I didn't think the doctors were taking these very seriously. It wasn't just patients like me who had been treated in the past, it was patients as young as ten years old, thirteen, nineteen, intersex youth that we work with in our organization who have had medical intervention and talk about their experiences in a way that is very similar to how a sexual abuse victim would talk about their experiences.

The host asked why it would cause psychological harm to fix, such as in the case with CAH, especially when it's the lack of an enzyme that's typically there in females.

I agreed that CAH was both complicated and as common as Dr. Bretan said, one of the most if not the most common intersex condition, so we were talking about a number of patients in this case. "And a good number of them, and the doctor could tell more specifically, have true medical issues and there's medical urgency around treating their condition. But that doesn't include surgery," and I was emphatic on that point, "and that doesn't include surgery certainly on reducing the size of their clitoris. But for medically necessary interventions, of course. I'm a parent as well, I have two adopted children, I would never want to prevent that from happening to my child. But when that's done for cosmetic reasons, sometimes under the guise of arguably preventing urinary tract infections or some other nonsense that has no good studies behind it, that's where we draw the line. Congenital Adrenal Hyperplasia patients, young children, need to be protected."

There was a caller in from Santa Monica who was intersex, and the host asked if she would support this bill. She said she did support it and wanted to reiterate that these are the only socially prescribed, medically unnecessary surgeries that are done to infants and children who have no say. She added that whatever psychological issues there were, it is really the family that needs to start at an early age to stop shaming the kids by even doing things such as surgeries and saying there is something wrong with the child. "Love the child as they are. Nature is beautiful in all of its forms and diversities."

After this is when Dr. Bretan got really condescending. Of course he started by saying he understood the points made by both me and the caller and that his heart went out to us. *Barf.*

"The issue, and Kimberly even pointed out, is one out of eight, the best case scenario? I don't agree with that. Even when you agree with her, that means 87 percent of the people with Congenital Adrenal Hyperplasia are going to benefit from that. It's much higher than that. The other part that she pointed out, and this is just untrue, that anesthesia causes developmental problems with brain development, is just not true. You'll have to show me that data! That's…huh! What data? We have very safe anesthesia, if necessary…that just does not exist. So we have safe anesthesia, we have multidisciplinary teams, we take this serious. There is far more psychological impairment if you don't let genetic females be raised to their fullest potential and be identified as they identify themselves, as females."

Uh, someone is really missing the point here. *As they identify themselves.*

"I get the other part," he concluded, "but that's a small portion." So the one person out of eight who gets screwed over by having this medically unnecessary surgery performed without their consent gets messed up, well, those are the what, the eggs that must be broken to make an omelette? Those are the necessary sacrifice to the gods of cosmetic urology and anyway, they don't matter as much as the ones who we can say agree with us?

He completely dismissed anyone, regardless of how many it might be, who suffers from having surgery that doesn't match their gender identity, not to mention the total dismissal of the physical and emotional harms that come from surgeries and medicalized experiences. I was rattled, but I felt firm in my convictions and even more convinced I was on the right side of this fight. I would continue to speak out and fight to help future babies.

Still, what bothered me the most was when he said there was far more psychological impairment if you don't let genetic females be raised to their fullest potential. *Fullest potential* is basically akin to what we have heard from another pediatric urologist, Larry Baskin from UCSF, who was one of the older and more influential of his field. He said almost the same phrase at one of the hearings the previous summer for SCR-110, that surgery was necessary for intersex girls to be "functioning members of society." These were Orwellian levels of horrifying authoritarianism given in a totally blasé tone.

Days later, I was contacted by the producer of a Connecticut NPR program called "Where We Live" who wanted to do an hour-long show called "Intersex Advocates Say Society Needs to Change, Not Them,"[13] featuring intersex stories and discussing the new legislation recently filed in Connecticut. I had learned of that bill filed only days before—it wasn't one that interACT was leading. I worked with the producer over the course of a few days to prepare, and I brought in Bonnie, a fantastic parent of one of our interACT Youth members, who lived in Connecticut. Bonnie was also a therapist who worked a few hours a week with families at one of the Hartford area hospitals.

I reiterated interACT's main points that we activists were not opposed to all surgeries, only medically unnecessary surgeries that are performed without consent, and how some doctors were suggesting abortion as an alternative to having an intersex baby, without providing parents with any information or resources to reach out to the intersex community or other parents of intersex children, highlighting just how far we have to go. Bonnie was absolutely stellar from the parents' point of view, and also from the psychological point of view.

I was almost blue in the face repeating these same talking points, but I would keep talking forever even if I had to actually turn blue to ensure that these harmful surgeries would end.

* * *

In April, filled with excitement and nervousness, I flew across the country to Sacramento to give my testimony in support of SB-201. I would be allotted two minutes to speak. I arrived on a gorgeous, sunny spring day, happy to leave the mounds of melting snow at home behind for a couple of days. Soon after checking into my hotel directly across from the California statehouse, I got a call from Senator Wiener to touch base and prepare me for the fact that we might not prevail. We needed five votes to get it passed out of committee, and we only had three votes firmed up so far. Furthermore, the chair of the committee, who had supported our resolution the previous year, refused to commit his support unless we got a fourth vote—then, he would most likely be the fifth, allowing SB-201 to move out of committee and onto its next hurdle in the Senate Judiciary. I understood this was a marathon and not a sprint. "My expectations are realistic. I really do appreciate your leadership with this issue."

The next morning, I met the other co-sponsors and speakers next door at the offices of the ACLU of California. Their lobbyist would be shepherding me, along with two ally doctors, two interACT Youth members, and another intersex adult around the capitol building all morning before the midday hearing. We were still trying to secure that much-needed last-minute vote. It was one of those moments when I took a beat and reflected on how far we'd come in a few short years. Regardless of the outcome today, I was testifying in support of a bill that, if passed, would protect hundreds of intersex babies in California.

I was so grateful to be flanked by incredible medical allies, including especially interACT board member Dr. Ilene Wong, a courageous urologist and outspoken critic of her peers, who were some of the worst perpetrators of the harms we were trying to stop. Early in her career, Dr. Wong was involved in surgery that removed the healthy testes of a young patient with CAIS, realizing only afterward that the young teenage patient had no idea that those testes had been producing necessary hormones and that she would have to take hormone replacement medication for the rest of her life. Dr. Wong never participated in another intersex surgery on a child again.

I first met Ilene a few years back at an AIS-DSD Support Group conference. She had come as an ally and was seeking consult on a young adult novel she was in the process of writing as a side project. Her main character was a teenager with CAIS. She spoke about the lack of intersex representation in literature. Her book, *None of the Above*,[14] was published a couple of years later and has become a popular YA novel. Dr. Wong is a rare gem and the first urologist actively speaking out about the harmful practices her colleagues are involved in.

It was time to take our seats across from the senate committee members. I sat between Senator Wiener and Ilene at the long table facing the committee members. I was the first to testify, all the committee members staring at me. But with Senator Wiener and Dr. Wong on either side of me, I felt supported and safe. On my bright blue blazer,

I wore an interACT pin on one side and a delicate silver orchid pin on the other. Hanne had given me that pin as a gift back in 2017, the year she came out and attended her first-ever AIS-DSD conference, held that year in Phoenix. She purchased the pin at the annual fundraiser auction. Her pin on my blazer felt like a symbol of all my Orchid siblings with me in this moment.

"My name is Kimberly Zieselman," I began. "I'm a lawyer, a parent, and the Executive Director of interACT: Advocates for Intersex Youth. I'm also an intersex woman."

My voice was steady—I'd been practicing this speech. And now, I was in business mode. Defender mode. I might have been wearing blue, but inside, I was dressed in red and black superhero latex, my XOXY shield at my side.

"When I was growing up, intersex traits were kept secret at all costs. I learned the truth about my body at age 41, after doctors lied to me and my family for decades. While some things have changed for kids like me, many haven't. Bodies like mine have existed throughout history, without any need for surgery. It was a fear of gay and transgender people that led to the first interventions on atypical genitalia. Women with large clitorises were a primary concern, for fear that they would pursue lesbian relationships. It's impossible to talk about where we are today without understanding this practice's historical roots in sexism and homophobia. Just as LGBTQ people fought against being classified as mental disorders, intersex people fight against being classified as physical disorders.

"I'm here on behalf of our youth who have attempted suicide when they learned their sexual dysfunction was caused by infant hypospadias surgery. I'm here on behalf of our youth who have lost sexual sensation to infant clitoral reductions, and our young people who wear diapers for incontinence because of infant vaginoplasties. Frankly, what hurts the most is not the physical pain but the knowledge that we were robbed of our own, most intimate choices. If opponents claim this is no longer happening, it is because their own definition of 'intersex' is intentionally narrow. A recent Public Records Act request by interACT shows that *over 4000* such surgeries were reimbursed by Medi-Cal in the last three years, with procedures to 1. relocate an already-functional urethra, and 2. create or alter a vaginal opening, among the most common. While not everyone uses the term 'intersex,' for myself and many others, including the youth I oversee, it has become a guiding light, a reclamation that our bodies are our own. The word has helped us heal from medical trauma and understand that we are not broken. Regardless of terminology, children with variations in their sex traits deserve to be centered in irreversible choices about *their* own bodies."

The testimony was over so quickly. I was careful to make as much eye contact with the senators as possible. While I was reading my remarks, I was conscious of who was smiling or nodding at me and who wasn't. Most weren't. I appreciated the two women senators who were giving me even a little bit of comforting feedback with their facial expressions.

Next, it was Ilene's two minutes. She spoke confidently into the microphone, opening with, "My name is Ilene Wong. I'm a Stanford-trained urologist, and I am here because I truly believe intersex care is one of the greatest ethical failures of modern medicine." She continued to be a badass for the rest of the hearing and fielded questions from committee members while also pointing out the many inaccuracies spun by the opposition's urologist.

After her testimony, it was time for the opposition's two witnesses to have their respective two minutes each. The first to speak was a 27-year-old woman named Adrienne. I recognized her from her testimony against the resolution the previous summer. She was brave and articulate and spoke about having been born with Congenital Adrenal Hyperplasia—a condition she claimed is not intersex. Both her parents and her partner sat in the audience behind us. She spoke about the medically necessary intervention she received as a child and how grateful she was to her parents and doctors. I listened closely to her testify in opposition to everything I and so many others in our community had been working toward for years. I was of course frustrated but also moved—moved by the fact that, in reality, she and I had much more in common than perhaps was obvious at the hearing. We had both suffered and overcome medical trauma due to our bodies being born outside of what was expected for a girl. We both had caring parents who were trying to do the right thing. We both were misled by doctors and were now struggling to find our own peace.

One of the hardest things for me doing this work is the rare occasion I hear other intersex people talking about the harm they think I and interACT are perpetrating by including them in the "intersex" category, claiming that we are not recognizing their conditions most often have an urgent medically necessary component. I am well aware that many born with CAH are also born with a life-threatening adrenal issue that needs to be managed with medication for their entire lives. I am also aware that in some extreme cases—as in Adrienne's—some genital surgery is necessary to allow the proper flow of urine and blood. Those have never been and will never be the interventions that interACT or I oppose. It hurts me to hear some intersex people accuse me and my organization of intentionally advocating for something that will harm them. We are trying to do the exact opposite. We are trying to give people with CAH the autonomy to make non-life-threatening decisions about their bodies, specifically clitoral recession or reduction surgery. There is rarely ever a reason to cut the clitoris of a baby or young child, yet this is what happens to most children born with CAH. And I have spoken to countless adults with CAH. And yes, most identify as female, but some identify as male or non-binary. Importantly, all the ones I have spoken with uniformly oppose these cosmetic surgeries and talk about the physical and psychological harms they have suffered for years as a result.

The urologist on the other side perpetuated the idea that CAH was not intersex, which shows exactly how much society is perpetuating harmful pressures to conform to a rigid binary that really is just fraudulent. At one point, Dr. Wong expressed her frustration with the other side's "intellectual dishonesty." That didn't go over well, and even a few committee members' facial reactions showed shock and disapproval. I thought her words were appropriate for what was being said. So what if they weren't kind. We weren't here to be kind to perpetrators of harm.

Near the end of the hearing, when the members would usually record their voice votes on whether or not to pass the bill out of committee, the chair surprised us all by calling for a five-minute recess. While the committee members filed out of the room, the rest of us stood up to stretch. The next thing I knew, I was walking over to Adriene. It was completely impulsive, but I had a need to connect with her. Luckily, she was receptive to my advance, and we shook hands. I quickly told her that I was sorry to hear what happened to her as I child. I also said I believed what was done to her was probably medically necessary and not the type of thing interACT is opposed to. "I think we have more in common than not," I said, and she nodded. I sensed that she too was relieved to break the ice. She then said that she didn't agree with what interACT was doing as she and others with CAH were not intersex and shouldn't be included in the bill. My heart was heavy, for her, for society, for my friends and loved ones who would disagree. So I said, "While I don't care what you or others choose to identify as or use as labels—I support and respect individual choices—in fact, people born with CAH fit the standard definition of intersex used globally." I explained that the way we use intersex in our advocacy is an umbrella term describing people born with one or more physical differences in their sex characteristics, such as genitals, reproductive organs, or hormones. Her body fit that description whether she chooses to use the label or not.

The urology associations and CARES, the parent-led, surgeon-funded group for families with CAH children, were working hard to misrepresent intersex and make sure they only applied the term intersex to those who had chromosomes that didn't match the gender with which they identify. Just because Adriene had XX chromosomes, which are typically female, didn't discount the fact that her genitals were an intersex trait, thus fitting the definition. I told her that I have XY chromosomes but have always identified as female; yet I also choose to identify as intersex because that describes my body. The recess was almost over. We agreed that it would be good to continue communicating. Since neither of us had business cards or pens on us, she promised to find my email on the interACT website. I hope she does.

We all took our seats when the committee members returned. Then, they announced that they had decided to defer their vote on the bill for another week and asked both sides to work together over the next few days on compromise language around a few key issues. Senator Wiener protested respectfully but agreed. Our time was then up, and the next bill on their docket was announced.

After the hearing, we assembled in Senator Wiener's office to debrief all that had been said. We decided it was worth making a few more senate office visits while we were all in town since the votes were still pending. We did, but without much success. Most senators and staff were unavailable. While waiting in the reception area of one of the senator's offices, I could hear his booming voice in his office off to the left. The door was open, and while we couldn't see anything, we could hear he had a few people in there with him for a meeting. Suddenly, I heard someone say, "…and she didn't find out until she was 41!" in a voice dripping with sarcasm. My heart sank—they were talking about me. Suddenly, we realized the senator was in there meeting with the urologists' lobbyist and the doctor who had testified in opposition—and possibly Adriene and her family. They clearly had that senator's vote, and he would not be speaking with us.

Back in the hallway, I recognized that I had been triggered and was feeling a sense of loss of control, almost as if I was a child again. I needed to be done for the day and told that group that was enough lobbying for me that day. They understood.

A week later, news broke that the bill had been essentially killed—for this year—due to opposition by the California Medical Association, the American Association of Clinical Urologists, the American Urological Association, and California Society of Plastic Surgeons, the California Urological Association, the Pediatric Endocrine Society, the Societies for Pediatric Urology, and the CARES Foundation.

Of course, urologists (still working with the PR firm that defended priests accused of sexual abuse) adhered to their own flawed definition of intersex. Of course this has confused and misled parents and law-makers in order to exempt intersex people born with CAH or hypospadias—the most common intersex traits and inevitably one of the most lucrative for those working in this sector. This might be at the heart of this; we were trying to take away a "guaranteed" surgery from them. The stupid thing is that older intersex people may eventually choose to undergo surgery—but the whole point of this is to make it the patient's choice, not the doctor's right to operate.

Regarding the Foundation, much of what they do is well intended and much needed—namely offering support and information to families about managing a child's medically necessary interventions related to their condition. But the sad fact is that CARES also does damage. The group is heavily influenced by a small group of doctors with a financial and career interest in performing surgeries on these babies and young children. Their leadership defends the practice of clitoral recessions and reductions on CAH babies in the name of "parental rights." They have ignored the decades of cries from CAH adults who have shared the harms they have suffered as a result. But, perhaps worst of all, as a result of the intersex community's increased activism and threat of legislation to protect these children, CARES has begun organizing opposition to intersex-affirming efforts, using incorrect and misleading information.

One of the problems is that CARES and the doctors who advise them usually focus incorrectly on just chromosomes as the sole marker for gender, pointing out that a baby with CAH is born with XX chromosomes and is thus biologically female—incorrectly arguing that they can therefore predict the baby's gender identity will be female. They use this line of "reasoning" to claim that invasive surgery, including a clitoral recession, is not harmful, despite that at least 10 percent of CAH children do not identify as female.

The intersex and the trans communities, if nothing else, have proven this is simply not true. Science has known for many years this is not true. But CARES and their advising doctors have been distorting the truth and dismissing reality. Our reality. My reality.

In one of their action alerts asking their membership to oppose our resolution that passed in California, they state that:

"LIMITING THE RIGHTS OF PARENTS TO MAKE MEDICAL DECISIONS FOR THEIR CHILDREN WILL LEAD TO THE DISINTEGRATION OF ALL PEDIATRIC MEDCAL CARE!"[15]

This is frankly the kind of fear mongering you see across many conservative forums. CARES fuels this incendiary narrative by listing the loss of rights these bills would incur. "This means," the alert reads, "that you and your doctor no longer get to decide on surgery for your child." This is a big point of contention, and honestly, parents should have no say in what genitals their children have. The alert continues, "This means that you and your children will be denied access to care." Not true—a blatant misstatement of our purpose. "This means that your genetically, biologically, female child with CAH must wait for surgery and may possibly suffer great physical and psychological trauma as a result of this delay." What is their data? Also, how about let's create a supportive and inclusive society in which parents don't ostracize their children and shame them for how they were born? How about an understanding medical community? *But oh, let's worry about how the grandparents feel when changing the baby's diapers. If they can't handle seeing a long clitoris, well then, let's just snip it off.* The mentality to me is unbelievable, and yet the fear mongering and misinformation campaign is at expert levels. They have convinced parents to fear genital differences. They also, again, wrongly believe that chromosomes are the ultimate dictator of gender.

No and no. In fact, that would be a *hell no*.

Days after I was in Sacramento giving my testimony, the Intersex Justice Project and the queer rights organization Voices4 organized another group of about 40 peaceful protestors outside a CARES Foundation gala, which was honoring pediatric endocrinologist Maria New, one of the most historically renowned perpetrators of harm on intersex babies. Dr. New was a strong proponent of giving pregnant women the dangerous steroid dexamethasone to prevent "behavioral masculinization," including "tomboyism," interest in male-typical hobbies and occupations, and homosexuality, bisexuality, and transgenderism.[16] She advocated a risky, very harmful treatment to essentially prevent CAH girls from being lesbians. On this night, at a swanky building on Fifth Avenue in Manhattan, CARES was presenting her with a lifetime achievement award.[17] I didn't know whether I wanted to scream, vomit, or kick something.

A mother walking into the CARES gala became wildly agitated and told the crowd that they didn't know what they were talking about. "My daughter's gender is *not* intersex!" she screamed. Someone even took video of this meltdown, which shocks and saddens me each time I see it. This whole night was another instance of erasure, and it felt shitty.

An upside, though, came two days after returning from California. I got an email from one of our interACT Youth members. They have been an interACT Youth member for years, and I met them at their first AIS-DSD conference when they were about 16.

"Hey!" they wrote, "I'm watching through your testimony from Monday again, and Kimberly, it was so moving. The strength and courage it takes to disclose in this setting is Olympian—I am deeply moved by how you advocate for intersex youth. I was so moved and my heart was so touched by hearing your testimony and how you work to protect children and young people. I really wanted to say how proud I am to work with you, to be a part of this organization, and to be a youth member with interACT. You're changing lives, Kimberly, and you're so effing important—we see your sacrifice and passion for this work; personally, you mean a lot to me, and I really look up to you. Thank you so much."

Pardon me while I ugly cry.

This came in just what I needed when I was feeling pretty triggered and discouraged after the hearing, and after lobbying all day in Sacramento. They reminded me why I do this. I was touched, and most importantly, it rekindled my hope.

We are on the right side of history.

We will win this.

CHAPTER 23

SHANGHAI CLOSURE

Despite the frenzy of activism of the last few years, I was still a wife and a mother, and that part of me was never absent. Alex and Charlotte were growing from the sweet lights of my life to amazing and empowered young women, and I was very much still a part of that.

Ever since the girls were old enough to understand, Steven and I had told them that someday we would take them back to China to show them where they were from. "Before high school," I would often say. Suddenly, they were in high school, and we realized it was time.

We pulled them out of school a couple of days before the start of winter break and flew to Shanghai to spend the whole week of school vacation. Usually, that time is spent with my family, but this year we were happy to break with tradition—and also forego all the hype that comes with the holidays. This would be a lasting memory for the girls. As a splurge, we stayed at the Fairmont Peace Hotel right on the Bund—the same beautiful, historic hotel where Steven and I stayed in 2001 when we adopted them. It was a perfect location for walking out your door and exploring. That was what we did every day for a week.

We had scheduled a visit to their orphanage in advance with the help of a local organization and guide. A couple of days after

Christmas, our guide met us at the hotel, and we all drove to the orphanage on the outskirts of the city. It was as huge as I remembered it, but now, it was a bit tired. Run down. I could see not much had been done to maintain the building. Paint chipped off the walls, and the floors were worn. The playgrounds were battered, and the clock tower with rotating cartoon characters tired and worn.

The girls, who were only nine months old when we got them, wouldn't have remembered how it was before, and Steven and I focused on the experience being a positive—albeit guaranteed emotional—day for Alexandra and Charlotte. We were greeted by a young woman who worked for the orphanage as a social worker—by her appearance, she must have been not even ten years older than my girls. I wondered what her background was, how she'd ended up there. Before I knew what was happening, she handed each of my girls a brightly colored gift bag. Inside each contained a small enamel pin with the colorful logo of the Shanghai Children's Home and a piece of paper that included a photo of each of them taken at just ten days old. Taken on the day they were brought to the orphanage. Photos we had never seen. Under these photos, the page was almost completely filled with Chinese text.

The photos were striking to see—these were the youngest, earliest images of our girls we had ever seen. That the girls had ever seen. They looked so tiny and vulnerable. Our heads were spinning with thoughts of what it must have been like for them. And for whomever had left them.

Our guide interpreted the text for us. "It describes when and where they were found." An address in the old part of the city not far from where the old, wretched orphanage used to be. One that had the Dying Rooms. The one where the girls had spent the first few months of their lives before the big relocation.

The guide translated the script from the paper while we all gazed at these early photos, and then the orphanage social worker, matter-of-factly, mentioned a note from their birth parents.

"Wait, what?" I said. "What note?" When we adopted the girls, I specifically had asked the orphanage director at the time if there was any note or anything at all left behind with the girls when they were found. I was told quite directly that there was not.

Steven gently touched my arm, subtly telling me to calm down and not agitate a delicate situation where we clearly had no power and where this woman held information precious to our daughters, no matter what the note actually said.

The orphanage worker shrugged, guessing the rules back then were different. She told our guide, who translated for us: "Things were just stricter back then under the old director." She then quickly went back to her office and returned with a photocopy of the note. All of these children, all of these years later, and a note allegedly from one or both of my daughters' birth parents was in a folder in a filing cabinet in one of the many rooms of the huge orphanage building. It had been purposely left with the girls in hopes that someday they would know that they had been loved and left only in the hopes of them having a better life.

I cried. Steven cried. My girls, my beautiful, wonderful girls, cried.

This moment was a huge one for them. Something so fundamental about their own personal history had been hidden from them and then nonchalantly revealed in an instant—dropped onto them with no warning.

I could relate so deeply in that moment.

This was absolutely an emotionally difficult moment for them. It was also a gift that had been given to them. A small but meaningful missing piece of their identity puzzle finally was snug in its place. It would take time for it to feel just right. It was an answer to the great question of *why*, one that had been guessed but could never be known without some evidence. There was a beginning to their story. There was love in that beginning.

Those poor parents to have given up so much and, in turn, they gave me so much. My daughters would find their way through all their feelings given time.

That afternoon, back in the hotel, we all processed the information and quietly enjoyed the comfort found being near each other. Being a family.

CHAPTER 24

WAR HERO

Days after the Sacramento hearing, a news story broke out about Revolutionary War Hero Casimir Pulaski, who fought for American Independence under George Washington and has many schools, roads, and bridges across the United States named after him. Researchers had just discovered evidence that he was most likely intersex.

I was checking my work email on a Saturday morning, and my computer pinged with a new email from a reporter at *The New York Times* wondering if I would be willing to talk to her about this new finding.

When *The New York Times* calls, you answer.

The next day, the article "Casimir Pulaski, Polish Hero of the Revolutionary War, Was Most Likely Intersex, Researchers Say"[1] was published, including my quotes near the end:

> Kimberly Zieselman, the Executive Director of interACT, an advocacy organization for children with intersex traits, said Pulaski's life showed what can happen when intersex people are allowed to live as they were born, without early surgical intervention.

"What's happening today is so wrong," Ms. Zieselman said. "You are erasing people like this person who went on, untouched, to be a war hero…This is what can happen if kids are left alone—natural and healthy as they are," she added.

In Pulaski's case, Ms. Zieselman said that the discovery highlighted the intersex community's fight against invisibility—first, by history, when it was common for people not to know they were intersex, and more recently, by surgeries that she said erase intersex traits and identity.

"Just imagine if Casimir Pulaski were born today," Ms. Zieselman said. He may have been raised as a girl, she said, making it unlikely that he would have joined the military and helped Washington.

I was particularly pleased with my final quote.

"Arguably, if urologists had tried to 'fix' Pulaski's body, the U.S. could still be a British Colony."

Imagine a world in which our kids' bodies are left alone, natural and healthy as they are. I like to picture lives not spent advocating or battling or suffering, but living, making choices, making mistakes, having all the experiences a person can have who doesn't have to worry about a label. We're not there yet, but I have hope.

For now, I am an intersex woman.
I am a wife and a mother.
And there's still a lot of work left to do.

XOXY,
Kimberly

Endnotes

Male Pseudo-Hermaphrodite
1. PTSD or Post Traumatic Stress Disorder is a psychiatric disorder that can occur in people who have experienced or witnessed a traumatic event. www.psychiatry.org/patients-families/ptsd/what-is-ptsd

Chapter 1
1. An inguinal hernia is when there is a protrusion of tissue—such as with part of the intestine—that protrudes through a weak spot in abdominal muscles. In men, this usually occurs in the groin. A double inguinal hernia is when both sides of the body or groin are herniated. The occurrence is more likely in men (>27%) than women (3%). While inguinal hernias are somewhat rare in females, they are common for girls with Androgen Insensitivity Syndrome.
2. Androgen Insensitivity Syndrome (AIS) results when an XY male has a defect in the X chromosome, rendering the body resistant to androgens (hormones). AIS can be complete or incomplete. Complete AIS (CAIS) inhibits development of the penis and other male sex organs and occurs in as many as 1 in 20,000 births. Partial AIS (PAIS) results in varying traits that may include failure of one or both testes to descend after birth.

Chapter 2
1. Vaginoplasty, which includes various procedures, is recognized by the UN as *intersex genital mutilation* when undertaken on an intersex person without their full knowledge or consent. This is common for intersex babies and children. Many procedures, such as vaginoplasty, clitoral reductions, phalloplasty, or orchiectomy, are done solely for social and cosmetic reasons and not to benefit the patient

medically. Additionally, many of these procedures leave scar tissue that reduce sexual sensation for the intersex person, reducing sexual pleasure and inhibiting the ability to reach orgasm. Sometimes, sex can be uncomfortable or even painful for the intersex person after surgical genital mutilation. These medical interventions commonly cause emotional and mental distress, or even PTSD.

Chapter 3

1. Most vaginoplasty or stretching has traditionally been performed to accommodate a potential male partner, with minimal consideration of the intersex patient's needs or pleasure. Recent progress is being made, however, and now patients can use more appropriate dilation kits and, in the best-case scenarios, they are counseled on how to properly use these kits.

2. For intersex people with AIS, the testes are able to convert some of the androgens to estrogen, a process called *aromatization*, helping the body to feminize, including to develop breasts and hips. Removing healthy testes in intersex patients disrupts the body's normal ability to convert hormones as needed. There is currently no adequate research available to help doctors prescribe adequate hormone replacement therapy to patients with intersex traits such as AIS.

Reckoning With the Truth

1. This group has since broadened to include all people with different gender identities and intersex conditions, as well as their families. The name, as of this writing, is the AIS-DSD Support Group, aisdsd.org. (The organization is in the process of changing its name again.)

2. Prior to the proliferation of social media sites, electronic mailing lists/elists/email lists such as Listserv were a popular and practical way to be in contact with a group.

3. Through my conversations with families over time, I have learned that siblings of kids with intersex conditions commonly experience some form of neglect.

Chapter 5

1. Type A describes a personality that is generally time-urgent, competitive and intense or aggressive with a focus on getting work done. www.simplypsychology. org/personality-a.html

2. Dissociative disorders are frequently linked with trauma and PTSD.

3. Psychogenic amnesia is a symptom of dissociation, sometimes called dissociation amnesia. Elevated stress levels or psychological trauma can trigger a "blocking out" of certain information, leaving gaps in memory. This is situation-specific amnesia, which is different from global amnesia, which refers to a loss of personal identity that can last for hours or even days.

4. Though not actually a disorder, Imposter Syndrome is the psychological phenomenon identified in 1978 by Pauline Clance and Suzanne Imes in which people doubt their accomplishments, convinced they don't deserve any of their success, despite external evidence or positive feedback. Imposter Syndrome carries a deep-seated fear of being viewed as or called out for being a fraud.

Orchids

1. Joining a peer support group is the best thing an intersex person or their family members can do for themselves. The AIS-DSD Support Group (aisdsd.org), for example, is the largest group in the United States for intersex people of all ages and their parents to get crucial information and support. Increasingly, such support groups are spreading to other countries as well—all these are vital resources.

Chapter 10

1. Being "501(c)(3)" means that a nonprofit organization has been approved by the US Internal Revenue Service as a tax-exempt, charitable organization. www.501c3.org/frequently-asked-questions/what-does-it-mean-to-be-a-501c3-organization

Chapter 12

1. The Resolve Project was completely separate from the other RESOLVE project I worked on during my run at The National Infertility Association.

Chapter 13

1. interACT Youth is the first program in the world for intersex young people to connect, get empowered, and advocate for themselves and others. It started as a small volunteer group called InterACT, sponsored by AIC, and it is now a fully funded program of interACT—AIC's current name (changed in 2016) in honor of the intersex youth at the core of its mission. See interactadvocates.org
2. GLAAD is an American non-governmental media monitoring organization founded by LGBT people in the media. www.glaad.org/about
3. www.mtv.com/shows/faking-it
4. Within over four-and-a-half years, the video accrued nearly 5 million views. https://youtu.be/cAUDKEI4QKI
5. https://interactadvocates.org/i-discovered-im-intersex-from-the-buzzfeed-video
6. www.buzzfeed.com/patrickstrudwick/this-woman-only-discovered-she-was-intersex-after-watching
7. www.ias.surrey.ac.uk/workshops/intersex
8. www.surrey.ac.uk/people/peter-hegarty
9. https://obamawhitehouse.archives.gov/blog/2015/12/07/making-art-make-change-championing-lgbt-artists-across-country

Chapter 14

1. So many people dealing with the same problems regarding IEPs and special accommodations for their children don't know where to begin, even if they have the means and the time to advocate for their children. The internet is a great resource, but there is so much information out there; how is it possible to sift through everything? Major cities will have special advocates and counseling available, and it is their job to help you figure out your options. And again, online communities will provide an invaluable resource. Join as many online groups for parents with children who have special learning needs as possible. Chances are good that someone has already been through the exact experience you're about to go through and can give you the best advice.

Out and Out Front

1. This debate was a major part of the history of intersex advocacy, so much so that interACT's current president, Georgiann Davis, wrote a book on the subject, *Contesting Intersex: The Dubious Diagnosis*, published in 2015. In fact, in Georgiann's book, my choice of terminology is even documented (using a pseudonym).
2. https://pediatrics.aappublications.org/content/118/2/e488
3. www.usatoday.com/story/opinion/2017/08/09/ intersex-children-no-surgery-without-consent-zieselman-column/539853001

Chapter 15

1. *Cisgender* or *cis* (cisgender as an adjective) is the term for someone who identifies exclusively as their sex assigned at birth. Cisgender does not, however, indicate gender expression, sexual orientation, hormonal makeup, physical anatomy, or how one is perceived in daily life.

Chapter 16

1. https://hslmcmaster.libguides.com/c.php?g=306726&p=2044095
2. https://owlspace-ccm.rice.edu/access/content/user/ecy1/Nazi%20Human%20 Experimentation/Pages/Hippocratic%20Oath-modern.html
3. https://medschool.ucla.edu/body.cfm?id=1158&action=detail&ref=22
4. www.statnews.com/2016/09/21/hippocratic-oath-medical-students-doctors
5. https://nibjournal.org/voices/normalizing-intersex
6. Institutional Review Board (IRB)—an administrative body set up to protect the rights and welfare of human research subjects recruited to participate in research activities conducted under the auspices of the institution with which it is affiliated.
7. http://alicedreger.com/DSD_human_rights
8. www.hrw.org/report/2017/07/25/i-want-be-nature-made-me/medically- unnecessary-surgeries-intersex-children-us
9. From the report: "an endocrinologist on a DSD team at a regional referral hospital said that while she observed many of her peers in DSD care speaking publicly about a decrease in medically unnecessary surgeries on intersex children: 'Most patients at our center have cosmetic surgery to their external genitalia.' She said: 'The main two groups that don't are the kids who are being raised female who have very mild virilization, and then the more developmentally delayed kids.' [Human Rights Watch interview with an endocrinologist, February 23, 2017.] This doctor also reported reviewing unpublished data indicating that medically unnecessary surgeries remain more widespread that many doctors acknowledge."
10. http://protomag.com/articles/boy-or-girl

Chapter 17

1. https://ihra.org.au
2. https://transactivists.org
3. https://oiieurope.org
4. http://stop.genitalmutilation.org
5. http://nnid.nl
6. http://sipduganda.org
7. www.oii.tw

8. http://xyspectrum.org
9. https://bilitis.org
10. www.ianz.org.nz
11. https://everydayfeminism.com/2015/03/9-ways-intersex-youth-want-to-be-supported
12. www.ohchr.org/EN/NewsEvents/Pages/Astepforwardforintersexvisibility.aspx
13. www.ohchr.org/EN/NewsEvents/Pages/DisplayNews.aspx?NewsID=16431
14. www.unfe.org/wp-content/uploads/2017/05/UNFE-Intersex.pdf
15. www.unfe.org/intersex-awareness
16. https://intersexday.org/en/origin-intersex-awareness-day
17. http://intersexday.org/en/max-beck-morgan-holmes-boston-1996
18. https://docs.google.com/document/u/1/d/16skW1o_
    ISP5pjdq9WUVcttJNgndO88W5cMZw3YwB3qc/
    pub?embedded=true
19. Public statement of UN and regional human rights experts, "End Violence
    and Harmful Medical Practices on Intersex Children and Adults, UN and
    Regional Experts Urge," www.ohchr.org/EN/NewsEvents/Pages/DisplayNews.
    aspx?NewsID=20739&LangID=E viewed 24 October 2016 (for Intersex
    Awareness Day).
20. https://2009-2017.state.gov/r/pa/prs/ps/2016/10/263578.htm

Chapter 18

1. www.usatoday.com/story/news/nation/2017/01/23/
   model-hanne-gaby-odiele-reveals-she-intersex/96622908
2. www.vogue.com/article/hanne-gaby-odiele-model-intersex-interview
3. Alas, it was beaten out narrowly by "Complicit," thanks to SNL's skit about Ivanka
   Trump in March of that year. www.dictionary.com/e/word-of-the-year-2017
4. www.teenvogue.com/story/
   intersex-video-periods-genital-mutilation-surgery-identity

Chapter 19

1. https://interactadvocates.org/promoting-intersex-rights-internationally/#inter-
   american-commission-on-human-rights
2. https://oiieurope.org/4th-international-intersex-forum-media-statement
3. https://oiieurope.org/malta-declaration
4. www.palmcenter.org/wp-content/uploads/2017/06/Re-Thinking-Genital-
   Surgeries-1.pdf
5. https://yogyakartaprinciples.org
6. http://yogyakartaprinciples.org/principle-32-yp10
7. http://yogyakartaprinciples.org/principle-37-yp10
8. www.washingtonpost.com/sf/style/2017/10/05/
   the-intersex-rights-movement-is-ready-for-its-moment

Chapter 20

1. www.statnews.com/2017/10/26/intersex-medical-care
2. https://intersexday.org/en/intersex-day-of-solidarity
3. https://phr.org/news/unnecessary-surgery-on-intersex-children-must-stop

4. www.aap.org/en-us/about-the-aap/aap-press-room/Pages/AAP-Recognizes-Intersex-Awareness-Day.aspx

5. www.hrw.org/report/2017/07/25/i-want-be-nature-made-me/medically-unnecessary-surgeries-intersex-children-us

6. www.intersexjusticeproject.org

7. www.state.gov/r/pa/prs/ps/2017/10/275098.htm

8. www.lambdalegal.org/press-release/case/39031

9. https://outrightinternational.org/about-us

10. www.instagram.com/voices4_

11. https://phr.org/people/lois-whitman-jd-ms

Chapter 21

1. www.jkp.com/uk/raising-rosie-1.html

2. https://kidshealth.org/en/parents/congenital-adrenal-hyperplasia.html

3. https://assets.ama-assn.org/sub/meeting/documents/i16-bot-07.pdf

Chapter 22

1. www.ohchr.org/EN/Issues/Discrimination/Pages/Biz4LGBTI.aspx

2. www.unfe.org/wp-content/uploads/2017/09/UN-Standards-of-Conduct.pdf

3. https://youtu.be/KxYg425My3Q

4. http://outandequal.org

5. www.nytimes.com/2018/10/21/us/politics/transgender-trump-administration-sex-definition.html

6. www.advocate.com/commentary/2018/10/26/intersex-people-wontbeerased-stand-trans-friends

7. https://leginfo.legislature.ca.gov/faces/billTextClient.xhtml?bill_id=201720180SCR110

8. www.them.us/story/california-legislation-intersex-rights

9. www.peoplesworld.org/article/intersex-justice-activists-call-on-hospitals-to-stop-unnecessary-surgeries-on-infants

10. https://leginfo.legislature.ca.gov/faces/billTextClient.xhtml?bill_id=201920200SB201

11. I've transcribed most of the interview as follows, and the audio recording is available to listen to on this website: www.scpr.org/programs/airtalk/2019/02/05/64157/should-ca-ban-nonconsensual-medically-unnecessary

12. https://link.springer.com/article/10.1007/s10508-015-0529-x

13. www.wnpr.org/post/intersex-advocates-say-society-needs-change-not-them

14. www.iwgregorio.com/books

15. CARES 5/28/2018 Email Action Alert. https://bit.ly/2GdarMC

16. www.thehastingscenter.org/preventing-homosexuality-and-uppity-women-in-the-womb

17. https://caresfoundation.z2systems.com/np/clients/caresfoundation/event.jsp?event=618&

Chapter 24

1. www.nytimes.com/2019/04/07/science/casimir-pulaski-intersex.html